Sources in Patterns of World History

Volume 2: Since 1400

Edited by

Carey Roberts

H. Micheal Tarver

Arkansas Tech University

New York Oxford
OXFORD UNIVERSITY PRESS

Oxford University Press, Inc., publishes works that further Oxford University's
objective of excellence in research, scholarship, and education.

Oxford   New York
Auckland   Cape Town   Dares Salaam   Hong Kong   Karachi
Kuala Lumpur   Madrid   Melbourne   Mexico City   Nairobi
New Delhi   Shanghai   Taipei   Toronto

With offices in
Argentina Austria Brazil Chile Czech Republic France Greece
Guatemala Hungary Italy Japan Poland Portugal Singapore
South Korea Switzerland Thailand Turkey Ukraine Vietnam

For titles covered by Section 112 of the US Higher Education Opportunity Act,
please visit www.oup.com/us/he for the latest information about
pricing and alternate formats.

Published by Oxford University Press, Inc.
198 Madison Avenue, New York, New York, 10016
http://www.oup.com

Oxford is a registered trademark of Oxford University Press

The editors acknowledge the work of several individuals in making this sourcebook possible, especially
Carolyn Neel, Carlos Marquez, John Derek Rowley, Antonio Contreras, Lyndsey Mosquito, Natasha Scruggs,
John Cotton, Kyla McIsaac, and Rod Williamson.

ISBN 978-0-19-984618-4

Printing number: 9 8 7 6 5 4

Printed in the United States of America
on acid-free paper

Table of Contents

Sources in
Patterns of World History

Primary Sources

How to Read Them and Why They Are Important in World History

Candace R. Gregory, Sacramento State University

Humans are first and foremost social animals. We have an intense need not only to be around our fellow humans, and to communicate our stories to others. In fact, it is our ability to communicate in a variety of complex and simple ways that most distinguishes us from other species. Although it is widely recognized by scientists and the general populace that many animals communicate basic information, and that scientists continue to discover that animal communication is more complex than we often assume, it is still true that no animal speaks about itself, and the world around it, more often and in more diverse ways than humans. Furthermore, no animal has created communicating technology as sophisticated as human beings have. From the first gestures and oral utterances, to the simple artistic efforts of the Paleolithic era (such as carved figures, rock paintings, and the use of abstract symbols), to the more advanced technology of writing, humans have always found ways to speak to one another. The age of digital communication illustrates this point well: our very culture is defined by ever evolving communication technology. Some may argue that in this current age we adapt to technology, where once we adapted technology to fit our needs. Whichever the case, the fact remains that we find more and more ways to communicate with one another.

Communication is thus the definitive pattern of human history, for people also communicate across time. The past speaks to the present through these communication technologies. Being able to listen to the past is the most important skill a historian must develop. History is not "what" happened in the past; rather, it is our interpretation of the "what" based on the sources of the past, including textual sources. Interpreting the sources is in essence the present speaking to the past; reading and interpreting sources is a conversation across time.

How to Use This Book

The sources in this reader were selected to work closely with the Patterns of *World History:* by Peter von Sivers, Charles A. Desnoyers, and George B. Stow. They have been chosen to illustrate the patterns and innovations that are explored in the textbook; however, the sourcebook can also be used on its own, for each document in it was also chosen to exemplify a key aspect of cultures and civilizations throughout world history.

There are no footnotes to distract the student from the text itself. Any names or terms not defined or explained in the text are explicated in the introduction or questions for each source. It is hoped that this will allow students to read the texts without feeling overly directed through them by cumbersome notes. Furthermore, limiting notes allows students to come to the sources as unfiltered as possible; the brief introductions that proceed each source are there to provide only the most necessary information to understand the origin of the source, and to suggest why that particular source is important for studying world history.

There are certain techniques that students should use when approaching primary sources that will help them navigate the source, and discern for themselves why that source is important to the study of history. Essentially, these are questions that need to be asked of every source, as if one were interviewing the source. However, it is important to note that reading the text in translation might mask information that could answer the questions differently or more accurately, and students must be aware that there are complications in reading sources in translation.

Question 1: What does the source say and what genre is the source?

The first task of the reader of any text, but particularly of sources written in the past, is to figure out what is going on. Because the majority of sources in this collection are excerpts, that is, brief selections from longer works, they are essentially taken out of context. Thus determining the actual story the document is trying to tell. Even though these excerpts are short, completing this task might require re-reading the document several times. Some of the documents are more philosophical in nature, and thus will not necessarily have a narrative plot of driven by characters or actions. Using primary sources in the classroom should always being with first ascertaining how the students understood the sources. Part of understanding the source is also figuring out what genre the text is written in. If it is a speech, there may not be actions within the text, or even characters.

Question 2: Who wrote the text?

Unfortunately, many sources from the past are anonymous. Yet, although the specific name of the author may not be known, a careful reader will often still be able to determine the kind of person who wrote it. Occupation, class, gender are possible characteristics of authorship that can be determined from within the source. Readers can often go past that, however, and determine more specific details about the identity of the author, such as religious or political beliefs, ethnic and linguistic background, and education. The most important aspect of the question of authorship is that of authorial bias. Readers must ask what are the deliberate or unintentional biases in the text?

Question 3: Where does the source come from?

There are several different meanings to this question. "Where" can refer to the geographic origin of a source, and it can also refer to the culture that produced the source. It could also mean from what class produced the source.

Question 4: When was the document or source created, and when was it written down?

These are two related question; sometimes the answer is the same (the source is created and written at the same time and by the same person, sometimes these two things happened at different times. Sometimes the distance between when the source was created and when it was written down is a crucial part of the story of how the document came to be. Because so many of the sources in this anthology come from the earliest days of culture and civilization, when orality was more common than writing, most sources were created long before they were written. This question is very important to answer, however, because to answer this question requires the reader to determine the full context of the document.

Question 5: Why was the source created and why was it finally written down?

Of all the questions to ask of the source, this is often the most difficult to answer. To answer this requires that the reader move beyond reading the source to empathizing with it, relating to it, and putting oneself into the mind of the creator and author. Finally, one must be aware that there is often more than one answer to the why of a source.

Let us walk through an example of how a historian approaches a source, ask the questions and determine the answers. Consider the following excerpt from Ezana, "The Destruction of Kush," which recounts the attack on Meröe by Aksum in 350 C.E.

Ezana, the son of Ella Amtda, a native of Halen, king of Aksum and of Hemer (Himyar), and of Raydan, and of Saba, and of Salhen, and of Seyamo, and of Bega, and of Kasu (the Meroites), King of Kings, the son of Ella Amida, who is invincible to the enemy. By the might of the Lord of Heaven, Who hath made me Lord, Who to all eternity, the Perfect One, reigns, Who is invincible to the enemy, no enemy shall stand before me, and after me no enemy shall follow. By the might of the Lord of all, I made war upon Noba, for the peoples had rebelled and had made a boast of it. And "they (the Axumites) will not cross the river Takkaze (Atbara)," said the peoples of Noba. And they were in the habit of attacking the peoples of Mangurto, and Khasa, and Barya, and the blacks, and of making war upon the Red peoples. And twice and thrice had they broken their solemn oaths, and had killed their neighbours mercilessly, and they had stripped bare and stolen the properties of our deputies and messengers which I had sent to them to inquire into their thefts. and had stolen from them their weapons of defence. And as I had sent warnings to them and they would not harken to me, and they refused to cease from their evil deeds, and then betook themselves to flight, I made war upon them. And I rose in the might of the Lord of the Land.

Question 6: What does the source say and what genre is the source?

The source is written as a kind of declaration by King Ezana of Aksum, justifying his attack on the city of Meroe. There are no events in the document, as it is a kind of speech (which is one of the genres of the text), although the text does list a series of events that has led to the current events, the war between Aksum and Meroe. But this text is more than just a declaration and a speech; notice that it often invokes the name of a deity: "By the might of the Lord of Heaven," "the Perfect One," and "By the might of the Lord of All." Thus the document is also a prayer who invoked the god of Ezana. Although the text does not specify what the religious system of Aksum is, or the specific identity of the god Ezana worships, the phrasing suggests Christianity and the Christian God. This interpretation is supported by knowledge external to the text itself; the fact that the kingdom of Aksum converted to Christianity in the fourth century.

Question 7: Who wrote the text?

The beginning of the excerpt indentifies Ezana, King of Aksum, and throughout the document the pronoun "me" is used. The implication is that Ezana is the author of the document. It is certainly possible that Ezana literally wrote the text, and it is reasonable for a student without much knowledge about that time period to read more from the document. However, if a reader is familiar with royal culture of fourth century East Africa, he or she might also consider that a Ezana dictated the text as is, or the gist of the text, to a professional writer (a scribe). The mere act of writing the text means that the scribe might have in some way "authored" the text. He (and it was most likely a he), certainly influenced the final form of the text.

Because the text was either written for or literally by Ezana, the King of Aksum, one of the biases at work in the source is that of Ezana. As the text concerns a war between Aksum and Meroe, the bias favors Aksum, and Ezana in particular.

Question 8: Where does the source come from?

In regard to this particular text, this question is easy to answer, as it is identified in the very beginning of the text: Aksum. It is also possible that it was written by a state or culture favorable to Aksum.

Question 9: When was the document or source created, and when was it written down?

There is no explicit statement of date in the source. To answer this question, a reader would have to turn to external knowledge of Aksum. The most important clue in the story is the figure of Ezana. Knowing his dates, and the dates of the conquest of Meroe by Aksum, helps to date the document to after 350 C.E. Reading the text in the original could help to date the written version, as the original language provided invaluable evidence of dating. Languages evolve, and change over time, and thus can be used to date texts.

Question 10: Why was the source created and why was it finally written down?

As suggested earlier, this is a more difficult question to answer. Ezana does not explicitly state why he has written, or caused to be written, this document. Because it is a declaration, and a prayer, something of the purpose might be discerned from the genre. Ezana lists many deeds, or rather, misdeeds, committed by the people of Meroe: "the peoples had rebelled and had made a boast of it," "they were in the habit of attacking the peoples," "twice and thrice had they broken their solemn oaths," and "they refused to cease from their evil deeds." Inevitably, the reader is led to think that the people of Meroe deserved to be conquered; they had earned their defeat. In addition, in the prayer aspects of the text, "By the might of the Lord of Heaven . . . no enemy shall stand before me," Ezana is using this text as an opportunity to acknowledge the power of his god, declare his own power as one chosen by his god.

Thus original texts have many layers of meaning. Beyond the questions, and method of reading, suggested here, readers must also consider that every primary source can be mined for factual details. Some of the details in this source are: Aksum had kings, those kings (or at least Ezana) controlled other lands than Aksum (Hemer, Raydan, Saba, Salhen, Seyamo, Bega, and Kasu are mentioned), and the people of Aksum believed their king to be an all-powerful creator. All primary sources should be read in various ways.

Chapter 15

The Rise of Empires in the Americas

600-1550

At their peak from the thirteenth through fifteenth centuries, Native American empires comprised some of the largest political territories in the world. They possessed advanced irrigation technology, vast armies, and enormous cities that rivaled the size of similar empires in Eurasia. They excelled at astronomy, engineering, and perhaps above all, the creation of trading networks that spanned thousands of miles. Their governments also undertook sophisticated planning efforts that directed most aspects of their economy, especially the all-important crop of corn, or *maize*. Because of the hierarchical nature of their states, once an outsider successfully toppled the leadership, organization and control dissipated throughout the empire. Without supervision, irrigation channels dried up, crops died, trade ceased, and the people, weakened by malnutrition, succumbed to foreign disease.

Within the course of a century following European contact, the vast empires of the Americas collapsed. Some civilizations, such as the Mound Builders of North America and the Mayans of Central America, had already disappeared centuries before. Nearly all of the empires revolved around the centralized production of agriculture, notably corn, even though extensive trade of the crop and other goods existed beyond the reaches of a given empire. Religion also played a valuable role in solidifying Native American states, and religious activity often remained inseparable from politics.

All Native American states and empires fluctuated in size and influence, much like pre-modern European states. However, not all Native Americans lived in a large metropolis or engaged in intercontinental trade. A significant number, perhaps even a majority in North America, lived in small tribal units or states that covered only a few hundred square miles. These groups facilitated shifting alliances with other tribes or states, migrated across vast distances, and occasionally shifted the balance of power between competing, larger empires. They seldom developed large, centralized governments, but they did build villages and even cities, especially in parts of North America. In the Caribbean, tribal connections expanded into sophisticated social structures on only the largest islands. The following documents illustrate both the advances of the American empires as well as the strict forms of political organization that held them together.

15.1 The Founding of Tenochtitlán

According to legend, the god Huitzilpochtli led the Aztecs (Mexica) to a location where an eagle sat atop a prickly pear cactus (tenochtli) growing out of a rock and told them to build their capital there. This image now graces the Mexican flag. The first printed record of this scene appeared in 1541 in the Codex Mendoza, a pictorial history of the Aztecs prepared for the first viceroy of New Spain, Antonio Mendoza.

Reading and Discussion Questions

1. Why would the Spanish viceroy have requested a history of the Aztecs?
2. Compare Tenochtitlán's founding myth with ones from other cities around the world. What purpose do founding myths serve?

Photo courtesy of the Library of Congress.

15.2 Human Sacrifice by the Aztecs

To the Christian invaders, no Aztec practice was more deplorable than ritual human sacrifice. However when analyzing the past, it is difficult to screen out contemporary moral perspectives when dealing with multiple cultures over vast time spans. The Aztec believed supernatural forces needed human blood and beating hearts for sustenance. The practice, which always took place at the temple, was a highly ritualized affair. The image shown here is a detail from a mid-sixteenth century Spanish document.

Reading and Discussion Questions

1. Consider why some societies practiced cannibalism. Consider both social and religious explanations.
2. Does the fact that this source comes from after the Spanish conquest affect the way you approach it? Why or why not?
3. How can you tell that the person who created this image likely never set foot in the Americas?

Photo courtesy of the Library of Congress.

15.3 Machu Picchu

The modern day photograph of Machu Picchu, listed as a World Heritage site by the United Nations, shows the ruins of an ancient capital of Inca civilization. Nestled high in the Andes Mountains, Machu Picchu's construction required advanced building techniques, a system of irrigation, and a considerable labor force.

Machu Picchu represents the peak of Inca civilization. Founded in the mid-1400s just before the Spanish arrived, the site was likely either a religious or political center for the Inca Empire. Building a city at such a high altitude and among such rocky terrain required considerable organizational and technological abilities, which often rivaled other contemporary civilizations. Its location also prevented significant outside contact and is why it remained largely unknown to most European explorers, who concentrated most of their efforts in lowland river basins and coastal plains. What happened to those who lived there still remains a mystery, but it is assumed the inhabitants succumbed to European diseases and the city was "lost" to the outside world.

Reading and Discussion Questions

1. What technological achievements were necessary to construct a city in such high and rocky terrain?
2. While it appears geographically isolated today, at its peak Machu Picchu served as a leading Inca city. How does it reflect the ability of the Inca government to supervise such a massive undertaking?
3. With the exception of local peoples living near the ruins, little was known of Machu Picchu until centuries after its collapse, and yet it thrived long after the Spanish destroyed similar Inca cities. How might its isolation have contributed to both its longevity and ultimate demise?

Photo courtesy of H. Micheal Tarver.

15.4 The Inca Census

Hailing from Extremadura, the same region of Spain as fellow conquistadores Hernán Cortès and Francisco Pizarro, Pedro Cieza de Léon (c. 1520-1554) was as much a scholar as a soldier. He recorded the events, places, and characters he encountered in the Andes, and, consequently, he is a major historical source for the time period and region under analysis. The following excerpt comes from *The Second Part of Cieza de Léon's Chronicle*, which was not published until the late nineteenth century. In this chapter, Cieza de Léon describes the annual census taken in each region as well as the storehouse economy practiced by the Inca.

Source: Pedro Cieza de Léon, *The Second Part of the Chronicle of Peru,* translated and edited by Clements R. Markham (London: Hakluyt Society, 1883), 57-59.

CHAPTER XIX.

How the Kings of Cuzco ordered that every year an account should be taken of all persons who died and were born throughout their dominions, also how all men worked, and how none could be poor by reason of the storehouses.

The Orejones who gave me information at Cuzco concurred in saying that formerly, in the time of the Kings, orders were given throughout all the towns and provinces of Peru, that the principal lords and their lieutenants should take note, each year, of the men and women who had died, and also of the births. For as well for the assessment of tribute, as for calculating the number of men that could be called upon to serve as soldiers, and for the defense of the villages, such information was needed. This was easily done, because each province, at the end of the year, was ordered to set down in the **quipus**, by means of the knots, all the men who had died in it during the year, as well as all who were born. In the beginning of the following year, the quipus were taken to Cuzco, where an account was made of the births and deaths throughout the empire. These returns were prepared with great care and accuracy, and without any fraud or deceit. When the returns had been made up, the lord and his officers knew what people were poor, the number of widows, whether they were able to pay tribute, how many men could be taken for soldiers, and many other facts which were considered, among these people, to be of great importance.

As this empire was of such vast extent, a fact which I have frequently pointed out in many parts of this work, and as in each province there were a great number of storehouses for provisions and other necessaries for a campaign, and for the equipment of soldiers, if there was a war these great resources were used where the camps were formed, without touching the supplies of allies, or drawing upon the stores of different villages. If there was no war, all the great store of provisions was divided amongst the poor and the widows. The poor consisted of those who were too old to work, or who were maimed, lame, or infirm; but those who were well and able to work received nothing. Then the storehouses were again filled from the obligatory tributes; and if, by chance, there came a year of great sterility, the storehouses were, in like manner, ordered to be opened, and the necessary provisions were given out to the suffering provinces. But as soon as a year of plenty came, the deficiencies so caused were made up. Although the tributes given to the Incas did not serve for other purposes than the above, yet they were well expended, and the kingdom was well supplied and cared for.

It was not permitted that any should be idle, or should profit by the labor of others, all being commanded to work. Each lord, on certain days, went to his farm, took the plough in his hand and made a furrow, besides working at other things. Even the Incas themselves did so, to give a good example to others; for they intended it

---

quipu: Inca counting device that consisted of bundles of knotted cords. Also spelled "khipu"

to be understood that there must not be any one so rich that, on account of his riches, he could affront the poor: and by this system, there was no one in the whole land, being in good health, who did not work. The infirm were fed and clothed from the storehouses. No rich man was allowed to wear more ornaments than the poor, nor to make any difference in his dress, except the lords and the *Curacas*. These, as well as the Orejones, to maintain their dignity, could use great freedom in this respect, and they were made much of, among all the nations.

Reading and Discussion Questions

1. In what ways were the Inca's storehouses similar to the modern concept of a social safety net? In what ways do they differ?
2. How did the regional storehouses function as both a political and military institution?
3. For what reason did the Inca leadership require a count of the births and deaths in each providence?
4. Does Cieza de Léon speak favorably of the Inca system? Explain why or why not.

Chapter 16

The Ottoman–Habsburg Struggle and European Overseas Expansion

1450–1600

In 1450, the Habsburgs were nearing the height of their power in Europe at the same time the Ottomans were expanding eastward, capturing Constantinople in 1453. The Ottomans started as mounted nomads, moving out of their steppe homeland in Central Asia around 1300 and within half a century had established themselves across Anatolia into southeastern Europe, conquering much of modern-day Bulgaria and expanding into Greece and the Balkans by 1400. In retrospect, it seems inevitable the Ottoman and Habsburgs would clash as their expansions put each in the direct path of the other.

Spanish monarchs considered Muslims to be enemies of Christianity as well as imperial threats. The Muslim invasions of the eighth century had pushed Iberian aristocrats to the Pyrenees Mountains; their reclamation of the lost lands took the aspect of a crusade, or holy war. In 1492, the conquest of the last Iberian Muslim lands was completed by the armies of Ferdinand II of Aragon and Isabella I of Castile, who took pride in their joint life, *Los Reyes Católicos*, the Catholic Monarchs. Habsburg power increased dramatically when the Habsburg lands merged with Spanish possessions through bedroom politics. Joanna (Joanna the Mad), the daughter of Isabella and Ferdinand, married Philip I of Castile (Philip the Handsome), the son of the Holy Roman Emperor Maximilian I. Joanna and Phillip's son inherited both the Spanish and Habsburg realms, ruling as Charles I of Spain and Charles V of the Holy Roman Empire. The Habsburgs were ambitious, tough, and related to almost every royal family in Europe, despite wars with France, uprisings in Spain, and the pressures of Protestants in Northern Europe who taxed Charles's resources.

16.1 The Tribute of Children

The notion of raising children to be warriors was not limited to the Ottomans, yet the idea of forming slave armies is surprising to modern readers. As the source below details, these children comprised the elite corps, whether as the backbone of the bureaucracy or officers and soldiers charged with defense and keeping order. The possible hazards—such as divided loyalty, loneliness for family and homeland, etc.—spring immediately to mind. Nevertheless, there are also distinct advantages. First, since these soldiers would not have ties to the "great families" of the state, they would be less likely to have mentors or benefactors outside the existing ruling structure to whom they might develop a stronger loyalty than to the existing sovereign. And, of course, one should never underestimate the *esprit de corps* that develops in elite military structures. Elite status is often psychologically addictive.

Source: Anonymous, "The Tribute of Children," in *The World's Story. A History of the World in Story, Song and Art*, edited by Eva March Tappan. Volume VI: *Russia, Austria-Hungary, The Balkan States and Turkey* (Boston: Houghton Mifflin Co, 1914), 491-494.

The advice of the vizier was followed; the edict was proclaimed; many thousands of the European captives were educated in the Mohammedan religion and arms, and the new militia was consecrated and named by a celebrated dervish. Standing in the front of their ranks, he stretched the sleeve of his gown over the head of the foremost soldier, and his blessing was delivered in the following words — "Let them be called Janissaries (*yingi cheri*, or new soldiers); may their countenances be ever bright; their hand victorious; their swords keen; may their spear always hang over the heads of their enemies; and, wheresoever they go, may they return with a white face." "White" and "black" faceare common and proverbial expressions of praise and reproach in the Turkish language. Such was the origin of these haughty troops, the terror of the nations, and sometimes of the sultans themselves. They were kept up by continual additions from the sultan's share of the captives, and by recruits, raised every five years, from the children of the Christian subjects. Small parties of soldiers, each under a leader, and each provided with a particular firearm, went from place to place. Wherever they came, the **protogeros** assembled the inhabitants with their sons. The leader of the soldiers had the right to take away all the youth who were distinguished by beauty or strength, activity or talent, above the age of seven. He carried them to the court of the grand seignior, a tithe, as it were, of the subjects. The captives taken in war by the pashas, and presented by them to the sultan, included Poles, Bohemians, Russians, Italians, and Germans.

These recruits were divided into two classes. Those who composed the one, especially in the earlier periods, were sent to Anatolia, where they were trained to agricultural labor, and instructed in the Mussulman faith; or they were retained about the seraglio, where they carried wood and water, and were employed in the gardens, in the boats, or upon the public buildings, always under the direction of an overseer, who with a stick compelled them to work. The others, in whom traces of a higher character were discernible, were placed in one of the four seraglios of Adrianople or Galata, or the old or new one at Constantinople [Istanbul]. Here they were lightly clad in linen or in cloth of Saloniki, with caps of Prusa cloth. Teachers came every morning, who remained with them until evening, and taught them to read and write. Those who had performed hard labor were made Janissaries. Those who were educated in the seraglios became *spahis* or higher officers of state. Both classes were kept under a strict discipline. The former especially were accustomed to privation of food, drink, and comfortable clothing, and to hard labor. They were exercised in shooting with the bow and **arquebus** by day, and spent the night in a long, lighted hall, with an overseer, who walked up and down, and permitted no one to stir. When they were received into the corps of the Janissaries, they were placed in cloister-like barracks, in which the different *odas* or *ortas* lived so entirely in common that the military dignitaries were called from their soups and kitchens. Here not only the younger continued to obey the elders in silence and submission, but all were governed with such strictness that no one was permitted to spend the night abroad, and whoever was punished was compelled to kiss the hand of him who inflicted the punishment.

The younger portion, in the seraglios, were kept not less strictly, every ten being committed to the care of an inexorable attendant. They were employed in similar exercises, but likewise in study. The grand seignior permitted them to leave the seraglio every three years. Those who chose to remain, ascended, according to their age in the immediate service of their master, from chamber to chamber, and to constantly greater pay, till they attained, perhaps, to one of the four great posts of the innermost chamber, from which the way to the dignity of a *beglerbeg*, or a *capitan deiri* (that is, an admiral), or even of a vizier, was open. Those, on the contrary, who took advantage of this permission, entered, each one according to his previous rank, into the four first corps of the paid spahis, who were in the immediate service of the sultan, and in whom he confided more than in his other bodyguards.

---

protogeros: village headman, obliged to offer hospitality to Ottoman officials

arquebus: forerunner of the rifle, an early firearm used in the 15th-17th centuries

Reading and Discussion Questions

1. The image of children being taken from their families seems heart-wrenching, yet the writer does not record resistance or tears when the boys are taken from their families. Why?
2. How is it that these captives are trusted with both the affairs of the state and its defense? Can a slave soldier be really trusted?
3. What is the basis for dividing the boys into two groups? Why does their training differ?
4. The boys are given a chance to leave the seraglio (apartments within a sultan's palace or other official building) every three years. Why would any stay?

16.2   A European Ambassador Reports on the Ottomans

Flemish diplomat Ogier Ghiselin de Busbecq (1522-1592) served as ambassador from Holy Roman Emperors Charles V (r. 1519-1556) and Ferdinand I (r. 1556-1564) to the court of Süleyman I. In the sixteenth-century, one of the Habsburg ambassador's primary duties was to assess the military and economic potential of the states he visited.

Source: Ogier Ghiselin de Busbecq, *The Life and Letters of Ogier Ghiselin de Busbecq*, edited by Charles Thornton Forster and F.H. Blackburne Daniell (London: C. Kegan Paul & Co., 1881), Volume I, 86-88.

At Buda I made my first acquaintance with the Janissaries; this is the name by which the Turks call the infantry of the royal guard. The Turkish state has 12,000 of these troops when the corps is at its full strength. They are scattered through every part of the empire, either to garrison the forts against the enemy, or to protect the Christians and Jews from the violence of the mob. There is no district with any considerable amount of population, no borough or city, which has not a detachment of Janissaries to protect the Christians, Jews, and other helpless people from outrage and wrong.

A garrison of Janissaries is always stationed in the citadel of Buda. The dress of these men consists of a robe reaching down to the ankles, while, to cover their heads, they employ a cowl which, by their account, was originally a cloak sleeve, part of which contains the head, while the remainder hangs down and flaps against the neck. On their forehead is placed a silvergilt cone of considerable height, studded with stones of no great value.

These Janissaries generally came to me in pairs. When they were admitted to my dining room they first made a bow, and then came quickly up to me, all but running, and touched my dress or hand, as if they intended to kiss it. After this they would thrust into my hand a nosegay of the hyacinth or narcissus; then they would run back to the door almost as quickly as they came, taking care not to turn their backs, for this, according to their code, would be a serious breach of etiquette. After reaching the door, they would stand respectfully with their arms crossed, and their eyes bent on the ground, looking more like monks than warriors. On receiving a few small coins (which was what they wanted) they bowed again, thanked me in loud tones, and went off blessing me for my kindness. To tell you the truth, if I had not been told beforehand that they were Janissaries, I should, without hesitation, have taken them for members of some order of Turkish monks, or brethren of some Moslem college. Yet these are the famous Janissaries, whose approach inspires terror everywhere. During my stay at Buda a good many Turks were drawn to my table by the attractions of my wine, a luxury in which they have not many opportunities of indulging. The effect of this enforced abstinence is to make them so eager for drink, that they swill themselves with it whenever they get the chance. I asked them to make a night of it, but at last I got tired of the game, left the table, and retired to my bedroom. On this my Turkish guests made a move to go, and great was their grief as they reflected that they were not yet dead drunk, and could still use their legs. Presently they sent a servant to request that I would allow them access to my stock of wine and lend them some silver cups. 'With my permission,' they said, 'they would like to continue their drinking bout through the night; they were not particular where they sat; any odd corner would do for them.' Well, I ordered them to be furnished with as much wine as they could drink, and also with the cups they asked for. Being thus supplied, the fellows never left off drinking until they were one and all stretched on the floor in the last stage of intoxication.

To drink wine is considered a great sin among the Turks, especially in the case of persons advanced in life: when younger people indulge in it the offence is considered more venial. Inasmuch, however, as they think that they will have to pay the same penalty after death whether they drink much or little, if they taste one drop of wine they must needs indulge in a regular debauch…

Reading and Discussion Questions

1. The ambassador's description of the drinking bouts of the Janissaries' seems rather dismissive. What would have been a purpose for including the episodes?
2. During this period, Western Europeans were concerned about the advance and expansion of the Ottoman Empire. From his descriptions, what do you infer about the ambassador's assessment of the dangers from the Ottomans?
3. In 1555, the first year of the ambassador's visit to the Ottomans, the Holy Roman Emperor, Charles V, relinquished both the crown and his ambition for a global Christian empire. Do you believe the political uncertainty in Europe contributed to the ambassador's assessment of the Janissaries?

16.3 An Ottoman Travel Journal

Travel journals have a long history, serving to record the wonders of strange lands as well as the travelers' adventures. In this passage below, Admiral Sidi Alui Reis (1498-1563) writes of being sent to secure 15 ships from Basra in Iraq, and return them to Egypt, which was then part of the Ottoman Empire. The admiral writes of visiting the holy sites and provides a description of a battle with a Portuguese fleet.

Source: Sidi Alui Reis, "The Mirror of Countries" (1556), printed in Charles F. Horne, ed., *The Sacred Books and Early Literature of the East,* (New York: Parke, Austin, & Lipscomb, 1917), Vol. VI: Medieval Arabia, 332-340.

When Sultan Suleyman had taken up his winter residence in Aleppo, I, the author of these pages, was appointed to the Admiralship of the Egyptian fleet, and received instructions to fetch back to Egypt the ships (15 galleys), which some time ago had been sent to Basra on the Persian Gulf. But, "Man proposes, God disposes." I was unable to carry out my mission, and as I realized the impossibility of returning by water, I resolved to go back to Turkey by the overland route, accompanied by a few tried and faithful Egyptian soldiers. I traveled through Gujarat, Hind, Sind, Balkh, Zabulistan, Bedakhshan, Khotlan, Turan, and Iran, i.e., through Transoxania, Khorassan, Khareem, and Deshti-Kiptchak; and as I could not proceed any farther in that direction, I went by Meshed and the two Iraqs, Kazwin and Hamadan, on to Bagdad.

Our travels ended, my companions and fellow-adventurers persuaded me to write down our experiences, and the dangers through which we had passed, an accurate account of which it is almost impossible to give; also to tell of the cities and the many wonderful sights we had seen, and of the holy shrines we had visited. And so this little book sees the light; in it I have tried to relate, in simple and plain language, the troubles and difficulties, the suffering and the distress which beset our path, up to the time that we reached Constantinople.

Considering the matter it contains this book ought to have been entitled, "A tale of woe," but with a view to the scene of action I have called it "Mirror of Countries," and as such I commend it to the reader's kind attention.

. . .

I, humble Sidi Ali bin Husein, also known as Kiatibi-Rumi (the writer of the West, i.e., of Turkey), most gladly accepted the post. I had always been very fond of the sea, had taken part in the expedition against Rhodes under the Sultan (Suleiman), and had since had a share in almost all engagements, both by land and by sea. I had fought under Khaireddin Pasha, Sinan Pasha, and other captains, and had cruised about on the Western (Mediterranean) sea, so that I knew every nook and corner of it. I had written several books on astronomy, nautical science, and other matters bearing upon navigation. My father and grandfather, since the conquest of Constantinople, had had charge of the arsenal a at Galata; they had both been eminent in their profession, and their skill had come down to me as an heirloom.

. . .

I had plenty of leisure to visit the mosque of Ali and the graves of Hasan Basri, Talha, Zobeir, Uns-bin-Malik, Abdurrahman-bin-Anf, and several martyrs and companions of the Prophet. One night I dreamed that I lost my sword, and as I remembered that a similar thing had happened to Sheik Muhieddin and had resulted in a defeat, I became greatly alarmed, and, just as I was about to pray to the Almighty for the victory of the Islam arms, I awoke. I kept this dream a secret, but it troubled me for a long time, and when later on Mustafa Pasha sent a detachment of soldiers to take the island of Huweiza (in which expedition I took part with five of my galleys), and the undertaking resulted in our losing about a hundred men all through the fickleness of the Egyptian troops, I fully believed this to be the fulfilment of my dream. But alas! there was more to follow — for:

What is decreed must come to pass,
No matter, whether you are joyful or anxious.

When at last the time of the monsoon came, the Pasha sent a trusty sailor with a frigate to Ormuz, to explore the neighborhood. After cruising about for a month he returned with the news that, except for four boats, there was no sign of any ships of the infidels in those waters. The troops therefore embarked and we started for Egypt.

WHAT TOOK PLACE IN THE SEA OF ORMUZ

On the first of Shawal we left the harhor of Basra, accompanied, as far as Ormuz, by the frigate of Sherifi Pasha. We visited on the way from Mehzari the grave of Khidr, and proceeding along the coast of Duspul (Dizful), and Shushter in Charik, I made pilgrimages to the graves of Imam Mohammed, Hanifi, and other saints.

From the harbor in the province of Shiraz we visited Rishehr (Bushir) and after reconnoitering the coasts and unable to get any clue as to the whereabouts of the enemy by means of the Tshekleva? I proceeded to Katif, situated near Lahsa 2 and Hadjar on the Arabian coast. Unable to learn anything there, I went on to Bahrein, where I interviewed the commander of the place, Reis Murad. But neither could he give me any information about the fleet of the infidels. There is a curious cuetom at Bahrein. The sailors, provided with a leather sack, dive down into the sea and bring the fresh water from the bottom for Reis Murad's use. This water is particularly pleasant and cold in the spring time, and Reis Murad gave me some. God's power is boundless! This custom is the origin of the proverb: "Maradj ul bahreia jaltakian," and hence also the name." Bahrein."

Next we came to Kis, i.e., old Ormuz, and Barhata, and several other small islands in the Green Sea, i.e., the waters of Ormuz, but nowhere could we get any news of the fleet. So we dismissed the vessel, which Mustafa Pasha had sent as an escort, with the message that Ormuz was safely passed. We proceeded by the coasts of Djilgar and Djadi, past the towns of Keimzar or Leime, and forty days after our departure, i.e., on the tenth of Ramazan, in the forenoon, we suddenly saw coming toward us the Christian fleet, consisting of four large ships, three galleons, six Portuguese guard ships, and twelve galleys (Kalita), 25 vessels in all. I immediately ordered the canopy to be taken down, the anchor weighed, the guns put in readiness, and then, trusting to the help of the Almighty, we fastened the filandra to the mainmast, the flags were unfurled, and, full of courage and calling upon Allah, we commenced to fight. The volley from the guns and cannon was tremendous, and with God's help we sank and utterly destroyed one of the enemy's galleons.

Never before within the annals of history has such a battle been fought, and words fail me to describe it.

The battle continued till sunset, and only then the Admiral of the infidel fleet began to show some signs of fear. He ordered the signal-gun to fire a retreat, and the fleet turned in the direction of Ormuz.

With the help of Allah, and under the lucky star of the Padishah, the enemies of Islam had been defeated. Night came at last; we were becalmed for awhile, then the wind rose, the sails were set and as the shore was near . . . until daybreak. The next day we continued our previous course. On the day after we passed Khorfakan, where we took in water, and soon after reached Oman, or rather Sohar. Thus we cruised about for nearly 17 days. When on the sixth of 'Riimazan, i.e., the day of Kadr-Ghedjesi, a night in the month of Ramazan, we arrived in the vicinity of Maskat and Kalhat, we saw in the morning, issuing from the harbor of Maskat, 12 large boats and 22 *gurabs*, 32 vessels in all, commanded by Captain Kuya, the son of the Governor. They carried a large number of troops.

The boats and galleons obscured the horizon with their mizzen sails (*Magistra*) and *Peneta* (small sails) all set; the guard-ships spread their round sails (*Chember-yelken*), and, gay with bunting, they advanced toward us. Full of confidence in God's protection we awaited them. Their boats attacked our galleys; the battle raged, cannon and guns, arrows and swords made terrible slaughter on both sides. The *Badjoalushlca* penetrated the boats and the *Shaikas* and tore large holes in their hulls, while our galleys were riddled through by the javelins (*Darda*) thrown down upon us from the enemy's turrets, which gave them the appearance of bristling porcupines; and they showered down upon us. . . .The stones which they threw at us created quite a whirlpool as they fell into the sea.

One of our galleys was set on fire by a bomb, but strange to say the boat from which it issued shared the like fate. God is merciful! Five of our galleys and as many of the enemy's boats were sunk and utterly wrecked, one of theirs went to the bottom with all sails set. In a word, there was great loss on both sides; our rowers were now insufficient in number to manage the oars, while running against the current, and to fire the cannon. We were compelled to drop anchor (at the stern) and to continue to fight as best we might. The boats had also to be abandoned.

Alemshah Reis, Kara Mustafa, and Kalfat Memi, captains of some of the foundered ships, and Derzi Mustafa Bey, the Serdar of the volunteers, with the remainder of the Egyptian soldiers and 200 carpenters, had landed on the Arabian shore, and as the rowers were Arabs they had been hospitably treated by the Arabs of Nedjd.

The ships (*gurabs*) of the infidel fleet had likewise taken on board the crews of their sunken vessels, and as there were Arabs amongst them, they also had found shelter on the Arabian coast. God is our witness. Even in the war between Khaiveddin Pasha and Andreas Doria no such naval action as this has ever taken place.

When night came, and we were approaching the bay of Ormuz, the wind began to rise. The boats had already cast two *Lenguvurta*, i.e., large anchors, the *Lushtas* were tightly secured, and, towing the conquered *gurabs* along, we neared the shore while the galleys, dragging their anchors, followed. However, we were not allowed to touch the shore, and had to set sail again. During that night we drifted away from the Arabian coast into the open sea, and finally reached the coasts of Djash, in the province of Kerman. This is a long coast, but we could find no harbor, and we roamed about for two days before we came to Kichi Mekran.

As the evening was far advanced we could not land immediately, but had to spend another night at sea. In the morning a dry wind carried off many of the crew, and at last, after unheard-of troubles and difficulties, we approached the harbor of Sheba.

Here we came upon a *Notak*, i.e, a brigantine (pirateship), laden with spoils, and when the watchman sighted us they hailed us. We told them that we were Mussulmans, whereupon their captain came on board our vessel; he kindly supplied us with water, for we had not a drop left, and thus our exhausted soldiers were invigorated. This was on Bairam day, and for us, as we had now got water, a double feast-day. Escorted by the said captain we entered the harbor of Guador. The people there were Beluchistanis and their chief was Malik Djelaleddin, the son of Malik Dinar. The Governor of Guador came on board our ship and assured us of his unalterable devotion to our glorious Padishah. He promised that henceforth, if at any time our fleet should come to Ormuz, he would undertake to send 50 or 60 boats to supply us with provisions, and in every possible way to be of service to us. We wrote a letter to the native Prince Djelaleddin to ask for a pilot, upon which a first-class pilot was sent us, with the assurance that he was thoroughly trustworthy and entirely devoted to the interests of our Padishah.

Reading and Discussion Questions

1. In Admiral Sidi Ali Reis's narrative, in what ways can you discern the growing power of the Portuguese at sea? Support your conclusion with examples.
2. Find and discuss examples of Adiral Reis's piety. Do you think there was a practical impact or did he separate his religious life from his military responsibilities?
3. To what can we attribute the Ottoman victory in the battle of the Sea of Ormuz?

16.4 The *Journal* of Christopher Columbus

Few figures in world history illustrate the clash of civilizations more dramatically than Christopher Columbus (1451-1506), the Italian-born explorer, whose voyage to the Americas ushered in an age of exploration, conquest, trade, and colonization. The story of Columbus's voyages is often portrayed as a catalyst to the expansion of European trade, political might, and the "Columbian Exchange" of biological material that ultimately claimed the life of millions of Native Americans. However, Columbus's first voyage was also characterized by hardened determination, willingness to risk great loss, and an insatiable curiosity. The following except from Columbus' journal is taken from the day his crew first spotted the Caribbean islands. It was not until subsequent voyages that Columbus realized he encountered vast continents and the indigenous populations were not natives of the Indian subcontinent.

Source: E. G. Bourne, ed., *The Northmen, Columbus and Cabot* (New York, 1906).

Wednesday, 10 October. Steered west-southwest and sailed at times ten miles an hour, at others twelve, and at others, seven; day and night made fifty-nine leagues' progress; reckoned to the crew but forty-four. Here the men lost all patience, and complained of the length of the voyage, but the Admiral encouraged them in the best manner he could, representing the profits they were about to acquire, and adding that it was to no purpose to complain, having come so far, they had nothing to do but continue on to the Indies, till with the help of our Lord, they should arrive there.

Thursday, 11 October. Steered west-southwest; and encountered a heavier sea than they had met with before in the whole voyage. Saw pardelas and a green rush near the vessel. The crew of the Pinta saw a cane and a log; they also picked up a stick which appeared to have been carved with an iron tool, a piece of cane, a plant which grows on land, and a board. The crew of the Nina saw other signs of land, and a stalk loaded with rose berries. These signs encouraged them, and they all grew cheerful. Sailed this day till sunset, twenty-seven leagues.

After sunset steered their original course west and sailed twelve miles an hour till two hours after midnight, going ninety miles, which are twenty-two leagues and a half; and as the Pinta was the swiftest sailer, and kept ahead of the Admiral, she discovered land and made the signals which had been ordered. The land was first seen by a sailor called Rodrigo de Triana, although the Admiral at ten o'clock that evening standing on the quarter-deck saw a light, but so small a body that he could not affirm it to be land . . . . At two o'clock in the morning the land was discovered, at two leagues' distance; they took in sail and remained under the square-sail lying to till day, which was Friday, when they found themselves near a small island, one of the Lucayos, called in the Indian language Guanahani. Presently they described people, naked, and the Admiral landed in the boat, which was armed, along with Martin Alonzo Pinzon, and Vincent Yanez his brother, captain of the Nina. The Admiral bore the royal standard, and the two captains each a banner of the Green Cross, which all the ships had carried; this contained the initials of the names of the King and Queen each side of the cross, and a crown over each letter Arrived on shore, they saw trees very green many streams of water, and diverse sorts of fruits. The Admiral called upon the two Captains, and the rest of the crew who landed, as also to Rodrigo de Escovedo notary of the fleet, and Rodrigo Sanchez, of Segovia, to bear witness that he before all others took possession (as in fact he did) of that island for the King and Queen his sovereigns, making the requisite declarations, which are more at large set down here in writing. Numbers of the people of the island straightway collected together. Here follow the precise words of the Admiral: "As I saw that they were very friendly to us, and perceived that they could be much more easily converted to our holy faith by gentle means than by force, I presented them with some red caps, and strings of beads to wear upon the neck, and many other trifles of small value, where-with they were much delighted, and became wonderfully attached to us. Afterwards they came swimming to the boats, bringing parrots, balls of cotton thread, javelins, and many other things which they exchanged for articles we gave them, such as glass beads, and hawk's bells; which trade was carried on with the utmost good will. But they seemed on the whole to me, to be a very poor people. They all go completely naked, even the women, though I saw but one girl.

Reading and Discussion Questions

1. How did Columbus know he was nearing land, and how did his sailors react to the possibility of reaching a destination?
2. What caused Columbus to think the native peoples of the Caribbean were peaceful and good-willed?
3. What in Columbus's journal indicates the key reasons for his voyage across the Atlantic?

Chapter 17

Renaissance, Reformation, and the New Science in Europe

1450–1700

From 1450 to 1700 Europeans experienced significant changes, due in part to developments such as the Renaissance, Reformation, and the progression of science. All aspects of European society changed from politics and religion to the emergence of new forms of economic life. While many aspects of European cultured continued unchanged, others were irrevocably altered due to the rise of capitalism, and the emergence of the modern fiscal-military state.

The Renaissance spanned from the end of the fourteenth century to the end of the sixteenth century and emphasized renewed interest in antiquity. The term "humanism" is often used to describe Renaissance education, which focused on self-fulfillment, philosophy, and the study of previously lost works from antiquity. The Renaissance was both a progenitor and a consequence of new developments in the sciences and the Protestant Reformation.

For centuries, the Catholic Church remained unchallenged in Western Europe, which allowed it to gain a significant amount of power. By the late Middle Ages the use of empirical evidence and reason had replaced faith as an avenue to learning. Men such as Martin Luther (1483-1546) and John Calvin (1509-1564), who disagreed with the theological tenets and practices of the Catholic Church, pressed their challenges and gained a large public following that lead to the Protestant Reformation. Consequently, the Catholic Church lost many of its followers and much of its power and authority over Western Europe.

During the Scientific Revolution, the development of new theories and knowledge of subjects such as physics, medicine, and biology transformed medieval thought and paved the way for future scientists. Knowledge and reason replaced superstitions and speculative theories about the natural world. Early sciences based on description were replaced with sciences based on mathematics. The works of scientists such as Galileo (1564-1642), Newton (1642-1727), and Leeuwenhoek (1632-1723) spurred European intellectuals and political leaders to champion the sciences as a means to further social, political, and economic progress. The Scientific Revolution focused intellectual and popular attention on empirical evidence rather than abstract theories. Techniques such as the scientific method, a system of investigation used to empirically retrieve scientific evidence, promised to scientists a way to question theories without prejudice and bias towards the experiment.

The sources that follow explore the evolving aspects of society during this period. With the Renaissance, Europeans focused on antiquity as well as the revival of subjects and works by previous philosophers and scientists. They reconstructed the old in order to move on to the new. During the Protestant Reformation, western Christianity underwent a schism. Northern Europe mostly embraced Protestantism, while southern Europe mostly remained loyal to Rome. This religious change adjusted the balance of power throughout Europe and the cultural unity formerly provided by Catholicism.

17.1   Marsilio Ficino, "Letter to Paul of Middelburg"

Marsilio Ficino (1433-1499) received a Renaissance education steeped in classical languages and philosophy that fostered a deep appreciation for humanism and antiquity. The first person to translate into Latin all of the works of the ancient Greek philosopher, Plato (423-347 BCE), Ficino also witnessed and wrote about the changes that took place in European art and culture. Ficino wrote a letter to Paul of Middelburg (1436-1534), a Dutch scientist and bishop of Fossombrone, explaining how a "golden age" was upon them. He wrote to Paul not only to demonstrate his knowledge of writing Latin, but also to explain a "breakthrough" in the arts. "Humanism" is a modern term used to describe Renaissance education, whereby the means of achieving self-fulfillment and virtue are stressed through the study of the classical literature, history, and languages. In the source below, Ficino argues that the Renaissance was a rediscovery of antiquity. In addition to mentioning Plato, he also discusses Federigo, Duke of Urbino (1422-1482) also known as Federico da Montefeltro), a condottieri (Italian mercenary) who popularized the importance of Renaissance education.

Source: *The Renaissance,* edited by Alison Brown. (London: Longman, 1999), 69.

Our Plato in *The Republic* transferred the four ages of lead, iron, silver and gold described by poets long ago to types of men, according to their intelligence … So if we are to call any age golden, it must certainly be our age which has produced such a wealth of golden intellects. Evidence of this is provided by the inventions of this age. For this century, like a golden age, has restored to light the liberal arts that were almost extinct: grammar, poetry, oratory, painting, sculpture, architecture, music, the ancient singing of songs to the Orphic lyre, and all this in Florence. The two gifts venerated by the ancients but almost totally forgotten since have been reunited in our age: wisdom with eloquence and prudence with the military art. The most striking example of this is Federigo, Duke of Urbino … and you too, my dear Paul, who seem to have perfected astronomy – and Florence, where Platonic teaching has been recalled from darkness into light. In Germany in our times have been invented the instruments for printing books: and, not to mention the Florentine machine which shows the daily motions of the heavens, tables have been invented which, so to speak, reveal the entire face of the sky for a whole century in one hour.

Reading and Discussion Questions
1. What does Ficino mean when he states that they were living in a "golden age"?
2. How might Ficino's depiction of European culture indicate an acceptance of the idea of human progress and beneficial change?
3. Ficino consistently and positively describes several different subjects that were changing during his life. Judging by his writing, why might he be considered a humanist?

17.2   Laura Cereta to Cardinal Ascanio Maria Sforza

Laura Cereta (1469-1499) was born into a wealthy family and lived in Brescia, Italy, where she received a Renaissance education and became a humanist. Modern scholars identify Cereta as a feminist because her writings stressed the education and training of women beyond what was widely acceptable for her time. She wrote a letter to Cardinal Ascanio Maria Sforza explaining her education, love for reading and writing, and the trials she faced as an aspiring female author, which she published as part of a larger volume in 1488. Cereta sought advice from a respected church official on what to do about the negative treatment she would receive if she were to continue writing. However opinionated her letter may be, it reveals the different educational expectations for men and women during this period.

Source: Cereta, Laura. *Collected Letters of a Renaissance Feminist.* translated and edited by Diana Robin. (Chicago: University of Chicago Press, 1997), pp. 101-2.

To Cardinal Ascanio Maria Sforza

Though I was untrained and scarcely exposed to literature, through my own intelligence and natural talents I was able to acquire the beginnings of an education. While my pleasure in embarking on such a journey of the mind and my love of study were strong at the outset, the weak seeds of my small talent have grown to such a degree that I have written speeches for public occasions, and these I embellished grandly, paintings pictures with words in order to influence people and stimulate their minds. My love of reading caused me to sample different kinds of subjects, and only in study did I feel a sense of inner contentment. And, although I remained ill-equipped for the task despite my passion for learning, I reached a decision that awakened in me a desire for fame and honor, as though my mind were challenging itself to scale new heights....

To get back to my story then, at the end of my childhood, when I was approaching adolescence and was becoming more mature in my understanding of literature, a nobler thought came to me. Accordingly, I devoted myself to other kinds of books, giving myself over to insomniac nights and study, like someone who has a passion for mathematics. If my intellect did not reveal to me things I longed for at that time, at least I had been allowed to cross the fourfold threshold to knowledge....

Now that I have availed myself of the counsel of religious texts, wherein writings about morality combine profundity with unity, I have found satisfaction in literature that would give me not smoke and darkness but something perfect, secure, and lasting. Since men receive an education in literature and other studies, however, so that they may benefit from the example of their forebears, the most elect men of diverse orders have said publicly that education has been wasted on me because it has benefited only me and not others.

I am happy to have the opportunity to express my opinion about something that may exonerate me from criticism. I preferred to please the crowd rather than myself. Stimulated by the desire for fame, I was drawn into a prodigious error in the course of my writing. Namely, the first thing that I wrote was a funeral oration composed to be read over the corpse of a donkey. This one humble oration stirred up the envy of a number of men, who cruelly sharpened the teeth of their spite against me, and as though their mouths had been swords, I was left trembling like a lamb among wolves. Full of their mockery of me, these men did not hesitate to dishonor me with their spittle, while I was hard-pressed by my wounds.

Reading and Discussion Questions

1. Why does Cereta stress the importance of receiving an education? Do you think it was for self-fulfillment or merely because it was socially acceptable?
2. Why might "elect men" have thought that an education was wasted on Cereta?
3. Cereta is writing to a Cardinal of the Catholic Church, seeking his advice. Why does she give him a brief biography of her life? Does it help her gain acceptance and understanding through the eyes of the church?

17.3 John Calvin, Prayer from *Commentary on Hosea*

John Calvin (1509-1564) was the principle leader of the Protestant Reformation in the non-German speaking areas of Western Europe, particularly France, Switzerland, and the Low Countries. While much of his influence depended upon his role as a pastor in Geneva (1541-1564), Calvin also authored several works, in which he translated and provided commentary on several books of the Bible. Among his works is the *Commentary on Hosea,* which is divided into chapters, lectures, and prayers. Below are three of his prayers from *Commentary on Hosea,* each offering summations of his interpretations of key portions of the book. Calvin argues in his *Commentary* that the people of Israel chose to worship other gods and idols, and God chose Hosea to lead the people toward the path of redemption. There were several key doctrinal differences between Calvin and Roman Catholicism, particularly election, faith as a gift from God rather than a human means of meriting grace and salvation, and the continued perseverance of all believers through a process of sanctification. In chapter 1, prayer lecture 3, Calvin mentions the Babylonian exile (586-538 BCE), which was the forced exile of Jews to Babylon (present day Iraq) by King Nebuchadnezzar II (634-562 BCE), the king of Babylon.

Source: Calvin, John. *Commentary on Hosea.* Translated by John Owen (Grand Rapids, Michigan: Christian Classics Ethereal Library, 1816).

Grant, Almighty God, that as we were from our beginning lost, when thou wert pleased to extend to us thy hand, and to restore us to salvation for the sake of thy Son; and that as we continue even daily to run headlong to our own ruin, — O grant that we may not, by sinning so often, so provoke at length thy displeasure as to cause thee to take away from us the mercy which thou hast hitherto exercised towards us, and through which thou hast adopted us: but by thy Spirit destroy the wickedness of our heart, and restore us to a sound mind, that we may ever cleave to thee with a true and sincere heart, that being fortified by thy defence [defense], we may continue safe even amidst all kinds of danger, until at length thou gatherest [gathers] us into that blessed rest, which has been prepared for us in heaven by our Lord Jesus Christ. Amen.

Grant, Almighty God, that as we have not only been redeemed from Babylonian exile, but have also emerged from hell itself; for when we were the children of wrath thou didst freely adopt us, and when we were aliens, thou didst in thine [your] infinite goodness open to us the gate of thy kingdom, that we might be made thy heirs through the Son, O grant that we may walk circumspectly before thee, and submit ourselves wholly to thee and to thy Christ, and not feign to be his members, but really prove ourselves to be his body, and to be so governed by his Spirit, that thou mayest [may] at last gather us together into thy celestial kingdom, to which thou daily invitest [invite] us by the same Christ our Lord. Amen.

Grant, Almighty God, that as thou hast not only of late adopted us as thy children, but before we were born, and as thou hast been pleased to sign us, as soon as we came forth from our mother's womb, with the symbol of that holy redemption, which has been obtained for us by the blood of thy only begotten Son, though we have by our ingratitude renounced so great a benefit, — O grant, that being mindful of our defection and unfaithfulness, of which eve are all guilty, and for which thou hast justly rejected us, we may now with true humility and obedience of faith embrace the grace of thy gospel now again offered to us, by which thou reconciles thyself to us; and grant that we may steadfastly persevere in pure faith, so as never to turn aside from the true obedience of faith, but to advance more and more in the knowledge of thy mercy, that having strong and deep roots, and being firmly grounded in the confidence of sure faith, we may never fall away from the true worship of thee, until thou at length receives us in to that eternal kingdom, which has been procured for us by the blood of thy only Son. Amen.

Reading and Discussion Questions

1. Judging by the prayers, why does Calvin believe it is God's responsibility to purify a person's heart?
2. Why would the Babylonian exile of the ancient Israelites be an important metaphor for Calvin to use in describing the Christian's life on earth?
3. Commentators often describe Calvin's view of humanity as pessimistic. What in the prayers offers Calvin

hope about the ability of human beings to do good?

4.   How might the prayers illustrate the doctrinal tensions between Roman Catholicism and Calvin's form of Protestantism?

17.4   Galileo Galilei. *Dialogue Concerning the Two Chief World Systems*

Galileo Galilei (1564-1642) is most well-known for his scientific arguments on the theory of motion, his discoveries in astronomy, and his improvements of the telescope. Due to his influence upon early scientific thought, historians and scientists often refer to him as "the Father of Modern Science." To promote his concerns about the development of the sciences, he wrote *Dialogue Concerning the Two Chief World Systems* in 1632. The book's story occurs over four days in which three philosophers named Salvati, Sagredo, and Simplicio argue about the accuracy of the Ptolemaic theory , the belief that the universe revolves around the earth, and the Copernican theory, the theory that the universe revolves around the sun. The Ptolemaic theory originated in the ancient world and continued to hold sway until the Middle Ages, when new theories surfaced to explain its aberrations and inconsistencies. With advances in astronomy made possible by improvements made to the telescope, the Copernican theory gained increased credibility as it more accurately predicted astronomical occurrences. Salvati, who is supposed to represent Galileo, argues for the diurnal motion of the earth (the daily motion of objects across the sky due to the earth's rotation) and for the Copernican scientific theory. Galileo wrote *Dialogue Concerning the Two Chief World Systems* because he believed that Copernicus's theories had been wrongfully accused as heretical by the Catholic Church, and he wished to contribute his own thoughts on the solar system.

Source: Galilei, Galileo. *Dialogue Concerning the Two Chief World Systems.* translated by Stillman Drake (Berkeley: University of California Press, 1953) 71-2.

SALV. It is obvious, then, that motion which is common to many moving things is idle and inconsequential to the relation of these movables among themselves, nothing being changed among them, and that it is operative only in the relation that they have with other bodies lacking that motion, among which their location is changed. Now, having divided the universe into two parts, one of which in necessarily movable and the other motionless, it is the same thing to make the earth alone move, and to move all the rest of the universe, so far as concerns any result which may depend upon such movement. For the action of such movement is only in the relation between celestial bodies and the earth, which relation alone is changed. Now if precisely the same effect follows whether the earth is made to move and the rest of the universe lay still, or the earth alone remains fixed while the whole universe shares one motion, who is going to believe that nature (which by general agreement does not act by means of many things when it can do so by means of few) has chosen to make an immense number of extremely large bodies move with inconceivable velocities, to achieve what could have been done by a moderate movement of one single body around its own center?

    . . .

    SALV. Every one of these variations which you recite to me is nothing except in relation to the earth. To see that this is true, remove the earth; nothing remains in the universe of rising and setting of the sun and moon, nor of horizons and meridians, nor day and night, and in a word from this movement there will never originate any changes in the moon or sun or any stars you please, fixed or moving. All these changes are in relation to the earth, all of them meaning nothing except that the sun shows itself now over China, then to Persia, afterward to Egypt, to Greece, to France, to Spain, to America, etc. And the same holds for the moon and the rest of the heavenly bodies, this effect taking place in exactly the same way if, without embroiling the biggest part of the universe, the terrestrial globe is made to revolve upon itself.

And let us redouble the difficulty with another very great one, which is this. If this great motion is attributed to the heavens, it has to be made in the opposite direction from the specific motion of all the planetary orbs, of which each one is incontrovertibly has its own motion from west to east, this being very gentile and moderate, and must then be made to rush the other way; that is, from east to west, with this very rapid diurnal motion. Whereas by making the earth itself move, the contrariety of motions is removed, and the single motion from west east accommodates all the observations and satisfies them all completely.

Reading and Discussion Questions

1. Based on your reading of this source, why did the church condemn Copernicus's and Galileo's works as heretical?
2. How does Galileo defend the Copernican theory?
3. How does he defend the theory of diurnal motion of the Earth?
4. How do his arguments show that descriptive science from earlier times was being replaced by new methods, based on analytical knowledge and mathematics?

17.5   Antony van Leeuwenhoek's "Animalcules"

Antony van Leeuwenhoek (1632-1723) was a Dutch scientist who made improvements to the microscope and was the first person to see living bacteria. Leeuwenhoek made over five hundred microscopic lenses throughout the course his lifetime. In 1683, he wrote a letter to the Royal Society of London for Improving Natural Knowledge (the Royal Society) stating that he had discovered living animalcules (bacteria) in the plaque between his teeth. Leeuwenhoek's discovery led him to find many other types of bacteria and lead modern scientists to refer to him as "The Father of Microbiology."

Source: Leeuwenhoek, Antony van. "Letter 39: 17 September, 1683." In *Antony van Leeuwenhoek and His "Little Animals,"* translated and edited by Clifford Dobell (New York: Dover Publications, Inc., 1960), 241-42.

While I was talking to an old man (who leads a sober life, and never drinks brandy or tobacco, and very seldom any wine), my eye fell upon his teeth, which were all coated over; so I asked him when he had last cleaned his mouth? And I got for answer that he'd never washed his mouth in all his life. So I took some spittle out of his mouth and examined it; but I could find in it nought but what I had found in my own and other people's. I also took some of the matter that was lodged between and against his teeth, and mixing it with his own spit, and also with fair water (in which there was no animalcules), I found an unbelievably great company of living animalcules, a-swimming more nimbly than any I had ever seen up to this time.

. . .

Moreover, the other animalcules were in such enormous numbers, that all the water (notwithstanding only a very little of the matter taken from between the teeth was mingled with it) seemed to be alive. The long particles too, as before described, were also in great plenty.

I have also taken the spittle, and the white matter that was lodged upon and betwixt the teeth, from an old man who makes a practice of drinking brandy every morning, and wine and tobacco in the afternoon; wondering whether the animalcules, with such continual boozing, could even remain alive. I judged that this man, because his teeth were so uncommon foul, never washed his mouth. So I asked him, and got for answer: "Never in my life with water, but it gets a good swill with wine or brandy every day." Yet I couldn't find anything beyond the ordinary in his spittle. I also mixed his spit with the stuff that coated his front teeth, but could make out nothing in it save very few of the least sort of living animalcules hereinbefore described time and again. But in the stuff I had hauled out from between his front teeth (for the old chap hadn't a back tooth in his head), I made out many more little animalcules, comprising two of the littlest sort.

Reading and Discussion Questions

1. What might have prompted Leeuwenhoek to test animalcules in several different solutions, and use samples from multiple people, including himself?
2. Judging from the way Leeuwenhoek tested his samples, how did he follow the scientific method?
3. How has Leeuwenhoek's discovery impacted science today?

17.6   Galileo's Views of the Moon

The first telescopic drawings of the Moon were made by Galileo in 1610. Using simple geometry, he showed the Moon to be a solid body, pitted with craters and dissected by mountains. This led him to later argue that the Earth was not unique.

Source: Courtesy of the Library of Congress

Reading and Discussion Questions

1. Galileo calculated the height of the lunar mountains by measuring the height cast by their shadows. How is this evidence of the New Science in action?

2. Why would Galileo's lunar discoveries contribute to his eventual disagreement with Aristotle's theory of an immutable universe?

3. Galileo's lunar discoveries were aided by the the telescope, an innovation in which he played a large part. How is the telescope a prime example of the origins-innovations-adaptations model that forms the core approach of *Patterns of World History*?

17.7   Peter the Great, "Correspondence with Alexis, 1715"

Peter the Great, Czar of Russia (r. 1672-1725) established greater links between his country and Western Europe, and introduced important reforms in the military and government with the goal of making Russia a European power. Borrowing from Western European shipbuilding techniques, Peter oversaw the construction of the first Russian naval fleet. He also made significant changes in the army, for example, putting in place programs to better train and organize the Russian nobles who served as government and military officers. Peter's ambitions for Russian territorial expansion led to numerous wars with Sweden, Poland, and the Ottoman Empire. His son Alexis, born in 1690, was his heir to the throne, but around 1715 Peter changed the terms of this succession so it passed over Alexis to Peter's grandson (Alexis's son). Alexis attempted to flee Russia in 1716, eventually returned, but his father, who believed he was plotting to assassinate him, ordered Alexis's arrest. Alexis died in 1718 as a result of his imprisonment and torture. When Peter died in 1725, a succession crisis and period of instability followed that finally ended with when Catherine the Great (r. 1729-1796), Peter's second wife, came to the throne.

Source: Polnoe sobranie zakonov rossikoi imperii, Vol. VI, No. 11, 1715

October 11, 1715

Declaration to My Son,

You cannot be ignorant of what is known to all the world, to what degree our people groaned under the oppression of the Swedes before the beginning of the present war.

By the usurpation of so many maritime places so necessary to our state. they had cut us off from all commerce with the rest of the world, and we saw with regret that besides they had cast a thick veil before the eyes of the clear-sighted. You know what it has cost us in the beginning of this war (in which God alone has led us, as it were, by the hand. and still guides us) to make ourselves experienced in the art of war, and to put a stop to those advantages which our implacable enemies obtained over us.

We submitted to this with a resignation to the will of God, making no doubt but it was he who put us to that trial, till he might lead us into the right way, and we might render ourselves worthy to experience, that the same enemy who at first made others tremble, now in his turn trembles before us, perhaps in a much greater degree. These are the fruits which, next to the assistance of God, we owe to our own toil and to the labor of our faithful and affectionate children, our Russian subjects.

But at the time that I am viewing the prosperity which God has heaped on our native country, if I cast an eye upon the posterity that is to succeed me, my heart is much more penetrated with grief on account of what is to happen, then I rejoice at those blessings that are past, seeing that you, my son, reject all means of making yourself capable of well-governing after me. I say your incapacity is voluntary, because you cannot excuse yourself with want of natural parts and strength of body, as if God had not given you a sufficient share of either: and though your constitution is none of the strongest, yet it cannot be said that it is altogether weak.

But you even will not so much as hear warlike exercises mentioned; though it is by them that we broke through that obscurity in which we were involved, and that we made ourselves known to nations, whose esteem we share at present. I do not exhort you to make war without lawful reasons: I only desire you to apply yourself to learn the art of it: for it is impossible well to govern without knowing the rules and discipline of it, was it for no other end than for the defense of the country.

I could place before your eyes many instances of what I am proposing to you. I will only mention to you the Greeks, with whom we are united by the same profession of faith. What occasioned their decay but that they neglected arms? Idleness and repose weakened them, made them submit to tyrants, and brought them to that slavery to which they are now so long since reduced. You mistake, if you think it is enough for a prince to have good generals to act under his order. Everyone looks upon the head; they study his inclinations and conform themselves to them: all the world owns this. My brother during his reign loved magnificence in dress, and great equipages of horses. The nation was not much inclined that way, but the prince's delight soon became that of his subjects. For they are inclined to imitate him in liking a thing as well as disliking it.

If the people so easily break themselves of things which only regard pleasure, will they not forget in time, or will they not more easily give over the practice of arms, the exercise of which is the more painful to them, the less they are kept to it?

You have no inclination to learn war. you do not apply yourself to it, and consequently you will never learn it: And how then can you command others, and judge of the reward which those deserve who do their duty. or punish others who fail of it? You will do nothing, nor judge of anything but by the eyes and help of others. like a young bird that holds up his bill to be fed.

You say that the weak state of your health will not permit you to undergo the fatigues of war: This is an excuse which is no better than the rest. I desire no fatigues, but only inclination, which even sickness itself cannot hinder. Ask those who remember the time of my brother. He was of a constitution weaker by far than yours. He was not able to manage a horse of the least mettle, not could he hardly mount it: Yet he loved horses. hence it came, that there never was, nor perhaps is there actually now in the nation a finer stable than his was.

By this you see that good success does not always depend on pain, but on the will.

If you think there are some, whose affairs do not fail of success, though they do not go to war themselves; it is true: But if they do not go themselves, yet they have an inclination for it, and understand it.

For instance, the late King of France did not always take the field in person; but it is known to what degree he loved war, and what glorious exploits he performed in it, which made his campaigns to be called the theatre and school of the world. His inclinations were not confined solely to military affairs, he also loved mechanics, manufactures and other establishments, which rendered his kingdom more flourishing than any other whatsoever.

After having made to you all those remonstrances, I return to my former subject which regards you.

I am a man and consequently I must die. To whom shall I leave after me to finish what by the grace of God I have begun, and to preserve what I have partly recovered? To a man, who like the slothful servant hides his talent in the earth, that is to say, who neglects making the best of what God has entrusted to him?

Remember your obstinacy and ill-nature, how often I reproached you with it, and even chastised you for it, and for how many years I almost have not spoke to you; but all this has availed nothing, has effected nothing. It was but losing my time: it was striking the air. You do not make the least endeavors. and all your pleasure seems to consist in staying idle and lazy at home: Things of which you ought to be ashamed (forasmuch as they make you miserable) seem to make up your dearest delight, nor do you foresee the dangerous consequences of it for yourself and for the whole state. St. Paul has left us a great truth when he wrote: If a man know not how to rule his own house, how shall he take of the church of God?

After having considered all those great inconveniences and reflected upon them, and seeing I cannot bring you to good by any inducement, I have thought fit to give you in writing this act of my last will, with this resolution however to wait still a little longer before I put it in execution to see if you will mend. If not, I will have you to know that I will deprive you of the succession, as one may cut off a useless member.

Do not fancy, that, because I have no other child but you, I only write this to terrify you. I will certainly put it in execution, if it please God; for whereas I do not spare my own life for my country and the welfare of my people, why should I spare you who do not render yourself worthy of either? I would rather choose to transmit them to a worthy stranger, than to my own unworthy son.

Peter

Reading and Discussion Questions

1. What were Peter the Great's views on war? What beliefs or ideas informed his views?
2. How did Peter the Great hope to increase the power and prestige of Russia?

Chapter 18

New Patterns in New Worlds: Colonialism and Indigenous Responses in the Americas

1500–1800

The economic impetus to gain control of the lucrative trade with Asia spurred Europeans to venture out into the Atlantic. The resulting explorations helped to create networks that spanned the globe. And what would become known as the Colombian Exchange would alter the course of natural evolution.

The Spanish—with a combination of advanced technology, ruthless diplomacy, and luck—conquered the two largest empires in the New World. Their conquest of the Aztecs and the Incas greatly enriched Spain and injected large amounts of silver into the global economy. The Portuguese would also amass an equally large colonial empire by conquering many disparate tribes and establishing sugar plantations and trading posts.

Less successfully, the English, Dutch, and French also sought to establish colonial empires in the sixteenth century. Colonies were often established to escape political persecution at home but also satisfy the demand for more land. After a halting start, trade in furs, tobacco, and other commodities led to rapid expansion and the displacement of the land's original occupants.

By the seventeenth century, most major European powers had colonial claims in the New World. The native peoples who had developed complex agriculture, religion, and societies were decimated by cross currents of the ensuing ecological exchange. The benefits of the ecological exchange that took place are debated to this day. The cataclysms that began as a search for alternate trade routes would eventually lead European kingdoms to establish a permanent presence across the globe.

18.1 Aztecs Recount the Beginning of the War with the Conquistadors

The Aztecs depended heavily upon religious devotion and ritual to maintain control over the diverse tribes of their empire. Aspects of their religious devotion involved considerable violence, which generated fear as much as piety. While Spanish conquistadors disliked much in Aztec culture, Aztec religion was the element they found most repugnant. When the opportunity arose, the conquistadors took action against religious forms they deemed demonic, and often murdered priests and those in authority. For their part, the Aztecs' religious practices often included violence levied against captured enemies and weaker tribes.

Source: From Miguel Leon Portilla, ed., The Broken Spears: *The Aztec Account of the Conquest of Mexico* (Boston: Beacon Press, 1962).

Massacre in the Main Temple

During this time, the people asked Motecuhzoma [Moctezuma or Montezuma] how they should celebrate their god's fiesta. He said: "Dress him in all his finery, in all his sacred ornaments."

During this same time, The Sun commanded that Motecuhzoma and Itzcohuatzin, the military chief of Tlatelolco, be made prisoners. The Spaniards hanged a chief from Acolhuacan named Nezahualquentzin. They also murdered the king of Nauhtla, Cohualpopocatzin, by wounding him with arrows and then burning him alive.

For this reason, our warriors were on guard at the Eagle Gate. The sentries from Tenochtitlán stood at one side of the gate, and the sentries from Tlatelolco at the other. But messengers came to tell them to dress the figure of Huitzilopochtli. They left their posts and went to dress him in his sacred finery: his ornaments and his paper clothing.

When this had been done, the celebrants began to sing their songs. That is how they celebrated the first day of the fiesta. On the second day they began to sing again, but without warning they were all put to death. The dancers and singers were completely unarmed. They brought only their embroidered cloaks, their turquoises, their lip plugs, their necklaces, their clusters of heron feathers, their trinkets made of deer hooves. Those who played the drums, the old men, had brought their gourds of snuff and their timbrels.

The Spaniards attacked the musicians first, slashing at their hands and faces until they had killed all of them. The singers-and even the spectators- were also killed. This slaughter in the Sacred Patio went on for three hours. Then the Spaniards burst into the rooms of the temple to kill the others: those who were carrying water, or bringing fodder for the horses, or grinding meal, or sweeping, or standing watch over this work.

The king Motecuhzoma, who was accompanied by Itzcohuatzin and by those who had brought food for the Spaniards, protested: "Our lords, that is enough! What are you doing? These people are not carrying shields or macanas. Our lords, they are completely unarmed!"

The Sun had treacherously murdered our people on the twentieth day after the captain left for the coast. We allowed the Captain to return to the city in peace. But on the following day we attacked him with all our might, and that was the beginning of the war.

Reading and Discussion Questions

1. According to the Aztecs, why did the Spanish attack their temple?
2. Why would the Spanish launch their attack first upon the unarmed performers in the Aztec religious ritual rather than the political leaders?
3. Why did the Aztec king supposedly not do more to prevent the Spanish from attacking the temple other than placing a few guards to protect it?

18.2 Letter from Hernando de Soto

Hernando de Soto (c. 1497–1542) was a Spanish conquistador from the Spanish region of Extremadura. In 1539 he set out with roughly 600 men, plus horses, chattel, and equipment. The trip would last beyond De Soto's death in 1542. In the course of the three years, the expedition would traverse much of what would become the southeastern United States. De Soto's relationship with the natives was cordial at best and often times fell far short of that. He was not above using torture and violence to achieve his ends.

Source: *Narratives of the Career of Hernando de Soto in the Conquest of Floria, as told by a Knight of Elvas and in a Relation by Luys Hernandez de Biedma, factor of the Expedition.* Edited with an Introduction by Edward Gaylord Bourne (New York: Allerton Book Co, 1904), 159-164.

VERY NOBLE GENTLEMEN:

Being in a new country, not very distant indeed from that where you are, still with some sea between, a thousand years appear to me to have gone by since anything has been heard from you; and although I left some letters written at Havana, to go off in three ways, it is indeed long since I have received one. However, since opportunity offers by which I may send an account of what it is always my duty to give, I will relate what passes, and I believe will be welcome to persons I know favourably, and are earnest for my success.

I took my departure from Havana with all my armament on Sunday, the XVIIIth of May, although I wrote that I should leave on the XXVth of the month. I anticipated the day, not to lose a favourable wind, which changed, nevertheless, for calms, upon our getting into the Gulf; still these were not so continuous as to prevent our casting anchor on this coast, as we did at the end of eight days, which was on Sunday, the festival of Espiritu Santo.

Having fallen four or five leagues below the port, without any one of my pilots being able to tell where we were, it became necessary that I should go in the brigantines and look for it. In doing so, and in entering the mouth of the port, we were detained three days; and likewise because we had no knowledge of the passage a bay that runs up a dozen leagues or more from the sea we were so long delayed that I was obliged to send my Lieutenant-General, Vasco Porcallo de Figueroa, in the brigantines, to take possession of a town at the end of the bay. I ordered all the men and horses to be landed on a beach, whence, with great difficulty, we went on Trinity Sunday to join Vasco Porcallo. The Indians of the coast, because of some fears of us, have abandoned all the country, so that for thirty leagues not a man of them has halted.

At my arrival here I received news of there being a Christian in the possession of a Cacique, and I sent Baltazar de Gallegos, with XL men of the horse, and as many of the foot, to endeavour to get him. He found the man a day's journey from this place, with eight or ten Indians, whom he brought into my power. We rejoiced no little over him, for he speaks the language; and although he had forgotten his own, it directly returned to him. His name is Juan Ortiz, an hidalgo, native of Sevilla.

In consequence of this occurrence, I went myself for the Cacique, and came back with him in peace. I then sent Baltazar de Gallegos, with eighty lancers, and a hundred foot-soldiers, to enter the country. He has found fields of maize, beans, and pumpkins, with other fruits, and provision in such quantity as would suffice to subsist a very large army without its knowing a want. Having been allowed, without interruption, to reach the town of a **cacique** named Urripacoxit, master of the one we are in, also of many other towns, some Indians were sent to him to treat for peace. This, he writes, having been accomplished, the Cacique failed to keep certain promises, whereupon he seized about 18 persons, among whom are some of the principal men; for in this way, it appears to him, he can best secure a performance. Among those he detains are some old men of authority, as great as can be among such people, who have information of the country farther on. They say that three days' journey from where they are, going by some towns and huts, all well inhabited, and having many maize-fields, is a large town called Acuera, where with much convenience we might winter; and that afterwards, farther on, at the distance of two days' journey, there is another town, called Ocale. It is so large, and they so extol it, that I dare not repeat all that is said. There is to be found in it a great plenty of all the things mentioned; and fowls, a multitude of turkeys, kept in pens, and herds of tame deer that are tended. What this means I do not understand, unless it be the cattle, of which we brought the knowledge with us. They say there are many trades among that people, and much intercourse, an abundance of gold and silver, and many pearls. May it please God that this may be

---

cacique: an Indian chief

so; for of what these Indians say I believe nothing but what I see, and must well see; although they know, and have it for a saying, that if they lie to me it will cost them their lives. This interpreter puts a new life into us, in affording the means of our understanding these people, for without him

I know not what would become of us. Glory be to God, who by His goodness has directed all, so that it appears as if He had taken this enterprise in His especial keeping, that it may be for His service, as I have supplicated, and do dedicate it to Him.

I sent eighty soldiers by sea in boats, and my General by land with 40 horsemen, to fall upon a throng of some thousand Indians, or more, whom Juan de Anasco had discovered. The General got back last night, and states that they fled from him; and although he pursued them, they could not be overtaken, for the many obstructions in the way. On our coming together we will march to join Baltazar de Gallegos, that we may go thence to pass the winter at the Ocale, where, if what is said to be true, we shall have nothing to desire. Heaven be pleased that something may come of this that shall be for the service of our Divine Master, and whereby I may be enabled to serve Your Worships, and each of you, as I desire, and is your due.

Notwithstanding my continual occupation here, I am not forgetful of the love I owe to objects at a distance; and since I may not be there in person, I believe that where you, Gentlemen, are, there is little in which my presence can be necessary. This duty weighs upon me more than every other, and for the attentions you will bestow, as befits your goodness, I shall be under great obligations. I enjoin it upon you, to make the utmost exertions to maintain the repose and well-being of the public, with the proper administration of justice, always reposing in the Licentiate, that every thing may be so done in accordance with law, that God and the King may be served, myself gratified, and every one be content and pleased with the performance of his trust, in such a manner as you, Gentlemen, have ever considered for my honor, not less than your own, although I still feel that I have the weight thereof, and bear the responsibility.

As respects the bastion which I left begun, if laboring on it have been neglected, or perhaps discontinued, with the idea that the fabric is not now needed, you, Gentlemen, will favor me by having it finished, since every day brings change ; and although no occasion should arise for its employment, the erection is provident for the well-being and safety of the town: an act that will yield me increased satisfaction, through your very noble personages.

That our Lord may guard and increase your prosperity is my wish and your deserving.

In this town and Port of Espiritu Santo, in the Province of Florida, July the IX., in the year 1539.

The servant of you, Gentlemen,

EL ADELANTADO DON HERNANDO DE SOTO.

Reading and Discussion Questions

1. How does de Soto describe the land? In what does he appear to be most interested?
2. Discuss the significance of the natives leaving the county upon de Soto's arrival.
3. How would you describe de Soto's diplomatic relations with the native peoples he meets? Use specific examples.

18.3 Coronado's Report to Viceroy Mendoza

Within a few years of Christopher Columbus's return to Spain from his first trip to the Americas, the Spanish quickly explored the new lands they had discovered. For three generations, Spanish explorers scoured river valleys, jungles, and mountain ranges from the lower plains of North America to the highlands of South America. They sought treasure, potential trading partners, and natives to proselytize. In many respects, they successfully accomplished all three goals, but not to the extent Spanish leaders and investors hoped. While episodes of intense conflict and battles occurred during the exploration period, contact between Europeans and Native Americans varied between violence and peaceful trade depending upon the tribe and the explorers. Francisco Vasquez de Coronado (1510–1554), who traveled through southwestern North America between 1540 and 1542 searching for the fabled "cities of gold," effectively illustrates the conquistador outlook. His depiction of encounters with local tribes illustrates a common pattern of violence, but also shows how Europeans often remained dependent upon natives for common necessities.

Coronado's description of Native American society and military tactics in southwestern North America shows how Native Americans equaled the might of the Spanish, especially when the Spanish failed to gain the assistance of native allies. Yet, their centralized states and economies could not repel Europeans and their Indian allies, who were anxious to overthrow their imperial masters. Their inability to resist European encroachments caused some Europeans to view Native Americans as backward, or at least primitive. Consequently, some Europeans believed the New World was a wilderness, if not an Edenic paradise filled with vast resources and friendly natives.

Source: Winship, George Parker. *The Journey of Coronado, 1540-1542, from the City of Mexico to the Grand Canyon of the Colorado and the Buffalo Plains of Texas, Kansas and Nebraska, as Told by Himself and His Followers* (Allerton Book Company, 1922), 167-169.

Coronado's Report to Viceroy Mendoza Sent from Cibola, August 3, 1540

. . . Ferrando Alvarado came back to tell me that some Indians had met him peaceably, & that two of them were with the army-master waiting for me. I went to them forthwith and gave them some paternosters and some little cloaks, telling them to return to their city and say to the people there that they could stay quietly in their houses and that they need not fear. After this I ordered the army-master to go and see if there were any bad passages which the Indians might be able to defend, and to seize and hold any such until the next day, when I would come up. He went, and found a very bad place in our way where we might have received much harm. He immediately established himself there with the force which he was conducting. The Indians came that very night to occupy that place so as to defend it, and finding it taken, they assaulted our men. According to what I have been told, they attacked like valiant men, although in the end they had to retreat in flight, because the army-master was on the watch and kept his men in good order. The Indians sounded a little trumpet as a sign of retreat, and did not do any injury to the Spaniards. The army-master sent me notice of this the same night, so that on the next day I started with as good order as I could, for we were in such great need of food that I thought we should all die of hunger if we continued to be without provisions for another day, especially the Indians, since altogether we did not have two bushels of corn, and so I was obliged to hasten forward without delay. The Indians lighted their fires from point to point, and these were answered from a distance with as good understanding as we could have shown. Thus notice was given concerning how we went and where we had arrived.

As soon as I came within sight of this city, I sent the army-master, Don Garcia Lopez, Friar Daniel and Friar Luis, and Ferrando Vermizzo, with some horsemen, a little way ahead, so that they might find the Indians and tell them that we were not coming to do them any harm, but to defend them in the name of our lord the Emperor. The summons, in the form which His Majesty commanded in his instructions, was made intelligible to the people of the country by an interpreter. But they, being a proud people, were little affected, because it seemed to them that we were few in number, and that they would not have any difficulty in conquering us. They pierced the gown of Friar Luis with an arrow, which, blessed be God, did him no harm. Meanwhile I arrived with all the rest of the horse and the footmen, and found a large body of the Indians on the plain, who began to shoot with their arrows. In obedience to the orders of Your Lordship and of the marquis, I did not wish my company, who were begging me for permission, to attack them, telling them that they ought not to offend them, and that what the enemy was doing was nothing, and that so few people ought not to be insulted. On the other hand, when the Indians saw that we did not move, they took greater courage, and grew so bold that they came up almost to the heels of our horses to shoot their arrows. On this account I saw that it was no longer time to hesitate, and as the priests approved the action, I charged them. There was little to do, because they suddenly took to flight, part running toward the city, which was near and well fortified, and others toward the plain, wherever chance led them. Some Indians were killed, and others might have been slain if I could have allowed them to be pursued. But I saw that there would be little advantage in this, because the Indians who were outside were few, and those who had retired to the city were numerous, besides many who had remained there in the first place.

Reading and Discussion Questions

1. On what basis did the Spaniards hope to achieve peaceful relations with the Indians? Why did such attempts prove unsuccessful in the long term?
2. What kinds of characteristics did the Spaniards appreciate about the Indians? What did they admire most?
3. In what ways were the Indians superior to the Spanish explorers? How did the native tribes use this to their advantage?

18.4 Increase Mather on King Philip's Death

When Plymouth, Massachusetts was established in 1620, it became the third permanent colony to be established in North America. As the settlements and populations along the coast grew, conflict between settlers and natives increased in frequency and intensity. These conflicts finally expressed themselves in what became known as King Philip's War. King Philip, sachem, or leader, of the Wampanoag tribe, led the fight against the Puritan settlers. The war raged from the summer of 1675 until King Phillip's death in the summer of 1676. The description of King Phillip's death is from Increase Mather (1639-1723), an influential Puritan preacher.

Source: From Increase Mather, *A Brief History of the War with the Indians of New England (1676): An Online Electronic Text Edition.* Edited by Paul Royster. Lincoln, Nebraska: University of Nebraska-Lincoln Faculty Publications: accessed on November 8, 2011 at: http://digitalcommons.unl.edu/libraryscience/31.

And in that very place where he first contrived and began his mischief, was he taken and destroyed, and there was he (like as Agag was hewed in pieces before the Lord) cut into four quarters, and is now hanged up as a monument of revenging Justice, his head being cut off and carried away to Plymouth, his Hands were brought to *Boston. So let all thine Enemies perish, O Lord!* When Philip thus slain, five of his men were killed with him, one of which was his chief Captains son, being (as the Indians testify) that very Indian, who shot the first gun at the English, when the War began. So that we may hope that the War in those parts will die with Philip.

Reading and Discussion Questions

1. What are the similarities between de Soto's and Mather's attitude toward the native people's? What are the differences if any?
2. What is the significance of Mather's use of Old Testament imagery to describe the King Phillip and the Indians?
3. What seem to be Mather's hopes for the colony? Do these seem to include a co-existence with the native cultures?

18.5 Reasons for Colonizing North America

Richard Hakluyt the Elder (c. 1553–1616) was one of the foremost geographers in early Elizabethan England. A contemporary of Sir Humphrey Gilbert and Sir Walter Raleigh, Hakluyt encouraged Queen Elizabeth I and her courtiers to support colonization efforts in the New World. England came late to the Western hemisphere, long after the French and a full century after the Spanish. Considered the weakest economy in Western Europe, much of England's economy depended upon the continental wool trade. When that was closed to English merchants, they sought support from the English crown for trade initiatives throughout the northern hemisphere, including around the Baltic Sea and Russia. Hakluyt proposed to shift English attention to North America, where he insisted the most lucrative trade would be found. His writings, which portrayed North America as a new Garden of Eden, encouraged hundreds of people to migrate. They soon discovered the New World would not welcome them with the warm climate, friendly natives, and bountiful harvests that Hakluyt promised. Nonetheless, the Edenic and agrarian imagery he used provided a rich tapestry for generations of British North Americans. Below are excerpts from 31 reasons Hakluyt gave for colonizing North America.

Source: Richard Hakluyt, "Inducements to the Liking of the Voyage Intended towards Virginia" (1585).

11. In the voyage we are not to cross the burnt zone, nor to pass through frozen seas encumbered with ice and fogs, but in temperate climate at all times of the year; and it requireth not, as the East Indies voyage doth, the taking in of water in divers places, by reason that it is to be sailed in five or six weeks; and by the shortness the merchant may yearly make two returns (a factory once being erected there), a matter in trade of great moment. . . .

13. By this ordinary trade we may annoy the enemies to Ireland and succour the Queen's Majesty's friends there, and in time we may from Virginia yield them whatsoever commodity, they now receive from the Spaniard; and so the Spaniards shall want the ordinary victual that heretofore they received yearly from thence, and so they shall not continue trade, nor fall so aptly in practice against this government as now by their trade thither they may. . . .

15. The great plenty of' buff hides and of many other sundry kinds of hides their now presently to be had, the tirade of whale and seal fishing and of divers other fishing in the great rivers, great hays, and seas there, shall presently defray the charge in good part or in all of the first enterprise, and so we shall be in better case than our men were in Russia, where many years were spent and great sums of it sums of money consumed before gain was found.

16. The great broad rivers of that main that we are to enter into, so many leagues navigable or portable into the mainland, lying so long a tract with so excellent and so fertile a soil on both sides, do seem to promise all things that the life of man doth require and whatsoever men may wish may wish that are to plant upon the same or to traffic in the same. . . .

20. Where there be many petty kings or lords planted on the rivers' sides, and by all likelihood maintain the frontiers of' their several territories by wars, we may by the aid of this river join with this king here, or with that king there, at our pleasure, and may so with a few men be revenged of any wrong offered by any of them; or may, if we will proceed with extremity, conquer, fortify, and plant in soils most sweet, most fertile, in and in the end bring them all in subjection and to civility.

21. The known abundance of fresh fish in the rivers, and the known plenty of fish on the sea-coast there, may assure us of sufficient victual in spite of the people, if we will use salt and industry. . . .

27. Since great waste woods be there of oak, cedar, pine, walnuts, and sundry other sorts, many of our waste people may be employed in making of ships, hoys, busses [types of ships], and boats, and in making of rosin, pitch, and tar, the trees natural for the same being certainly known to be near Cape Breton and the Bay of Menan, and in many other palaces thereabout. . . .

29. Sugar-canes may be planted as well as they are now in the South of Spain, and besides the employment of our idle people, we may receive the commodity cheaper and not enrich the infidels or our doubtful friends, of whom now we receive that commodity. . . .

31. This land that we propose to direct our course to, lying in part in the 40th degree of latitude, being in like heat as Lisbon in Portugal doth, and in the more southerly part, as the most southerly coast of Spain doth, may by our diligence yield unto us, besides wines and oils and sugars, oranges, lemons, figs, raisins, almonds, pomegranates, rice, raw silks such as come from Granada, and divers commodities for dyers, as **anil** and **cochineal**, and sundry other colors and materials. Moreover, we shall not only receive many precious commodities besides from thence, but also shall in time find ample vent of the labor of our poor people at home, by sale of hats, bonnets, knives, fish-hooks, copper kettles, beads, looking-glasses, bugles, and a thousand kinds of other wrought wares that in short time may be brought in use among the people of that country, to the great relief of the multitude of our poor people and to the wonderful enriching of this realm. And in time, such league and intercourse may arise between our stapling seats there, and other ports of our North America, and of the islands of the same, that incredible things, and by few as yet undreamed of, may speedily follow, tending to the impeachment of our mighty enemies and to the common good of this noble government.

Reading and Discussion Questions

1. In what ways does Hakluyt portray the New World as a new Garden of Eden?
2. What geopolitical and economic conditions shape Hakluyt's reasons for colonization, and how would a presence in North America assist the English with both foreign and domestic issues?
3. Given Hakluyt's sensational account of North America, a place he never visited, how might colonists have reacted when they reached Virginia?

---

anil: blue dye obtained from the indigo plant
cochineal: a scaly insect bred for dye in pre-colonial and colonial times

Chapter 19

African Kingdoms, the Atlantic Slave Trade, and the Origins of Black America

1450–1800

The great African kingdoms of Mali and Songhay illustrate important themes of global history on the eve of the modern era. Few places in the world possessed such an abundance of natural resources, most notably gold, and which beckoned European and Arab explorers and traders with the lure of material wealth. But just as important, the metropolitan cities of sub-Saharan Africa, such as Timbuktu, Goa, and Jenno-Jeno served as centers of learning that rivaled most universities in Europe, the Middle East and even Asia. In another sense, African kingdoms exhibited significant changes in this period that showed global connections among world civilizations. For example, the African slave trade transported Africans to Europe, the Middle East, India, and the Americas. As a result, aspects of African culture were also transplanted to those areas.

The expansion of African kingdoms also explains why non-Africans were so interested in expanding their trading relations with the continent. In particular, religion and natural resources account for most of the urge for expansion and trade. Muslims moved into West Africa seeking new converts. Contact with Africans revealed the rich natural resources of the continent. The African slave trade which had existed among African tribes for centuries, rapidly expanded as Arabs moved deeper into the continent. European explorers, hoping to find vast treasure troves of gold described by travelers, former slaves, and merchants, commenced setting up fortifications and trading posts along the Atlantic coast. Unable to successfully gain a foothold to mine gold, Europeans, led first by the Portuguese then the Dutch, established a lucrative slave trade. As depicted in source 19.4, European slave galleys then transported Africans across the Atlantic in the dreaded Middle Passage to the Americas in one of the most tragic events in human history.

The following sources provide first-hand accounts of African kingdoms, which sparked the imagination of both European and Arab travelers. Several of the accounts come from Europeans caught up in the African slave trade. Whether as slaves or masters, the accounts offer a glimpse of early modern African culture, its wealth, and social organization. The sources also demonstrate the importance of religion, most notably Islam, to the development of Africa's most impressive empires.

19.1 Leo Africanus on Timbuktu

Born El Hasan ben Muhammed el-Wazzan-ez-ZayyatiI in Granada, Leo Africanus (ca. 1485-1554) and his Moorish family were expelled from the Iberian Peninsula by King Ferdinand and Queen Isabella. They settled in Morocco, where he finished his studies before accompanying his uncle on diplomatic missions in north Africa, the Ottoman Empire, Egypt, and Arabia. He was captured by Spanish pirates in 1518 and presented to Pope Leo X, who recognized the young man's incredible intellectual abilities and learned experiences. Baptized with the name

"Johanniss Leo de Medici," he wrote a history and survey of Africa based on his travels. His description of African cities such as Timbuktu influenced countless generations of Europeans, whose knowledge of Africa remained largely limited to Leo's writings. At the time he wrote his description, Timbuktu's status as a center for learning and trade was already in decline.

Source: Leo Africanus, *History and Description of Africa,* translated by John Pory (London: Hakluyt Society, 1896)

The houses of Timbuktu are huts made of clay-covered wattles with thatched roofs. In the center of the city is a temple built of stone and mortar, built by an architect named Granata, and in addition there is a large palace, constructed by the same architect, where the king lives. The shops of the artisans, the merchants, and especially weavers of cotton cloth are very numerous. Fabrics are also imported from Europe to Timbuktu, borne by Berber merchants.

The women of the city maintain the custom of veiling their faces, except for the slaves who sell all the foodstuffs. The inhabitants are very rich, especially the strangers who have settled in the country; so much so that the current king has given two of his daughters in marriage to two brothers, both businessmen, on account of their wealth. There are many wells containing sweet water in Timbuktu; and in addition, when the Niger is in flood canals deliver the water to the city. Grain and animals are abundant, so that the consumption of milk and butter is considerable. But salt is in very short supply because it is carried here from Tegaza, some 500 miles from Timbuktu. I happened to be in this city at a time when a load of salt sold for eighty ducats. The king has a rich treasure of coins and gold ingots. One of these ingots weighs 970 pounds.

The royal court is magnificent and very well organized. When the king goes from one city to another with the people of his court, he rides a camel and the horses are led by hand by servants. If fighting becomes necessary, the servants mount the camels and all the soldiers mount on horseback. . . . This king makes war only upon neighboring enemies and upon those who do not want to pay him tribute. When he has gained a victory, he has all of them—even the children—sold in the market at Timbuktu. . . .

The king is a declared enemy of the Jews. He will not allow any to live in the city. If he hears it said that a Berber merchant frequents them or does business with them, he confiscates his goods. There are in Timbuktu numerous judges, teachers and priests, all properly appointed by the king. He greatly honors learning. Many hand-written books imported from Barbary are also sold. There is more profit made from this commerce than from all other merchandise.

Instead of coined money, pure gold nuggets are used; and for small purchases, cowrie shells which have been carried from Persia, and of which 400 equal a ducat. Six and two-thirds of their ducats equal one Roman gold ounce.

The people of Timbuktu are of a peaceful nature. They have a custom of almost continuously walking about the city in the evening (except for those that sell gold), between 10 PM and 1 AM, playing musical instruments and dancing. The citizens have at their service many slaves, both men and women.

Reading and Discussion Questions

1. To what degree might the relative peaceful nature of the inhabitants of Timbuktu contribute to their material wealth? Would the harsh rule of king enhance or diminish the inhabitants' personal wealth?
2. How would one reconcile the abundance of trade in a city like Timbuktu with harsh treatment of slaves and the exclusion of the Jews? To what degree did personal liberty depend upon the overall wealth of the city?
3. What geographic conditions contributed to Timbuktu's greatness, particularly with regard to trade?

19.2 "Krotoa" from the *Journal of Jan van Riebeeck*

Krotoa (1642-1674) was an African interpreter for Jan van Riebeeck, the early leader of the Dutch Cape Town colony in southern Africa. She came from the Khoikhoi tribe, served as a translator for Dutch authorities, and helped negotiate cultural exchange between native Africans and Dutch colonists. Named "Eve" by the Dutch, she eventually married Pieter van Meerhoff, a surgeon working for the Dutch East India Company. Krotoa lived between two vastly different cultures, but navigated both worlds with apparent ease. Her importance to the Dutch did not go unnoticed given her status among both native Africans and European merchants. Sadly, Krotoa fell victim to alcoholism following the death of her husband and was banished from the colony.

Source: Riebeeck, Jan van. *Journal of Jan van Riebeeck. Volume II, III, 1656-1662.* Edited by H. B. Thom and translated by J. Smuts. Cape Town: A.A. Balkema, 1954.

31 October 1657:

"The Commander [Jan van Riebeeck] spent the day entertaining the Saldanhars [a Khoikhoi tribe from the interior] and questioning them about various things through the medium of a certain girl, aged 15 or 16, and by us called Eva, who has been in the service of the Commander's wife from the beginning and is now living here permanently and is beginning to speak Dutch well."

21 June 1658:

"Fine weather with N.W. breeze. The freeman Jan Reijnierssen came to complain early in the morning that during the night all his male and female slaves had run away, taking with them 3 or 4 blankets, clothing, rice, tobacco, etc. We thereupon called the new interpreter Doman, now called Anthony, who had returned from Batavia with the Hon. Cuneus, and asked him why the Hottentots would not search for the runaway slaves, to which he coolly replied that he did not know. The Commander, not trusting him, then called the interpreter Eva alone into his office and privately asked her whether our blacks were not being harboured by the Hottentots. On this she asked whether such was the Commander's opinion, and being answered in the affirmative, she (speaking good Dutch) said these words, namely: "I tell you straight out, Mijnheer Van Riebeeck, Doman is no good. He told the Hottentots everything that was said in Mijnheer's room the day before yesterday. When I told him that it was wrong to do so, he replied: 'I am a Hottentot and not a Dutchman, but you, Eva, try to curry favour with the Commander, etc.'" She added: "Mijnheer, I also believe that the Fat Captain of the Kaapmans harbours the slaves." On being asked what the chief would do with the slaves, Eva replied: "He will present them to the Cochoquas to retain their friendship, and they in turn will deliver the slaves to the Hancumquas living far from here and cultivating the soil in which they grow daccha [also dagga, of the cannabis family], a dry herb which the Hottentots chew, which makes them drunk and which they highly esteem."

26 January 1661:

"The interpreter Eva has remained behind to live in the Commander's house again, laying aside her skins and adopting once more the Indian way of dressing. She will resume her services as an interpreter. She seems to have grown tired of her own people again; in these vacillations we let her follow her own will so that we may get the better service from her. But she appears to have become already so accustomed to the Dutch diet and way of life that she will never be able to give it up completely.

Reading and Discussion Questions

1.   Through what avenues did Krotoa move between Dutch and African cultures?

2.   How did Krotoa use her privileged status as an interpreter to shape Dutch attitudes toward Africans?
3.   How dependent did Krotoa become upon Dutch culture and the perceived advantages it help over her African tribal ways of life?

19.3   The Arab Slave Trade

The Arab, or Oriental slave trade, lasted until the twentieth century even though it followed a different pattern than European slavery. Europeans mainly captured Africans to work as slaves on their plantations in the Americas. They thus sought primarily young males. The Arab slave trade typically involved large numbers of women, who were used either as wet nurses or sex slaves in the Middle East. Occasionally, large numbers of men were enslaved and trained to be warriors. The sultan of Morocco, Moulay Ismail Ibn Sharif (ca. 1645-1727), was exceptional not only in how he used African slaves but also in his excessive cruelty towards them. Unlike most enslaved warriors who were used outside their native lands, Moulay's Abid al-Bukhari were used almost exclusively in their indigenous territories. Thomas Pellow (b. 1704), an English sailor and occasional mercenary, was captured by Barbary pirates in 1715 while still a cabin boy on an English ship and spent twenty years in Moulay's service. Like hundreds of Europeans taken as part of the "Christian slave trade," Pellow labored to build Moulay's palace. After he escaped slavery, he published a sensational account of his ordeal.

Source: Thomas Pellow. *The Adventures of Thomas Pellow, of Penryn, Mariner.* MacMillan and Co., 1890.

The manner of his [Moulay's] eating did not differ from the ordinary Moors. His other travelling utensils were two or three guns, a sword or two, and two lances, because one broke once as he was murdering. Both the swords and lances were carried with their points upwards. These were all carried by lusty fellows; his boys carried short Brazil sticks, knotted cords for whipping, a change of clothes to shift when bloody, and a hatchet, two of which he took in a Portuguese ship, and the first time they were brought to him, killed a negro without any provocation, to try if they were good.

Although the natives of his dominions are whites, yet they are not so much esteemed by him as the blacks and the copper-colored, to whom he commits the guard of his person, and was so fond of their breed, that he took care to mix them himself, by matching them to the best-complexioned of his female subjects."

Thus he took care to lay the foundation of his tawny nurseries, to supply his palace as he wanted, into which they were admitted very young, are taught to worship and obey that successor of their Prophet, and being nursed in blood from their infancy, become the executioners and ministers of their wrath, whose terrible commands they put in execution with as much zeal and fury as if they had received them immediately from Heaven. … They were so ready to murder and destroy—even while young—that the Alcaydes trembled at the very sight of them, and the Emperor seemed to take a great deal of pleasure, and placed much of his safety in them, for they surrounded him almost wherever he was. They are of all ranks and degrees; some were the sons of his chief Alcaydes, others picked up by chance, or taken from a large negro town joining to Mequinez, which the Emperor had filled with families of blacks and tawnies for his use. If they were well looked and strong, they needed no other quality; some who had relations that were able were fed, clothed, and lodged by them; others who had not were lodged in the outskirts of the palace, in great rooms, where they pigged an hundred or two together. They wore only a short and small coat without sleeves, which did not reach to their knees; their heads were shaved and always exposed to the sun, for he affected to breed them hard. …

He beat them in the cruelest manner imaginable, to try if they were hard; sometimes you should see forty or fifty of them all sprawling in their blood, none of them daring to rise till he left the place where they were lying, and if they were discountenanced and out of heart at this usage, they were of a bastard breed, and must turn out of his service. I never heard that he killed but three of them, one for a heinous crime, and two for hiding a piece of bread

Reading and Discussion Questions

1. How did the harshness of this case of Arab slavery compare to the rigors of European slavery of Africans?
2. To what degree did Islam shape Moulay's use of slavery and solidify his control over those he enslaved?
3. What strategy did Moulay employ in using the enslaved warriors against their native tribes and peoples?

19.4   An Account of the Atlantic Slave Trade

Alexander Falconbridge (d. 1792) served as a surgeon aboard several slave galleys during the 1780s. He knew firsthand of the difficult experiences suffered by slaves and sailors alike during the Middle Passage from the coast of Africa to the West Indies. Unwilling to continue his service, Falconbridge joined the English abolitionist movement and widely spoke of his life on board the slave ships. His popularity in abolitionist circles lead to a short-lived career governing a colony of freedmen in Sierra Leone and to the publication of his reminiscences.

Source: Alexander Falconbridge, *An Account of the Slave Trade on the Coast of Africa* (London: 1788).

After permission has been obtained for *breaking trade,* as it is termed, the captains go ashore, from time to time, to examine the negroes that are exposed to sale, and to make their purchases. The unhappy wretches thus disposed of, are bought by the black traders at fairs, which are held for that purpose, at the distance of upwards of two hundred miles from the sea coast; and these fairs are said to be supplied from an interior part of the country. Many negroes, upon being questioned relative to the places of their nativity have asserted, that they have travelled during the revolution of several moons, (their usual method of calculating time) before they have reached the places where they were purchased by the black traders. At these fairs, which are held at uncertain periods, but generally every six weeks, several thousands are frequently exposed to sale, who had been collected from all parts of the country for a very considerable distance round. While I was upon the coast, during one of the voyages I made, the black traders brought down, in different canoes, from twelve to fifteen hundred negroes, which had been purchased at one fair. They consisted chiefly of men and boys, the women seldom exceeding a third of the whole number. From forty to two hundred negroes are generally purchased at a time by the black traders, according to the opulence of the buyer, and consist of those of all ages, from a month, to sixty years and upwards.] Scare any age or situation is deemed an exception, the price being proportionable. Women sometimes form a part of them, who happen to be so far advanced in their pregnancy, as to be delivered during their journey from the fairs to the coast; and I have frequently seen instances of the deliveries on board ship. The slaves purchased at these fairs are only for the supply of the markets at Bonny, and Old and New Calabar.

There is great reason to believe, that most of the negroes shipped off from the coast of Africa, are *kidnapped.* But the extreme care taken by the black traders to prevent the Europeans from gaining any intelligence of their modes of proceeding; the great distance inland from whence the negroes are brought; and our ignorance of their language, (with which, very frequently, the black traders themselves are equally unacquainted) prevent our obtaining such information on this head as we could wish....

It frequently happens, that those who kidnap others, are themselves, in their turns, seized and sold. A negroe in the West Indies informed me, that after having been employed in kidnapping others, he had experienced this reverse. And he assured me, that it was a common incident among his countrymen.

Continual enmity is thus fostered among the negroes of Africa, and all social intercourse between them is destroyed; which most assuredly would not be the case, had they not these opportunities of finding a ready sale for each other....

Reading and Discussion Questions

1. To what degree does Falconbridge's account of the slave trade illustrate the divisions between various African peoples?
2. The prevalence of tropical diseases often hindered Europeans traveling inland. How did native Africans use this to their advantage?
3. How did European enslavement of Africans differ from the pattern generally followed by Arab slave traders?

19.5   Phillis Wheatly, "To the Right Honourable William, Earl of Dartmouth..."

Phillis Wheatley was born in Senegal on the west coast of Africa in 1753. At the age of seven, she was captured, enslaved, and shipped to America. Once there, she was purchased by the Wheatleys of Boston, Massachusetts, who gave her an education that helped her develop her considerable intellectual gifts. At age thirteen, she published her first book of poems. So many white people found it difficult to believe that a black woman could write sophisticated poetry, that Wheatley was forced to prove her abilities in court in 1772. After an exhaustive examination by some of Boston's most famous men, the court concluded that she was, indeed, the author of the poems published under her name. The Earl of Dartmouth, to whom Wheatley addressed the poem included below, helped with the publication of her work in England.

Source: Phillis Wheatley, Poems on Various Subjects, Religious and Moral (London, 1773), 73-75.

Hail, happy day, when, smiling like the morn, Fair Freedom rose New-England to adorn: The northern clime beneath her genial ray, Dartmouth, congratulates thy blissful sway: Elate with hope her race no longer Each soul expands, each grateful bosom burns, While in thine hand with pleasure we behold The silken reins, and Freedom's charms unfold. Long lost to realms beneath the northern skies She shines supreme, while hated faction dies: Soon as appear'd the Goddess long desir'd, Sick at the view, she languish'd and expir'd; Thus from the splendors of the morning light The owl in sadness seeks the caves of night. No more, America, in mournful strain Of wrongs, and grievance unredress'd complain, No longer shall thou dread the iron chain, Which wanton Tyranny with lawless hand Had made, and with it meant t' enslave the land. Should you, my lord, while you peruse my song, Wonder from whence my love of Freedom sprung, Whence flow these wishes for the common good, By feeling hearts alone best understood, I, young in life, by seeming cruel fate Was snatch'd from Afric's fancy'd happy seat: What pangs excruciating must molest, What sorrows labour in my parent's breast? Steel'd was that soul and by no misery mov'd That from a father seiz'd his babe belov'd: Such, such my case. And can I then but pray Others may never feel tyrannic sway? For favours past, great Sir, our thanks are due, And thee we ask thy favours to renew, Since in thy pow'r, as in thy will before, To sooth the griefs, which thou did'st once deplore. May heav'nly grace the sacred sanction give To all thy works, and thou forever live Not only on the wings of fleeting Fame, Though praise immortal crowns the patriot's name, But to conduct to heav'ns refulgent fane, May fiery coursers sweep th' ethereal plain, And bear thee upwards to that blest abode, Where, like the prophet, thou shalt find thy God.

Reading and Discussion Questions

1. Does the poem reveal anything about the nature of Wheatley's education? Why would the Wheatleys have educated her the way they did?
2. What strategies does Wheatley employ to get the Earl of Dartmouth to take action? What did she hope to achieve?

19-6 Slave Market, Pernambuco, Brazil, 1824

This engraving, part of a travelogue kept by the British writer Maria Graham (1785-1824) and published in 1824 as *Journal of a Voyage to Brazil*, shows the slave market at Pernambuco, on the northeast coast.

Reading and Discussion Questions

1. How would you describe this scene? How would you characterize the conditions of the slaves?
2. What details suggest that the artist had a negative view of slavery?

Source: Library of Congress

The Mughal Empire: Muslim Rulers and Hindu Subjects

Chapter 20

1400–1750

During the Mughal Empire in India (1526– 1739), the orientation of Muslim rulers to Islam and their attitude towards other religions fluctuated depending on the ruler. Although the Mughals were Sunni Muslims with an attraction to the Islamic mysticism of the Sufis, in 1540 the Persian Safavid ruler forced the Mughal Emperor Humayun to convert to Shi'a Islam to obtain Persian military support. Humayun's son Akbar (1542-1605) built impressive Islamic mosques yet sought truth in all religions. During the reigns of his son Jahangir (1569-1627) and grandson Shah Jahan (1592-1666), the Mughals shifted towards a more conservative, exclusive form of Islam, culminating in the strict orthodoxy and intolerance of Aurangzeb (1618-1707).

Judaism and Christianity enjoyed a special status in Islam, named in the Quran as *dhimmi* or "People of the Book," having a legitimate revelation from God. Islam allowed them a kind of second-class citizenship, but they had to pay the *jiziya*, a tax or tribute provided for in the Quran assessed on the *dhimmi* living under Islamic rule. After Islam conquered Iran and portions of India, some found a basis to argue that Zoroastrians and even Hindus and Buddhists could be included in this category. This was always subject to debate, since Muhammad did not explicitly identify these other religions.

It was under Akbar that religious openness reached its zenith. Akbar married a Hindu Rajput princess, and in1564 he exempted Hindus from paying the hated *jiziya*. His historian and chief minister, Abu'l Fazl, provided a summary and defense of the beliefs and customs of Hindu believers that likely reflected Akbar's own views. Akbar sought to reconcile the varying religious traditions of his empire, and even reached out to Catholic authorities in Goa, asking them to send learned priests to inform him of the doctrines of Christianity. Akbar regarded the *ulama* (Islamic doctors of jurisprudence) as arrogant, intolerant, and petty minded, and he took steps to limit their influence in his court. He exiled troublesome clerics, giving them a one-way ticket to pilgrimage. He obtained a ruling that the Emperor had a right to *ijtihād* (the making of a decision in Islamic law by personal effort independent of any school or jurisprudence) when there was a difference of opinion amongst the *ulama*. During the reigns of Jahangir and Shah Jahan, the power of the *ulama* remained diminished compared to the influence it had enjoyed under previous Islamic regimes in India.

Within a year of becoming Emperor in 1658, Aurangzeb had banned music, public consumption of alcohol, and gambling, in accordance with Sharia law. He then outlawed Hindu religious fairs, and forbid the construction of new Hindu temples. In 1679, Aurangzeb reinstituted the *jiziya* on non-Muslims. Akbar and Aurangzeb represent the two extremes of the continuum of the Mughal's orientation to Islam and towards Hinduism. Hindus tend to regard Akbar as the greatest Mughal ruler and Aurangzeb as the worst, while for most Muslims it is the opposite. First-hand accounts which illustrate the Mughal's policies have been selected from their court historians, critics from within their courts, and foreign observers who were allowed near access.

20.1 *The Ain-i-Akbari*

Abu'l Fazl Allami (1551-1602) was the leading vizier, historian and biographer in the court of the Indian Mughal Emperor Akbar (1542-1605). His *Akbarnama* is the primary authority for the dates and events associated with the reign of Akbar. The third volume of this work is the *Ain-i-Akbari* (Institutes of Akbar), and details the administration of the Mughal Empire. He was the second son of Shaikh Mubarak Nagawri, a distinguished Sufi scholar. Faizi, his older brother and poet laurate of the empire, presented Abu'l Fazl to the royal court in 1574. Abu'l Fazl's criticism of the narrow-mindedness of the *'ulamā'* (doctors of Islamic religion and law) gained the favor of the Emperor. In the passage below, Abu'l Fadl describes Hindu beliefs and customs.

Source: Abul Fazl Allami, *The Ain-i-Akbari* Vol. 3, trans. Col. .S. Jarrett, (Asiatic Society of Bengal, 1891), 8-9

Shall I tell of heroic valour or weave romances of their vivacity of intellect and their lore? The inhabitants of this land are religious, affectionate, hospitable, genial and frank. They are fond of scientific pursuits, inclined to austerity of life, seekers after justice, contented, industrious, capable in affairs, loyal, truthful and constant. The true worth of this people shines most in the day of adversity and its soldiers know not retreat from the field. When the day is doubtful, they dismount from their steeds and resolutely put their lives to hazard, accounting the dishonor of flight more terrible than death, while some even disable their horses before entering the fight.

They are capable of mastering the difficulties of any subject in a short space of time and surpass their instructors, and to win the Divine favor they will spend body and soul and joyfully devote their lives thereunto.

They one and all believe in the unity of God, and as to the reverence they pay to images of stone and wood and the like, which simpletons regard as idolatry, it is not so. The writer of these pages has exhaustively discussed the subject with many enlightened and upright men, and it became evident that these images of some chosen souls nearest in approach to the throne of God, are fashioned as aids to fix the mind and keep the thoughts from wandering, while the worship of God alone is required as indispensable. In all their ceremonial observances and usage they ever implore the favour of the world-illumining sun and regard the pure essence of the Supreme Being as transcending the idea of power in operation.

Brahma...they hold to be the Creator; Vishnu, the Nourisher and Preserver; and Rudra, called also Mahadeva, the Destroyer. Some maintain that God who is without equal, manifested himself under these three divine forms, without thereby sullying the garment of His inviolate sanctity, as the Nazarenes hold of the Messiah. Others assert that these were human creatures exalted to these dignities through perfectness of worship, probity of thought and righteousness of deed. The godliness and self-discipline of this people is such as is rarely to be found in other lands.

They hold that the world had a beginning, and some are of opinion that it will have an end, as will be mentioned hereafter.

Reading and Discussion Questions

1. A common Islamic charge against Hindus is that they are polytheists. How does Abu'l Fazl frame the Hindu beliefs to address this charge?
2. How effective would Abu'l Fazl's comparison of Hindu beliefs to the Christian doctrine of the Trinity be to orthodox Sunni Muslims?
3. Orthodox Islam also condemns the Hindus for idol worship. How does Abu'l Fazl explain this aspect of the Hindu religion?

20.2 *Journey to the Court of Akbar*

In 1579, the Indian Mughal Emperor Akbar requested that Church authorities in Goa send two learned priests to instruct him in the doctrines of Christianity. Realizing an opportunity to convert the emperor to Christianity, Church officials sent two Jesuit missionaries, among whom was Father Antonio Monserrate (1536-1600), a Spanish priest. Monserrate spent approximately three years in India from 1580-1582.

Akbar appointed Monserrate as a tutor in Portuguese and Christian ethics to his second son, Prince Murad. Monserrate spent time in the emperor's court at the capital city Fatehpur Sikri participating in theological discussions with Muslim Divines. Monserrate later accompanied Akbar's expedition against his rebellious half-brother Muhammad Hakim of Kabul.

Monserrate returned to Goa in 1582 without converting Akbar to Christianity. Dispatched to Abyssinia in 1588, he took the records of his observations during the Indian mission with him, intending to finalize them for Church officials. However, Arabs seized the ship and imprisoned him in Sanaa, where they allowed him to complete the manuscript in 1590. Ransomed in 1596, he returned to Goa with the manuscript, but it was lost to history until a British scholar discovered it in Calcutta in 1906.

In the excerpt below, Monserrate describes the Emperor Akbar. He refers to Akbar as Zelaldinus Equebar (a form of Jalal-ud-din Akbar), shortened to Zelaldinus. He uses the Turkish term Musalman for Muslim. Monserrate refers to several different peoples in the first paragraph by archaic names: Sauromates are a Scythian tribe; Sinae refers to the Chinese, and Niphones to the Japanese.

Source: Monserrate, *The Commentary of Father Monserrate, S.J., on his Journey to the Court of Akbar,* trans. J.S. Hoyland, (Oxford: Oxford University Press, 1922), 196-198

This Prince is of a stature and of a type of countenance well-fitted to his royal dignity, so that one could easily recognize, even at the first glance, that he is the King. He has broad shoulders, somewhat bandy legs well-suited for horsemanship, and a light-brown complexion. He carries his head bent towards the right shoulder. His forehead is broad and open, his eyes so bright and flashing that they seem like a sea shimmering in the sunlight.

His eyelashes are very long, as also are those of the Sauromates, Sinae, Niphones, and most other north-Asiatic races. His eyebrows are not strongly marked. His nose is straight and small, though not insignificant. His nostrils are widely opened, as though in derision. Between the left nostril and the upper lip there is a mole. He shaves his beard, but wears a moustache like that of a Turkish youth who has not yet attained to manhood (for on reaching manhood they begin to affect a beard). Contrary to the custom of his race he does not cut his hair; nor does he wear a hat, but a turban, into which he gathers up his hair. He does this, they say, as a concession to Indian usages, and to please his Indian subjects.

. . .

It is hard to exaggerate how accessible he makes himself to all who wish audience of him. For he creates an opportunity almost every day for any of the common people or of the nobles to see him and converse with him; and he endeavors to show himself pleasant-spoken and affable, rather than severe, toward all who come to speak with him. It is very remarkable how great an effect this courtesy and affability has in attaching to him the minds of his subjects. For in spite of his very heterodox attitude towards the religion of Muhammad, and in spite also of the fact that Musalmans regard such an attitude as an unforgivable offence, Zelaldinus has not yet been assassinated. He has an acute insight, and shows much wise foresight both in avoiding dangers and in seizing favorable opportunities for carrying out his designs. Yet all these fine qualities both of body and mind lose the greater part of their splendor because the luster of the True Faith is lacking.

...

According to the instructions of the worthless Muhammad and the custom of the Musalmans, the orthodox must wear a long robe coming down to the calf, together with shoes very low at the ankle. Their dress must be made of wool, linen or cotton: and must be white. The shoes must be of a certain fixed pattern. However, Zelaldinus is so contemptuous of the instructions given by the false law-giver, that he wears garments of silk, beautifully embroidered in gold. His military cloak comes down only as far as the knee, according to the Christian fashion; and his boots cover his ankles completely.

Reading and Discussion Questions

1. Politicians frequently act and talk in a manner to appeal to different constituencies. From the excerpt, what evidence is there that Akbar was a practitioner of this art?
2. Why would Akbar be inclined to participate in a council composed of Muslim, Christian, Hindi, Sikh and Hindu priests?
3. Why was Monserrate so meticulous in his description of Akbar?

20.3 Jahangir Debates with the Hindus

The Indian Mughal Emperor Akbar despaired of producing a male heir after several children born to him died in infancy. Akbar sought the prayers and blessings of Shaikh Salim Chrishti, a Sufi saint and scholar renowned in India. The sage assured the monarch he would have three sons, and soon Akbar's wife, a Rajput Princess, was pregnant. When a son was born in 1569, they named him Salim after the Shaikh, and Akbar built the city of Fatehpur Sikri to commemorate his gratitude for this event. Akbar later fathered two additional sons, Prince Murad and Prince Daniyal.

Prince Salim alienated his father by arranging the assassination of Akbar's beloved vizier Abu'l Fazl in 1602 because he opposed the accession of Salim to the throne. It took the intervention of Akbar's mother to reconcile them after this murder. Salim forcibly took the throne shortly after Akbar's death in 1605, and took the name Jahangir, "seizer of the world." Jahangir (1569-1627) left a diary in which he describes himself as a devout Muslim, but many contemporaries had difficulty classifying his beliefs. The passage below gives Jahangir's account of his discussions with the Hindu Brahmins.

Source: Jahangir, *Tuzuk-i-Jahangiri*, tr. Alexander Rogers, ed. Henry Beveridge (Oriental Translation Fund, 1909-14).

One day I observed to the Pandits, that is, the wise men of the Hindus, "If the doctrines of your religion are based on the incarnation of the Holy Person of God Almighty in ten different forms by the process of metempsychosis, they are virtually rejected by the intelligent. This pernicious idea requires that the Sublime Cause, who is void of all limitations, should be possessed of length, breadth, and thickness. If the purpose is the manifestation of the Light of God in these bodies, that of itself is existent equally in all created things, and is not peculiar to these ten forms. If the idea is to establish some one of God's attributes, even then there is no right notion, for in every faith and code there are masters of wonders and miracles distinguished beyond the other men of their age for wisdom and eloquence." After much argument and endless controversy, they acknowledged a God of Gods, devoid of a body or accidents, and said, "As our imagination fails to conceive a formless personality (*zāt-i-mujarrad*), we do not find any way to know Him without the aid of a form. We have therefore made these ten forms the means of conceiving of and knowing Him." Then said I, "How can these forms be a means of your approaching the Deity?"

My father always associated with the learned of every creed and religion, especially with Pandits and the learned of India, and although he was illiterate, so much became clear to him through constant intercourse with the learned and wise, in his conversations with them, that no one knew him to be illiterate, and he was so acquainted with the niceties of verse and prose compositions that his deficiency was not thought of.

Reading and Discussion Questions

1. How does Jahangir's consideration of the Hindu belief of incarnation of the Godhead reflect a more ortho-dox Muslim position than Abu'l Fazl's?
2. Whom does Jahangir portray as the winner of the debate?
3. Jahangir was quite proud of his education and literacy. How might the last paragraph be taken as a back-handed compliment, meant to demean Akbar?

20.4 Summary of the Reasons Which Led Akbar To Renounce Islam

Mulla 'Abd-al-Qadir Bada'uni (1540-1615) was a Sunni Muslim who entered the Mughal Emperor Akbar's court in 1574, the same year as Abu'l Fazl. Both had studied under Abu'l Fazl's father, Shaikh Mubarak. The range of Bada'uni's theological learning caught Akbar's eye, and Akbar at first thought Bada'uni was a Sufi. Eventually Bada'uni revealed himself to be "a sun dried *Mullah*" [a mullah is a Muslim cleric] compared to the liberal Abu'l Fazl. Akbar valued Bada'uni's literary abilities despite his rigid orthodoxy, and he commissioned Bada'uni to trans-late the Hindu epics, the *Ramayana* and the *Mahabharata*. He composed the *Muntakhab-ut-Tawrick* ("Selection of Chronicles" or "Abstract of Histories), a frank and critical history of Akbar's reign not made public until after Ak-bar's death. The orthodox Bada'uni resented the reforms of Akbar, and his elevation of Hindus to high offices in the administration. He was also jealous of his rivals in Abu'l Fazl and his brother Faizi. In the source below, Bada'uni gives a summary of the reasons Akbar came to renounce Islam.

Source: "Bada' oní's Summary of the Reasons Which Led Akbar To Renounce the Islam" quoted by S. Jarrett in *The Ain-i-Akbari* Vol. 1, (Asiatic Society of Bengal), 179-180

The principal reason is the large number of learned men of all denominations and sects that came from various countries to court, and received personal interviews. Night and day people did nothing but enquire and inves-tigate; profound points of science, the subtleties of revelation, the curiosities of history, the wonders of nature, of which large volumes could only give a summary abstract, were ever spoken of. His Majesty collected the opinions of everyone, especially of such as were not Muhammadans, retaining whatever he approved of, and re-jecting everything which was against his disposition, and ran counter to his wishes. From his earliest childhood to his manhood, and from his manhood to old age, His Majesty has passed through the most various phases, and through all sorts of religious practices and sectarian beliefs, and has collected everything which people can find in books, with a talent of selection peculiar to him, and a spirit of enquiry opposed to every [Islamic] principle. Thus a faith based on some elementary principles traced itself on the mirror of his heart, and as the result of all the influences which were brought to bear on His Majesty, there grew, gradually as the outline on a stone, the conviction in his heart that there were sensible men in all religions, and abstemious thinkers, and men endowed with miraculous powers, among all nations. If some true knowledge was thus everywhere to be found, why should truth be confined to one religion, or to a creed like the Islam, which was comparatively new, and scarcely a thousand years old; why should one sect assert what another denies, and why should one claim a preference without having superiority conferred on itself.

Moreover **brahmins** managed to get frequent private interviews with His Majesty. As they surpass other learned men in their treatises on morals, and on physical and religious sciences, and reach a high degree in their knowledge of the future, in spiritual power and human perfection, they brought proofs, based on reason and testimony, for the truth of their own, and the fallacies of other religions, and inculcated their doctrines so firmly, and so skillfully represented things as quite self-evident which require consideration, that no man, by expressing his doubts, could now raise a doubt in His Majesty, even if mountains were to crumble to dust, or the heavens were to tear asunder.

Hence His Majesty cast aside the Islamitic revelations regarding resurrection, the day of judgment, and the details connected with it, as also all ordinances based on the tradition of our prophet. He listened to every abuse which the courtiers heaped on our glorious and pure faith, which can be so easily followed; and eagerly seizing such opportunities, he showed in words and gestures, his satisfaction at the treatment which his original religion received at their hands.

Reading and Discussion Questions

1. What does this source reveal about Akbar's approach to religion?
2. What would have been the consequences of making Bada'uni's history public while Akbar lived?
3. Muslims regard Islam as the final revelation of God's word. How did the Hindu Brahmins counter this claim?

20.5 Akbar on Proper Behavior

The Mughal Emperor Akbar's second son, Prince Murad, was born in 1570 and was tutored in the Emperor's court from a young age. Once they reached adulthood, Akbar gave his sons military and administrative duties, and Murad was made governor of the province of Malwa at the age of twenty-one. In 1595, after three Muslin Shiite rulers in the Deccan region in southern India refused to recognize Akbar as Emperor, Akbar put Murad in command of a Mughal military force sent to the Deccan to force them to acknowledge his sovereignty over them. The poor performance of the army in the Deccan was in part due to Murad's drunkenness, and in 1599, Abu'l Fazl was dispatched by Akbar to relieve him of command. Murad died of *delirium tremens* (a severe form of alcohol withdrawal) in camp soon after Abu'l Fazl arrived. All three of Akbar's sons were alcoholics. The following passage gives a transcription of a letter which Akbar sent to Murad when he was appointed Governor of Malwa.

Source: Abul Fazl, Akbar-Nama, tr. H. Beveridge (Asiatic Society, 1907-39), Vol. 3, 912

The first step is to enquire into what is God's Will, in order that right actions may be performed. After that, outward purification is to be pursued. Food and clothing are not to be made ends. Profundity of view is to be exercised. Tyrannous actions are to be abstained from. The rules of moderation and of fitting season are not to be departed from. Every member (of the body) is to be kept to its proper office. Much speaking and laughing are to be avoided. Sleep is not to exceed one-third part of the day and night. There must be an endeavour to improve the army, and the country, to provide for the safety of the roads, and the obedience of the refractory; and thieves and robbers must be put down. Then attention is to be paid to internal improvement. Lust and wrath must be subjected to the commands of Wisdom, for the Creator has placed two sentinels in the palace of the

---

Brahmins: members of the Hindu priestly caste

body. The one sees that proper things are done; the other that evil things are abstained from. The children of men out of somnolent intellect have given these two a loose rein, and have made what should be the adornment of life the supplier of death. Do not neglect the knowledge of what is right, and support the power of the ruler (Reason). Preserve the equability of the four humours, and keep far from excess and defect which constitute evil. Use justice and discretion in this daily market of hypocrisy and double-facedness. The worship of the choosers of bypaths who have severed the links of association is one thing, and that of those who are bound in the improvement of the world is another. Though the idea of both is development, yet the former never departs from awakedness, while insouciance is suitable to the latter. Study the actions of every one, and be not disturbed by seeing improprieties. Let not love or hate, or threats or encouragements, transgress bounds. A frown will effect with many, what in other men requires a sword and dagger. Let not difference of religion interfere with policy, and be not violent in inflicting retribution. Adorn the confidential council with men who know their work. If apologies be made, accept them. Be not stiff in your own opinions. Do not consider any one suitable for this employment (the giving of advice) except a far-seeing, right-thinking and disinterested person. Do not make ease your rule, and do not reject help in the day of (your) distress. Do not be dismayed by much ill-success. Choose the observance of your promises above all advantage to yourself, and live so that the crowds of foreigners be not distressed. Especially see to it that merchants have a good opinion of you for their report carries far. Expect from every one service in proportion to his ability. Be not deceived in your inquiries by glozing words.

Reading and Discussion Questions

1. What evidence is there in the source that Akbar is concerned about the potential for overindulgence and dissolution?
2. How does the passage reflect Akbar's own record as Emperor, and his concern that religion and revenge might distract his son from effective ruling?
3. What kind of paternal demands and high expectations might the sons of Emperor Akbar have experienced? Why might alcoholism be so tempting given easy access to opium and spirits because of their royal status?

20.6 The Habits and Manners of Aurangzeb

Shah Jahan's (1592-1666) heir apparent was his favorite and eldest son, Dara Shikoh (1616-1659). Dara Shikoh was a mystic who took after Akbar's universalism. In 1655 he wrote a book on of the parallels between Islam and Hinduism entitled *Majma-'ul'Bahrain* (The Meeting Point of the Two Oceans). Two years later, he commissioned a translation into Persian of the *Upanishads* (Hindu sacred texts, composed between 400-200 BCE) which he entitled *Sirr-i-Akbar* (The Great Secret). Dara found the only difference between the Sufis and the "Indian monotheists" was in their terminology. His religious eclecticism horrified and antagonized the orthodox, and his brother Aurangzeb labeled him as "chief of the atheists" and said he had "not even the semblance" of a Muslim. In 1658, Aurangzeb defeated Dara's forces in battle, and deposed and imprisoned Shah Jahan in the Agra fort. In 1659, a local chieftain betrayed Dara, and Aurangzeb arranged to have his brother paraded through Delhi clothed in rags on a filthy elephant. Aurangzeb convened a council of priests and nobles who sentenced Dara to death as an apostate from Islam. Guards entered his prison cell and killed him, and then paraded his corpse through the streets.

The *Mirat-i-alam* is a work in Persian attributed to Bakhtawar Khan (died 1684), the superintendent of eunuchs under Aurangzeb. A favorite eunuch of Aurangzeb, he held the rank of a thousand (indicating he was among the highest-ranking court officials).The translator of the *Mirat-i-alam* makes a convincing case that the author of this book was in fact Muhammad Baqá (d. 1683), a poet and scholar. Baqá was a lifelong friend of Bakhtawar Khan, to whom he owed his position in court, and likely wrote the book in his friend's name as a form of flattery. The

Mirat-i-alam, a combination of history and biography written in 1668,contains an account of the first ten years of Aurangzeb's reign, and the selection below is a description of the "habits and manners of the Emperor Aurangzeb" (explanatory notes added in brackets [ ]):

Source: Bakhtawar Khan, "Mirat-i-Alam," *The History of India as told by its own Historians*, Henry Miers Elliot, ed. John Dowson. (London, 1877), 156-159

The Emperor, a great worshipper of God by natural propensity, is remarkable for his rigid attachment to religion. He is a follower of the doctrines of the Imam Abu Hanífa [founder of a school of Islamic Jurisprudence] (may God be pleased with him!), and establishes the five fundamental doctrines of the *Kanz* [a famous work containing containing questions and decisions according to the doctrines of Abu Hanifa]. Having made his ablutions, he always occupies a great part of his time in adoration of the Deity, and says the usual prayers, first in the *masjid* [mosque or place of public prayer] and then at home, both in congregation and in private, with the most heartfelt devotion. He keeps the appointed fasts on Fridays and other sacred days, and he reads the Friday prayers in the *Jámi' masjid* [chief mosque]with the common people of the Muhammadan faith. He keeps vigils during the whole of the sacred nights, and with the light of the favor of God illumines the lamps of religion and prosperity. From his great piety, he passes whole nights in the Mosque which is in his palace, and keeps company with men of devotion. In privacy he never sits on a throne. … During the whole month of Ramazán [ninth month of Islamic calendar] he keeps fast, says the prayers appointed for that month, and reads the holy Koran in the assembly of religious and learned men, with whom he sits for that purpose during six, and sometimes nine hours of the night. During the last ten days of the month, he performs worship in the mosque, and although, on account of several obstacles, he is unable to proceed on a pilgrimage to Mecca, yet the care which he takes to promote facilities for pilgrims to that holy place may be considered equivalent to the pilgrimage.

. . .

The duties of preserving order and regularity among the people are very efficiently attended to, and throughout the empire, notwithstanding its great extent, nothing can be done without meeting with the due punishment enjoined by the Muhammadan law. Under the dictates of anger and passion he never issues orders of death. In consideration of their rank and merit, he shows much honor and respect to the Sayyids, saints and learned men, and through his cordial and liberal exertions, the sublime doctrines of Hanifa and of our pure religion have obtained such prevalence throughout the wide territories of Hindustan as they never had in the reign of any former king.

Hindu writers have been entirely excluded from holding public offices, and all the worshipping places of the infidels and the great temples of these infamous people have been thrown down and destroyed in a manner which excites astonishment at the successful completion of so difficult a task. His Majesty personally teaches the sacred *kalima* [Islamic declaration of faith] to many infidels with success, and invests them with *khil'ats* [a special, honorific robe] and other favors.

Reading and Discussion Questions

1. What would the reaction of the Hindus, Sikhs, and other religions of India likely be to the reign of Aurangzeb? What impact would his rule have upon the leaders, priests and legal experts of the non-Muslim religions?
2. Contrast the likely influence of the orthodox *ulama* (doctors of Islamic jurisprudence) under Aurangzeb with that during Akbar's reign.
3. How might the history of the Mughals have turned out if Dara had triumphed over Aurangzeb?

Chapter 21

Regulating the "Inner" and the "Outer" Domains: China and Japan

1500-1800

Improved navigation methods as well as enhanced production techniques by 1500 introduced a new set of problems to lands like China and Japan that previously had been able to control contact with the outside world. Although these societies reacted differently, both took strong measures to regulate contact and trade, while also reinforcing the "inner and outer" domains of their own societies.

As the Chinese struggled to rebuild their social and economic structures after the loss of population resulting from the bubonic plague and expulsion of the Mongol Yuan dynasty, they focused on improving agricultural production and maintaining social order. Nevertheless, the luxury goods from China were highly coveted across Europe and Asia. As pressures disrupted the inner equilibrium, both Japan and China acted to stabilize existing social arrangements and control contact with the new strangers and their doors. Chinese merchants enjoyed the benefits of new markets for porcelain, tea, and silk, but the authorities were concerned about the social disruption. They reacted by controlling access and limiting the new foreigners to specific ports.

The Portuguese reached Japan in 1543, followed soon by Francis Xavier, a Jesuit missionary. Initially, Christianity seemed simply another type of Buddhism. Nobunaga (1534–1582) was well disposed toward the missionaries, as was his successor, Toyotomi Hideyoshi (1536–1598), who once remarked that only the insistence on monogamy prevented him from converting to Christianity. However, Hideyoshi became concerned that Japanese conversions might result in divided loyalty and issued an order in 1587 expelling monks. Both Christian missionaries and traders (Dutch, Portuguese, English, and Spanish) seemed to divide the loyalty of the Japanese. In 1587, Hideyoshi crucified six Franciscan missionaries and 18 converts and began restricting access. By 1630, the Japanese were prohibited from traveling overseas. The Japanese acted to eliminate foreign incursions, limiting even contacts with the Dutch whose presence was generally considered non-threatening.

21.1   The Seclusion of Japan

By 1630, Japanese were prohibited from going overseas. The Shimabara Rebellion (1637-1638), during which peasants, many of whom were Christian, rebelled against a brutal daimyo, intensified the perception that Christianity would ultimately destroy the existing order if allowed to expand unchecked. The Edict of 1635 was designed to eliminate dangerous foreign influences from Japan.

Source: Tokugawa Iemitsu, "Closed Country Edict of 1635"

1. Japanese ships are strictly forbidden to leave for foreign countries.

2. No Japanese is permitted to go abroad. If there is anyone who attempts to do so secretly, he must be executed. The ship so involved must be impounded and its owner arrested, and the matter must be reported to the higher authority.

3. If any Japanese returns from overseas after residing there, he must be put to death.

4. If there is any place where the teachings of the [Catholic] priests is practiced, the two of you must order a thorough investigation.

5. Any informer revealing the whereabouts of the followers of the priests must be rewarded accordingly. If anyone reveals the whereabouts of a high ranking priest, he must be given one hundred pieces of-silver. For those of lower ranks, depending on the deed, the reward must be set accordingly.

6. If a foreign ship has an objection (to the measures adopted) and it becomes necessary to report the matter to Edo, you may ask the Omura domain to provide ships to guard the foreign ship. . . .

7. If there are any Southern Barbarians who propagate the teachings of the priests, or otherwise commit crimes, they may be incarcerated in the prison. . . .

8. All incoming ships must be carefully searched for the followers of the priests.

9. No single trading city shall be permitted to purchase all the merchandise brought by foreign ships.

10. Samurai are not permitted to purchase any goods originating from foreign ships directly from Chinese merchants in Nagasaki.

11. After a list of merchandise brought by foreign ships is sent to Edo, as before you may order that commercial dealings may take place without waiting for a reply from Edo.

12. After settling the price, all white yarns brought by foreign ships shall be allocated to the five trading cities and other quarters as stipulated.

13. After settling the price of white yarns, other merchandise [brought by foreign ships] may be traded freely between the [licensed] dealers. However, in view of the fact that Chinese ships are small and cannot bring large consignments, you may issue orders of sale at your discretion. Additionally, payment for goods purchased must be made within twenty days after the price is set.

14. The date of departure homeward of foreign ships shall not be later than the twentieth day of the ninth month. Any ships arriving in Japan later than usual shall depart within fifty days of their arrival. As to the departure of Chinese ships, you may use your discretion to order their departure after the departure of the Portuguese galeota.

15. The goods brought by foreign ships, which remained unsold, may not be deposited or accepted for deposit.

16. The arrival in Nagasaki of representatives of the five trading cities shall not be later than the fifth day of the seventh month. Anyone arriving later than that date shall lose the quota assigned to his city.

17. Ships arriving in Hirado must sell their raw silk at the price set in Nagasaki, and are not permitted to engage in business transactions until after the price is established in Nagasaki.

You are hereby required to act in accordance with the Provisions set above. It is so ordered.

Reading and Discussion Questions

1. Under what circumstances can you imagine that a state would find it necessary to issue such draconian laws against contact with outsiders?
2. Reading the list, do you believe that the Shogunate is more concerned with religious or intellectual contamination or with the activities of merchants? Why?
3. Why would the Shogunate believe it advisable to prohibit foreign merchants from leaving their wares with Japanese merchants for a possible future sale?

21.2 Buddhist World Map, 1710

Compiled during Japan's age of national isolation (1636-1854), this world map is representative of Buddhist cosmology. Drawn in 1710 by the Japanese monk Hotan (1654-1738), the map is centered on India and shows the mythical Anukodatchipond, which represents the center of the universe and from which four rivers flow in the four cardinal directions.

Reading and Discussion Questions

1. What does this map say about the way the world beyond Asia is viewed in traditional Buddhist cosmology?
2. Can you locate Japan on the map? Is its size on the map in proportion to its actual size?

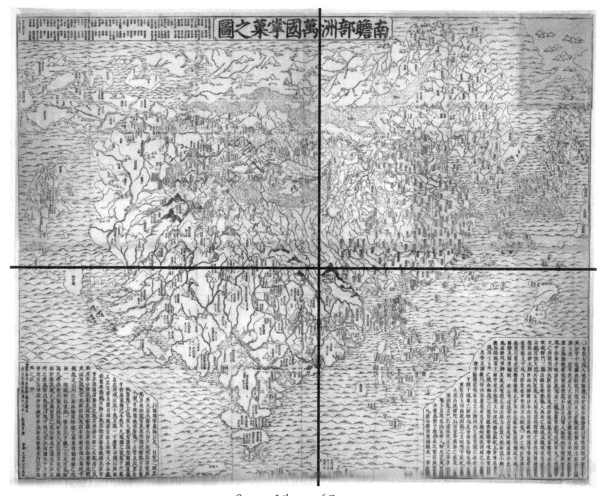

Source: Library of Congress

21.3   The Philosophy of Wang Yang-Ming

The slow dissolution of the Ming dynasty (1368-1529) called forth dynamic new interpretations of Confucianism and of the duties of a Confucian scholar. Wang Yang-Ming (1472-1529) believed that knowledge without action could not be true knowledge, and might well be more damaging than action devoid of knowledge. His dynamic approach was in direct opposition to the traditions of the meditative sages, but was a vital reaction to the increasing chaos of the late Ming period.

Source: *The Philosophy of Wang Yang-Ming,* translated from the Chinese by Frederick Goodrich Henke (London: The Open Court Publishing, 1916), 53-58.

The Teacher replied: This separation is due to selfishness and does not represent the original character of knowledge and practice. No one who really has knowledge fails to practice it. Knowledge without practice should be interpreted as lack of knowledge. Sages and virtuous men teach men to know how to act, because they wish them to return to nature. They do not tell them merely to reflect and let this suffice. The Great Learning exhibits true knowledge and practice, that men may understand this. For instance, take the case of loving what is beautiful and despising a bad odor. Seeing beauty is a result of knowledge; loving the beautiful is a result of practice. Nevertheless, it is true that when one sees beauty one already loves it. It is not a case of determining to love it after one sees it. Smelling a bad odor involves knowledge; hating the odor involves action. Nevertheless, when one perceives the bad odor one already hates it. One does not determine to hate it after one has smelt it. A man with his nostrils stuffed may see the malodorous object before him, but does not smell it. Under such circumstances it is a case of not perceiving it, rather than of disliking it. No one should be described as understanding filial piety and respectfulness, unless he has actually practiced filial piety toward his parents and respect toward his elder brother. Knowing how to converse about filial piety and respectfulness is not sufficient to warrant anybody s being described as understanding them. Or it may be compared to one's understanding of pain. A person certainly must have experienced pain before he can know what it is. Likewise to understand cold one must first have endured cold; and to understand hunger one must have been hungry. How, then, can knowledge and practice be separated? This is their original nature before selfish aims have separated them. The sage instructs the individual that he must practice before he may be said to have understanding. If he fails to practice, he does not understand. How thoroughly important a task this is!

. . .

The Teacher said: "But thereby you have lost the meaning of the ancients. I have said that knowledge is the purpose to act, and that practice implies carrying out knowledge. Knowledge is the beginning of practice; doing is the completion of knowing. If when one knows how to attain the desired end, one speaks only of knowing, the doing is already naturally included; or if he speaks of acting, the knowing is already included. That the ancients after having spoken of knowledge also speak of doing, is due to the fact that there is a class of people on earth who foolishly do as they wish and fail to understand how to deliberate and investigate. They act ignorantly and recklessly. It is necessary to discuss knowledge so that they can act correctly. There is another class of people who vaguely and vainly philosophize but are unwilling to carry it out in practice. This also is merely an instance of estimating shadows and echoes. The ancients of necessity discussed doing, for only then can such people truly understand. The language of the ancients is of necessity directed toward rectifying prejudices and reforming abuses. When one comprehends this idea, a word is sufficient. Men of the present, however, make knowledge and action two different things and go forth to practice, because they hold that one must first have knowledge before one is able to practice. Each one says, I proceed to investigate and discuss knowledge; I wait until knowledge is perfect and then go forth to practice it, Those who to the very end of life fail to practice also fail to understand. This is not a small error, nor one that came in a day. By saying that knowledge and practice are a unit, I am herewith offering a remedy for the disease. I am not dealing in abstractions, nor imposing my own ideas, for the nature of knowledge and practice is originally as I describe it, In case you comprehend the purport, no harm is done if you say they are two, for they are in reality a unit. In case you do not comprehend the purport thereof and say they are one, what does it profit? It is only idle talk."

. . .

The Teacher said: "Nature is the original character of the mind (one's mental constitution). Heaven is the source of nature. To exhaust one's mind means to exhaust one's nature. Only he who is possessed of the most complete sincerity is able to exhaust his nature and understand the nourishing power of heaven and earth. He who preserves his mental constitution has not exhausted it. Knowledge of heaven is as the knowledge of the Chihchou and Chihhsien, whose knowledge of the territory they govern is a thing in line with their duty. It implies considering one's self as one with Heaven. Serving Heaven is like the son serving his parents, and the minister serving the prince. It must be done reverently if it is to be perfect.

. . .

The Teacher said: "Yes. The controlling power of the body is the mind. The mind originates the idea, and the nature of the idea is knowledge. Wherever the idea is, we have a thing. For instance, when the idea rests on serving one's parents, then serving one's parents is a thing; when it is on serving one's prince, then serving one's prince is a thing; when it is occupied with being benevolent to the people and kind to creatures, then benevolence to the people and kindness to creatures are things; when it is occupied with seeing, hearing, speaking, moving, then each of these becomes a thing. I say there are no principles but those of the mind, and nothing exists apart from the mind. The Doctrine of the Mean says : Without sincerity there would be nothing. The Great Learning makes clear that the illustrating of illustrious virtue consists merely in making one's purpose sincere, and that this latter has reference to investigating things."

The Teacher spoke again saying: "The examine of examining into the nature of things, just as the rectify of the great man can rectify the mind of the prince , of Mencius, has reference to the fact that the mind is not right. Its object is to reinstate the original Tightness. But the idea conveyed is that one must cast out the wrong in order to complete the right, and that there should be no time or place in which one does not harbor heaven-given principles. This includes a most thorough investigation of heaven-given.

Reading and Discussion Questions

1. Do you believe that Wang is correct in his assertion that knowledge that is not translated into action is invalid as knowledge? Why?
2. What does Wang mean when he says that those "who fail to practice fail to understand"?
3. What does Wang consider to be the nature of human beings? What evidence or passage supports your conclusion?

21.4 Qianlong, Letter to George III

Qianlong (r. 1735-1796) was the fourth emperor of China's Qing Dynasty. Born in 1711 with the name Hung-li, Qianlong was the longest reigning emperor in Chinese history. He expanded Chinese territorial control to its greatest extent, defeating Mongols and Turks in the north and conquering the northwestern province of Xinjiang. Qianlong also pushed Chinese power into southeast Asia, conquering Burma and Annam. His reign marked the height of Chinese power and prestige, but also the rise of corruption that would eventually help bring the dynasty to its downfall.. He died in 1799.

In 1793, he rejected a British proposal to develop trade and diplomatic relations. King George III's ambassador, Lord Macartney (1737-1806) had been instructed to deliver a personal letter from the king to the emperor requesting permission to post a representative to the imperial court and allow the expansion of trade with China which, for all foreign countries, could only be conducted under strict regulation at the southern port of Canton. The request was unprecedented and, as far as the emperor was concerned, impossible to grant. The indifference to diplomatic niceties of the Son of Heaven conveyed in the emperor's refusal played its part in the hardening the British attitude toward China, though it was to take another 50 years before China's weakness in the face of real military power was revealed in the Opium War.

Source: Qianlong, Letter to George III, 1793 (Boston: Houghton Mifflin, 1913)

...I have perused your **memorial**: the earnest terms in which it is couched reveal a respectful humility on your part, which is highly praiseworthy. In consideration of the fact that your Ambassador and his deputy have come a long way with your memorial and tribute, I have shown them high favor and have allowed them to be introduced into my presence. To manifest my indulgence, I have entertained them at a banquet and made them numerous gifts. I have also caused presents to be forwarded to the Naval Commander and six hundred of his officers and men, although they did not come to Peking, so that they too may share in my all-embracing kindness.

As to your entreaty to send one of your nationals [namely, Lord Macartney] to be accredited to my Celestial Court and to be in control of your country's trade with China, this request is contrary to all usage of my dynasty and cannot possibly be entertained. It is true that Europeans, in the service of the dynasty, have been permitted to live at Peking, but they are compelled to adopt Chinese dress, they are strictly confined to their own precincts and are never permitted to return home. You are presumably familiar with our dynastic regulations. Your proposed Envoy to my Court could not be placed in a position similar to that of European officials in Peking who are forbidden to leave China, nor could he, on the other hand, be allowed liberty of movement and the privilege of corresponding with his own country; so that you would gain nothing by his residence in our midst.

...Supposing that your Envoy should come to our Court, his language and national dress differ from that of our people, and there would be no place in which to bestow him. It may be suggested that he might imitate the Europeans permanently resident in Peking and adopt the dress and customs of China, but it has never been our dynasty's wish to force people to do things unseemly and inconvenient. Besides, supposing I sent an Ambassador to reside in your country, how could you possibly make for him the requisite arrangements?

Europe consists of many other nations besides your own: if each and all demanded to be represented at our Court, how could we possibly consent? The thing is utterly impracticable. How can our dynasty alter its whole procedure and system of etiquette, established for more than a century, in order to meet your individual views?

If it be said that your object is to exercise control over your country's trade, your nationals have had full liberty to trade at Canton for many a year, and have received the greatest consideration at our hands. Missions have been sent by Portugal and Italy, preferring similar requests. The Throne appreciated their sincerity and loaded

---

memorial: in the sense used here, a diplomatic request or petition

them with favors, besides authorizing measures to facilitate their trade with China. You are no doubt aware that, when my Canton merchant, Wu Chao-ping, was in debt to the foreign ships, I made the Viceroy advance the monies due, out of the provincial treasury, and ordered him to punish the culprit severely. Why then should foreign nations advance this utterly unreasonable request to be represented at my Court? Peking is nearly two thousand miles from Canton, and at such a distance what possible control could any British representative exercise?

If you assert that your reverence for Our Celestial dynasty fills you with a desire to acquire our civilization, our ceremonies and code of laws differ so completely from your own that, even if your Envoy were able to acquire the rudiments of our civilization, you could not possibly transplant our manners and customs to your alien soil.

Therefore, however adept the Envoy might become, nothing would be gained thereby.

...I have but one aim in view, namely, to maintain a perfect governance and to fulfill the duties of the state: strange and costly objects do not interest me. If I have commanded that the tribute offerings sent by you, O King, are to be accepted, this was solely in consideration for the spirit which prompted you to dispatch them from afar. Our dynasty's majestic virtue has penetrated unto every country under heaven, and kings of all nations have offered their costly tribute by land and sea. As your Ambassador can see for himself, we possess all things. I set no value on objects strange or ingenious, and have no use for your country's manufactures. This then is my answer to your request to appoint a representative at my Court, a request contrary to our dynastic usage, which would only result in inconvenience to yourself. I have expounded my wishes in detail and have commanded your tribute Envoys to leave in peace on their homeward journey. It behoves you, O King, to respect my sentiments and to display even greater devotion and loyalty in future, so that, by perpetual submission to our Throne, you may secure peace and prosperity for your country hereafter...

[The emperor's follow-up communication on the subject follows]:

You, O King, from afar have yearned after the blessings of our civilization, and in your eagerness to come into touch with our converting influence have sent an Embassy across the sea bearing a memorial. I have already taken note of your respectful spirit of submission, have treated your mission with extreme favor and loaded it with gifts, besides issuing a mandate to you, O King, and honoring you with the bestowal of valuable presents.

Thus has my indulgence been manifested.

Yesterday your Ambassador petitioned my Ministers to memorialize me regarding your trade with China, but his proposal is not consistent with our dynastic usage and cannot be entertained. Hitherto, all European nations, including your own country's barbarian merchants, have carried on their trade with Our Celestial Empire at Canton. Such has been the procedure for many years, although Our Celestial Empire possesses all things in prolific abundance and lacks no product within its own borders. There was therefore no need to import the manufactures of outside barbarians in exchange for our own produce. But as the tea, silk, and porcelain which the Celestial Empire produces are absolute necessities to European nations and to yourselves, we have permitted, as a signal mark of favor, that foreign hongs (Chinese business associations) should be established at Canton, so that your wants might be supplied and your country thus participate in our beneficence. But your Ambassador has now put forward new requests which completely fail to recognize the Throne's principle to 'treat strangers from afar with indulgence', and to exercise a pacifying control over barbarian tribes, the world over. Moreover, our dynasty, swaying the myriad races of the globe, extends the same benevolence toward all.

Your England is not the only nation trading at Canton. If other nations, following your bad example, wrongfully importune my ear with further impossible requests, how will it be possible for me to treat them with easy indulgence? Nevertheless, I do not forget the lonely remoteness of your island, cut off from the world by intervening wastes of sea, nor do I overlook your excusable ignorance of the usages of Our Celestial Empire. I have consequently commanded my Ministers to enlighten your Ambassador on the subject, and have ordered the departure of the mission. But I have doubts that, after your Envoy's return he may fail to acquaint you with my view in detail or that he may be lacking in lucidity, so that I shall now proceed to take your requests seriatim [one by one] and to issue my mandate on each question separately. In this way you will, I trust, comprehend my meaning.

Reading and Discussion Questions

1. How would you describe the tone of the emperor's letter?
2. Does the emperor's letter give any indication of the rising military and economic power of Britain?

Nation–States and Patterns of Culture in Europe and North America

Chapter 22

1750-1871

The period between 1776 and 1914 is sometimes referred to by historians as "the long nineteenth century." The many revolutions that occurred in the period provided the basic contours of the modern world. The almost unfathomable amount of change in Western society during this period remains a fiercely contested arena of historical debate.

The ideas which undergirded the period had their roots in the Enlightenment, which drove both revolution and reaction. Men like John Locke, Adam Smith, and Jean Jacques Rousseau bequeathed to subsequent generations a revolutionary set of ideals. The first political expression of these ideas manifested itself in the American Revolution. The American experiment in governance by the people was soon replicated by the French, though with a greatly different outcome. The former led to half a century of economic expansion (though at the expense of North American natives and African slaves) while the latter led to violence, centralization, and the return of tyranny. When the dust settled from these very modern revolutions, Europe and North America were forever changed.

Europe after the Napoleonic era Europe continued to reverberate with change. New ideologies and artistic movements sought to grapple with the problems of industrialization, individualism, and ideals of human perfectibility. Meanwhile, a conservative backlash in politics sought to reestablish some semblance of tradition. This push, exemplified by Prince Clemens von Metternich, culminated in yet more revolutions: those of 1848. While these failed, the dialectical forces culminated in new philosophies of realism and cultural nationalism. These forces were strong enough to create new nation-states. Conflicts over nationalist ambitions, the second phase of industrialization, and the struggle over colonial empires led to the breakdown of the "Concert of Europe."

The alliances that emerged would carry the continent, and eventually the world, to war. In the roughly 150 years covered in this chapter, absolute monarchy would fall to middle-class liberalism, which in turn would be challenged by the forces ethnic nationalism.

22.1   Jean Jacques Rousseau, and *The Social Contract*

The political philosophy of Jean-Jacques Rousseau (1712–1778) exerted enormous influence on both the Enlightenment and the revolutions that swept the western world in late eighteenth and first of the nineteenth centuries. In *The Social Contract* (1762), Rousseau articulated his concepts of will and power. He also provided commentary on various styles of governments. His work greatly influenced not only republican forms of government in general, but the French Revolution in particular.

Source: Jean Jacques Rousseau, *The Social Contract, Or Principles of Political Right.* Book III, Part 4, 1762.

He who makes the law knows better than anyone else how it should be executed and interpreted. It seems then impossible to have a better constitution than that in which the executive and legislative powers are united; but this very fact renders the government in certain respects inadequate, because things which should be distinguished are confounded, and the prince and the Sovereign, being the same person, form, so to speak, no more than a government without government.

It is not good for him who makes the laws to execute them, or for the body of the people to turn its attention away from a general standpoint and devote it to particular objects. Nothing is more dangerous than the influence of private interests in public affairs, and the abuse of the laws by the government is a less evil than the corruption of the legislator, which is the inevitable sequel to a particular standpoint. In such a case, the State being altered in substance, all reformation becomes impossible, A people that would never misuse governmental powers would never misuse independence; a people that would always govern well would not need to be governed.

If we take the term in the strict sense, there never has been a real democracy, and there never will be. It is against the natural order for the many to govern and the few to be governed. It is unimaginable that the people should remain continually assembled to devote their time to public affairs, and it is clear that they cannot set up commissions for that purpose without the form of administration being changed.

In fact, I can confidently lay down as a principle that, when the functions of government are shared by several tribunals, the less numerous sooner or later acquire the greatest authority, if only because they are in a position to expedite affairs, and power thus naturally comes into their hands.

Besides, how many conditions that are difficult to unite does such a government presuppose! First, a very small State, where the people can readily be got together and where each citizen can with ease know all the rest; secondly, great simplicity of manners, to prevent business from multiplying and raising thorny problems; next, a large measure of equality in rank and fortune, without which equality of rights and authority cannot long subsist; lastly, little or no luxury — for luxury either comes of riches or makes them necessary; it corrupts at once rich and poor, the rich by possession and the poor by covetousness; it sells the country to softness and vanity, and takes away from the State all its citizens, to make them slaves one to another, and one and all to public opinion.

This is why a famous writer has made virtue the fundamental principle of Republics; for all these conditions could not exist without virtue. But, for want of the necessary distinctions, that great thinker was often inexact, and sometimes obscure, and did not see that, the sovereign authority being everywhere the same, the same principle should be found in every well-constituted State, in a greater or less degree, it is true, according to the form of the government.

It may be added that there is no government so subject to civil wars and intestine agitations as democratic or popular government, because there is none which has so strong and continual a tendency to change to another form, or which demands more vigilance and courage for its maintenance as it is. Under such a constitution above all, the citizen should arm himself with strength and constancy, and say, every day of his life, what a virtuous Count Palatinesaid in the Diet of Poland: *Malo periculosam libertatem quam quietum servitium.*

Were there a people of gods, their government would be democratic. So perfect a government is not for men.

Reading and Discussion Questions
1. Why does Rousseau say there has never been a real democracy?
2. What, according to Rousseau, is the fundamental principle of all Republics? Is this principle evident in today's democracies?

3. List three reasons Rousseau says democracy is not meant for men (by which he means humans, not males).

22.2 Olympe de Gouges, *Declaration of the Rights of Woman and the Female Citizen*

Olympe de Gouges (1748-1793 CE) was a French feminist, writer, and playwright. De Gouges wrote plays that dealt with a variety of sensitive subjects, such as divorce and sexual relations. Taking the Revolution's Declaration of the Rights of Man and of the Citizen as a guide, de Gouges wrote a similar document on the rights of women, advocating equal rights for men and women. Her opposition to the execution of the king and his family in 1793 exposed her to radical revolutionaries during the Great Terror. As a result, she was guillotined for her opposition to the revolutionary National Convention.

Source: Olympe de Gouges, *Declaration of the Rights of Woman and the Female Citizen* (1791).

TO THE QUEEN: MADAME

Little accustomed the language which one speaks to royalty, I will not employ the adulation of courtiers by dedicating this unusual production to you. My goal, Madam, is to speak to you frankly. I did not wait for the present time of freedom to express myself thus. I declared myself with the same energy when the blindness of despots punished such a noble audacity.

But when all the Empire held you responsible for its calamities, I alone, in a time of disorder and storm, had the force to take your defense. I never could persuade myself that a Princess, high within the state, had all the defects of lowness.

Yes, Madame, when I saw the sword raised against you, I threw my observations between that sword and you, but today when I see who is observed near the crowd of useless hirelings, and [when I see] that she is restrained by fear of the laws, I will tell you, Madame, what I did not say then.

If the foreigner bears arms into France, you are no longer in my eyes this falsely accused Queen, this attractive Queen, but an implacable enemy of the French. Oh, Madame, bear in mind that you are mother and wife; employ all your credit for the return of Princes. This credit, if wisely applied, strengthens the father's crown, saves it for the son, and reconciles you to the love of the French. This worthy negotiation is the true duty of a queen. Intrigue, cabals, bloody projects will precipitate your fall, if it is possible that you are capable of such plots.

Madame, may a noble function characterize you, excite your ambition, and fix your attentions. Only one whom chance has elevated to an eminent position can assume the task of lending weight to the progress of the Rights of Woman and of hastening its success. If you were less well informed, Madame, I might fear that your individual interests would outweigh those of your sex. You love glory; think, Madame, the greatest crimes immortalize one as much as the greatest virtues, but what a different fame in the annals of history! The one is ceaselessly taken as an example, and the other is eternally the execration of the human race.

It will never be a crime for you to work for the restoration of customs, to give your sex all the firmness of which it is capable. This is not the work of one day, unfortunately for the new regime. This revolution will happen only when all women are aware of their deplorable fate, and of the rights they have lost in society.

Madame, support such a beautiful cause; defend this unfortunate sex, and soon you will have half the realm on your side, and at least one-third of the other half.

Those, Madame, are the feats by which you should show and use your credit. Believe me, Madame, our life is a pretty small thing, especially for a Queen, when it is not embellished by people's affection and by the eternal delights of good deeds.

If it is true that the French arm all the powers against their own Fatherland, why? For frivolous prerogatives, for chimeras. Believe, Madame, if I judge by what I feel - the monarchical party will be destroyed by itself, it will abandon tyrants, and all hearts will rally around the fatherland to defend it.

There are my principles, Madame. In speaking to you of my fatherland, I lose sight of the purpose of this dedication. Thus, any good citizen sacrifices his glory and his interests when he has none other than those of his country.

I am with the most profound respect, Madame,

Your most humble and most obedient servant,

de Gouges.

THE RIGHTS OF WOMAN

Man, are you capable of being just? It is a woman who poses the question, you will not deprive her of that right at least. Tell me, what gives you sovereign empire to oppress my sex? Your strength? Your talents? Observe the Creator in his wisdom; survey in all her grandeur that nature with whom you seem to want to be in harmony, and give me, if you dare, an example of this tyrannical empire. Go back to animals, consult the elements, study plants, finally glance at all the modifications of organic matter, and surrender to the evidence when I offer you the means; search, probe, and distinguish, if you can, the sexes in the administration of nature. Everywhere you will find them mingled; everywhere they cooperate in harmonious togetherness in this immortal masterpiece.

Man alone has raised his exceptional circumstances to a principle. Bizarre, blind, bloated with science and degenerated - in a century of enlightenment and wisdom - into the crassest ignorance, he wants to command as a despot a sex which is in full possession of its intellectual faculties, he pretends to enjoy the Revolution and to claim his rights to equality in order to say nothing more about

DECLARATION OF THE RIGHTS OF WOMAN AND THE FEMALE CITIZEN

Preamble

The mothers, daughters, sisters, representatives of the nation, ask to constitute a National Assembly. Considering that ignorance, forgetfulness or contempt of the rights of women are the sole causes of public miseries, and of corruption of governments, they have resolved to set forth in a solemn declaration, the natural, unalterable and sacred rights of woman, so that this declaration being ever present to all members of the social body, may unceasingly remind them of their rights and their duties; in order that the acts of women's power, as well as those of men, may be judged constantly against the aim of all political institutions, and thereby be more respected for it, in order that the complaints of women citizens, based henceforth on simple and indisputable principles, may always take the direction of maintaining the Constitution, good morals and the welfare of all.

In consequence, the sex superior in beauty and in courage in maternal suffering recognizes and declares, in the presence of and under the auspices of the supreme Being, the following rights of woman and of the woman citizen:

1.   Woman is born free and remains equal to man in rights. Social distinctions can be based only on common utility.

2.   The aim of every political association is the preservation of the natural and imprescriptible rights of man and woman. These rights are liberty, prosperity, security and above all, resistance to oppression.

3.   The source of all sovereignty resides essentially in the Nation, which is nothing but the joining together of Man and Woman; no body, no individual, can exercise authority that does not emanate expressly from it.

4.   Liberty and justice consist in giving back to others all that belongs to them; thus the only limits on the exercise of woman's natural rights are the perpetual tyranny by which man opposes her; these limits must be reformed by the laws of nature and of reason.

5.   The laws of nature and reason forbid all actions that are harmful to society; all that is not forbidden by these wise and divine laws cannot be prevented, and no one can be constrained to do what they do not prescribe.

6.   Law must be the expression of the general will: all citizens, men and women alike, must personally or through their representatives concur in its formation; it must be the same for all; all citizens, men and women alike, being equal before it, must be equally eligible for all high offices, positions and public employments, according to their abilities, and without distinctions other than their virtues and talents.

7.   No woman can be an exception: she will be accused, apprehended and detained in cases determined by law; women, like men, will obey the rigorous rule.

8.   The law must establish only those penalties which are strictly and clearly necessary, and no woman can be punished by virtue of a law established and promulgated prior to the offense, and legally applied to women.

9.   When a woman is declared guilty, full severity is exercised by the law.

10.   No one ought to be disturbed for one's opinions, however fundamental they are; since a woman has the right to mount the scaffold, she must also have the right to address the House, providing her interventions do not disturb the public order as it has been established by law.

11.   The free communication of ideas and opinions is one of the most precious rights of woman, since this freedom ensures the legitimacy of fathers towards their children. Every woman citizen can therefore say freely: I am a mother of a child that belongs to you, without being forced to conceal the truth because of barbaric prejudice; except to be answerable for abuses of this liberty as determined by law.

12.   The guarantee of the rights of woman and of the rights of the woman citizen is a necessary benefit; this guarantee must be instituted for the advantage of all, and not for the personal benefit of those to whom it is entrusted.

13.   For the upkeep of public forces and for administrative expenses, the contribution of woman and man are equal; a woman shares in all the labors required by law, in the painful tasks; she must therefore have an equal share in the distribution of offices, employments, trusts, dignities and work.

14.   Women and men citizens have the right to ascertain by themselves or through their representatives the necessity of public taxes. Women citizens will not only assume an equal part in pro-viding the wealth but also in the public administration and in determining the quota, the assessment, the collection and the duration of the impost.

15.   The mass of women, joined together to contribute their taxes with those of men, have the right to demand from every public official an accounting of his administration.

16.   Any society in which the guarantee of rights is not assured, nor the separation of powers determined, has no Constitution: the Constitution is null if the majority of the individuals of whom the nation is comprised

have not participated in its drafting.

17.   Ownership of property is for both sexes, mutually and separately; it is for each a sacred and inviolable right; no one can be deprived of it as a true patrimony from nature, unless a public necessity, legally established, evidently demands it, and with the condition of a just and prior indemnity.

AFTERWORD

Women, wake up! The alarm bell of reason is making itself heard throughout the universe; recognize your rights. The powerful empire of nature is no longer beset by prejudices, fanaticism, superstition and lies. The torch of truth has dispelled all clouds of stupidity and usurpation. The enslaved man multiplied his forces but has had to resort to yours to break his chains. Once free he became unjust to his female companion. O women! women, when will you stop being blind? What advantages have you received from the revolution? A more pronounced scorn, a more marked contempt? During the centuries of corruption, your only power was over the weaknesses of men. Your empire is destroyed, what then is left to you? The conviction that men are unjust. The claiming of your patrimony based on the wise laws of nature. The good word of [Jesus Christ] the Lawgiver of the Marriage at Cana? Are you afraid that our French lawmakers, correctors of this morality, so long tied up with the politics which is no longer in style will say to you: "Women, what is there in common between you and us?" Everything, you would have to reply. If they persisted in their weakness, in putting forth this inconsistency which is a contradiction of their principles, you should courageously oppose these male pretensions of superiority with the forces of reason; unite under the banner of philosophy, unfold all the energy of your character and you will soon see these proud men, your servile adorers, crawling at your feet, but proud to share with you the treasures of the Supreme being. Whatever the obstacles that oppose us may be, it is in your power to free us, you have only to will it...Since it is now a question of national education, let us see if our wise lawmakers will think wisely about the education of women.

Women have done more harm than good. Constraint and dissimulation have been their lot. What force had robbed them of, ruse returned to them. Poison and the sword were both subject to them; they commanded in crime as in fortune. The French government, especially, depended throughout the centuries on the nocturnal administration of women; the cabinet kept no secret from their indiscretion; ambassadorial post, command, ministry, presidency, pontificate, college of cardinals; finally, anything which characterises the folly of men, profane and sacred, all have been subject to the cupidity and ambition of this sex, formerly contemptible and respected, and since the revolution, respectable and scorned.

In this sort of contradictory situation, what remarks could I not make! I have but a moment to make them, but this moment will fix the attention of the remotest posterity. Under the Old Regime, all was vicious, all was guilty; but could not the amelioration of conditions be perceived even in the substance of vices? A woman only had to be beautiful or amiable; when she possessed these two advantages, she saw a hundred fortunes at her feet. If she did not profit from them, she had a bizarre character or a rare philosophy which made her scorn wealth; then she was deemed to be like a crazy woman; the most indecent made herself respected with gold; commerce in women was a kind of industry in the first class [of society], which, henceforth, will have no more credit. If it still had it, the revolution would be lost, and under the new relationships we would always be corrupted; however, reason can always be deceived [into believing] that any other road to fortune is closed to the woman whom a man buys, like the slave on the African coasts. The difference is great; that is known. The slave is commanded by the master; but if the slave has lost all her charms, what will become of this unfortunate woman? The victim of scorn, even the doors of charity are closed to her; she is poor and old, they say; why did she not know how to make her fortune? Reason finds other examples that are even more touching. A young, inexperienced woman, seduced by a man whom she loves, will abandon her parents to follow him; the ingrate will leave her after a few years, and the older she has become with him, the more inhuman is his inconstancy; if she has children, he will likewise abandon them. If he is rich, he will consider himself excused from sharing his fortune with his noble victims. If some involvement binds him to his duties, he will deny them, trusting that the laws will support him. If he is married, any other obligation loses its rights. What laws remain to extirpate vice all the way to its root? The law of dividing wealth and public administration between men and women. It can easily be seen that one who is born into a rich family gains very much from such equal sharing. But the one born into a poor family with merit and virtue - what is her lot? Poverty and opprobrium. If she does not precisely excel in music or painting, she cannot be admitted to any public function when she has all the capacity for it. I do not to give only a sketch of things; I will go more deeply into this in the new edition of all my political writings, with notes, which I propose to give to the public in a few days.

I take up my text again on the subject of morals. Marriage is the tomb of trust and love. The married woman can with impunity give bastards to her husband, and also give them the wealth that does not belong to them. The woman who is unmarried has only one feeble right; ancient and inhuman laws refuse to her for her children the right to the name and the wealth of their father; no new laws have been made in this matter. If it is considered a paradox and an impossibility on my part to try to give my sex an honorable and just consistency, I leave it to men to attain glory for dealing with this matter; but while we wait, the way can be prepared through national education, the restoration of morals, and conjugal conventions.

FORM FOR A SOCIAL CONTRACT BETWEEN MAN AND WOMAN

We, _____ and _____, moved by our own will, unite ourselves for the duration of our lives, and for the duration of our mutual inclinations, under the following conditions: We intend and wish to make our wealth communal, meanwhile reserving to ourselves the right to divide it in favor of our children and of those to whom we might have a particular inclination, mutually recognizing that our property belongs directly to our children, from whatever bed they come, and that all of them without distinction have the right to bear the name of the fathers and mothers who have acknowledged them, and we are charged to subscribe to the law which punishes the renunciation of one's own blood. We likewise obligate ourselves, in case of separation, to divide our wealth and to set aside in advance the portion the law indicates for our children, and in the event of a perfect union, the one who dies will divest himself of half his property in his child's favour, and if one dies childless, the survivor will inherit by right, unless the dying person has disposed of half the common property in favour of one whom he judged deserving.

That is approximately the formula for the marriage act I propose for execution. Upon reading this strange document, I see rising up against me the hypocrites, the prudes, the clergy, and the whole infernal sequence. But how it [my proposal] offers to the wise the moral means of achieving the perfection of a happy government! I am going to give in a few words the physical proof of it. The rich, childless Epicurean finds it very good to go to his poor neighbour to augment his family. When there is a law authorising a poor man's wife to have a rich one adopt their children, the bonds of society will be strengthened and morals will be purer. This law will perhaps save the community's wealth and hold back the disorder which drives so many victims to the almshouses of shame, to a low station, and into degenerate human principles where nature has groaned for so long. May the detractors of wise philosophy then cease to cry out against primitive morals, or may they lose their point in the source of their citations.

Moreover, I would like a law which would assist widows and young girls deceived by the false promises of a man to whom they were attached: I would like, I say, this law to force an inconstant man to hold to his obligations or at least [to pay] an indemnity equal to his wealth. Again, I would like this law to be rigorous against women, at least those who have the effrontery to have recourse to a law which they themselves had violated by their misconduct, if proof of that were given. At the same time, as I showed in Le Bonheur primitif de l'Homme, in 1788, that prostitutes should be placed in designated quarters. It is not prostitutes who contribute the most to the depravity of morals, it is the women of society. In regenerating the latter, the former are changed. This link of fraternal union will first bring disorder, but in consequence it will produce at the end a perfect harmony.

I offer a foolproof way to elevate the soul of women; it is to join them to all the activities of man; if man persists in finding this way impractical, let him share his fortune with woman, not at his caprice, but by the wisdom of laws. Prejudice falls, morals are purified, and nature regains all her rights. Add to this the marriage of priests and the strengthening of the king on his throne, and the French government cannot fail.

It would be very necessary to say a few words on the troubles which are said to be caused by the decree in favor of colored men in our islands. There is where nature shudders with horror; there is where reason and humanity have still not touched callous souls; there, especially, is where division and discord stir up their inhabitants. It is not difficult to divine the instigators of these incendiary fermentations; they are even in the midst of the National Assembly; they ignite the flame in Europe which must inflame America. Colonists make a claim to reign as despots over the men whose fathers and brothers they are; and, disowning the rights of nature, they trace the source of [their rule] to the scantiest tint of their blood. These inhuman colonists say: our blood flows in their veins, but we will shed it all if necessary to glut our greed or our blind ambition. It is in these places nearest to nature where the father scorns the son; deaf to the cries of blood, they stifle all its attraction; what can be hoped from the resistance opposed to them? To constrain [blood] violently is to render it terrible; to leave [blood] still enchained is to direct all calamities towards America. A divine hand seems to spread liberty abroad throughout the realms of man; only the law has the right to curb this liberty if it degenerates into license, but it must be equal for all; liberty must hold the National Assembly to its decree dictated by prudence and justice. May it act the same way for the state of France and render her as attentive to new abuses as she was to the ancient ones which each day become more dreadful. My opinion would be to reconcile the executive and legislative power, for it seems to me that the one is everything and the other is nothing - whence comes, unfortunately perhaps, the loss of the French Empire. I think that these two powers, like man and woman, should be united but equal in force and virtue to make a good household.

Reading and Discussion Questions

1. Does the Declaration give women any real responsibilities or does it simply ascribe to them the same rights as men?
2. How many of the rights that de Gouges advocates for women have been achieved?
3. In article 11, the "free communication of ideas and opinions" is held to be one of the most precious rights of women. What, specifically, is de Gouges referring to?

22.3   Charles Maurice Talleyrand to Louis XVIII

Charles Maurice de Talleyrand (1754-1838) was one of the most skilled diplomats of the 19th century, if not of all time. He served, in one capacity or another, under several French rulers, including Louis XVI, Napoleon, Louis XVIII, Charles X, and Louis-Philippe. He was in instrumental in the restoration of the Bourbon dynasty and served as the French ambassador to the Congress of Vienna. In this letter to Louis XVIII (r. 1814-1824), he reports on his secret treaty with England and Austria that ended the anti-French coalition.

Source: Talleyrand to Louis XVIII, January 4, 1815, in James Harvey Robinson, ed., *Readings in European History*, 2 Vols., (Boston: Ginn and Co., 1904-1905), II: 534-536.

Vienna, January 4, 1815

Sire:

I have received the letter of the 23d of last month with which your Majesty deigned to honor me. On the 21st of the present month, the anniversary of a day of horror and eternal mourning, a solemn expiatory service will be celebrated in one of the principal churches of Vienna. . . . Everything in this sad ceremony must be proportioned to the grandeur of its object, the splendor of the crown of France, and the quality of those who are to be present. All the members of the Congress will be invited, and I am sure that they will come. . . .

The news of the signature of peace between England and the United States of America was announced to me on New Year's day by a note from Lord Castlereagh.

I hastened to offer him my congratulations, and I also congratulated myself on the event, feeling that it may influence both the disposition of the minister and the resolution of those with whose pretensions we have had to contend hitherto. Lord Castlereagh showed me the treaty. It does not touch the honor of either of the two parties concerned and consequently it will satisfy both.

This happy intelligence was only the precursor of a still more fortunate event. The spirit of the coalition, and the coalition itself, had survived the Peace of Paris. My correspondence up to the present time has supplied your Majesty with repeated proofs of this. If the plans which, on arriving here, I found had been formed, had been carried into execution, France might have stood alone in Europe without being in good relations with any one single power for half a century to come. All my efforts were directed to the prevention of so great a misfortune, but my most ardent hopes did not reach the height of a complete success.

But now, sire, the coalition is dissolved, and forever. Not only does France no longer stand alone in Europe, but your Majesty is already in an alliance such as it seemed that fifty years of negotiation could not have procured for her. France is now in concert with two of the greatest powers and three states of the second order, and will soon be in concert with all the states which are guided by other than revolutionary principles and maxims. Your Majesty will be, in reality, the head and soul of that union, formed for the defense of the principles which your Majesty has been the first to proclaim.

So great and happy a change is only to be attributed to that special favor of Providence which was so clearly indicated by the restoration of your Majesty to the throne. Under God, the efficient causes of this change have been:

My letters to Monsieur de Metternich and Lord Castlereagh and the impressions which they have produced;

The suggestions which I gave Lord Castlereagh relative to a union with France and of which I gave your Majesty an account in my last letter;

The pains I have taken to lull his distrust by exhibiting perfect disinterestedness in the name of France;

The peace with America, which, by releasing him from difficulty on that side, has left him more liberty of action and given him greater courage;

Lastly, the pretensions of Russia and Prussia, as set forth in the Russian project of which I have the honor to subjoin a copy; and especially the manner in which those pretensions were advanced and argued in a conference between their plenipotentiaries and those of Austria. The arrogant tone of that insolent and nonsensical document so deeply offended Lord Castlereagh that, departing from his habitual calmness, he declared that the Russians were claiming to lay down the law and that England was not disposed to accept that from anybody.

Reading and Discussion Questions

1. What does Talleyrand tell Louis XVIII about the opinion of the French when he arrived at the Congress? Why would the French occupy such a position?
2. Talleyrand reports "the coalition is dissolved." To whom does he attribute the change in allegiance? Does this square with Enlightenment thinking?
3. Does Talleyrand announce a balance of power in Europe? If not, what is he reporting to the Louis XVIII?

22.4   Abraham Lincoln's First Inaugural Address

When Abraham Lincoln (1809-1865) delivered his Inaugural Address, the United States was on the verge of disunion. Seven southern states had summoned conventions and voted to secede from the union. The secessionist states wasted no time in forming a general government and had inaugurated a president of their own—all before Lincoln's inauguration. Lincoln thus assumed the presidency confronted with the gravest crisis that the U.S. had ever faced. The following selections from Lincoln's address reveal his understanding of the nature of the union of American states and ideals about democracy.

Source: http://www.bartleby.com/124/pres31.html

It is seventy-two years since the first inauguration of a President under our National Constitution. During that period fifteen different and greatly distinguished citizens have in succession administered the executive branch of the Government. They have conducted it through many perils, and generally with great success. Yet, with all this scope of precedent, I now enter upon the same task for the brief constitutional term of four years under great and peculiar difficulty. A disruption of the Federal Union, heretofore only menaced, is now formidably attempted.

I hold that in contemplation of universal law and of the Constitution the Union of these States is perpetual. Perpetuity is implied, if not expressed, in the fundamental law of all national governments. It is safe to assert that no government proper ever had a provision in its organic law for its own termination. Continue to execute all the express provisions of our National Constitution, and the Union will endure forever, it being impossible to destroy it except by some action not provided for in the instrument itself.

Again: If the United States be not a government proper, but an association of States in the nature of contract merely, can it, as a contract, be peaceably unmade by less than all the parties who made it? One party to a contract may violate it-break it, so to speak-but does it not require all to lawfully rescind it?

Descending from these general principles, we find the proposition that in legal contemplation the Union is perpetual confirmed by the history of the Union itself. The Union is much older than the Constitution. It was formed, in fact, by the Articles of Association in 1774. It was matured and continued by the Declaration of Independence in 1776. It was further matured, and the faith of all the then thirteen States expressly plighted and engaged that it should be perpetual, by the Articles of Confederation in 1778. And finally, in 1787, one of the declared objects for ordaining and establishing the Constitution was "to form a more perfect Union."

But if destruction of the Union by one or by a part only of the States be lawfully possible, the Union is less perfect than before the Constitution, having lost the vital element of perpetuity.

It follows from these views that no State upon its own mere motion can lawfully get out of the Union; that resolves and ordinances to that effect are legally void, and that acts of violence within any State or States against the authority of the United States are insurrectionary or revolutionary, according to circumstances.

I therefore consider that in view of the Constitution and the laws the Union is unbroken, and to the extent of my ability, I shall take care, as the Constitution itself expressly enjoins upon me, that the laws of the Union be faithfully executed in all the States. Doing this I deem to be only a simple duty on my part, and I shall perform it so far as practicable unless my rightful masters, the American people, shall withhold the requisite means or in some authoritative manner direct the contrary. I trust this will not be regarded as a menace, but only as the declared purpose of the Union that it will constitutionally defend and maintain itself.

In doing this there needs to be no bloodshed or violence, and there shall be none unless it be forced upon the national authority. The power confided to me will be used to hold, occupy, and possess the property and places belonging to the Government and to collect the duties and imposts; but beyond what may be necessary for these objects, there will be no invasion, no using of force against or among the people anywhere. Where hostility to the United States in any interior locality shall be so great and universal as to prevent competent resident citizens from holding the Federal offices, there will be no attempt to force obnoxious strangers among the people for that object. While the strict legal right may exist in the Government to enforce the exercise of these offices, the attempt to do so would be so irritating and so nearly impracticable withal that I deem it better to forego for the time the uses of such offices.

The mails, unless repelled, will continue to be furnished in all parts of the Union. So far as possible the people everywhere shall have that sense of perfect security which is most favorable to calm thought and reflection. The course here indicated will be followed unless current events and experience shall show a modification or change to be proper, and in every case and exigency my best discretion will be exercised, according to circumstances actually existing and with a view and a hope of a peaceful solution of the national troubles and the restoration of fraternal sympathies and affections.

That there are persons in one section or another who seek to destroy the Union at all events and are glad of any pretext to do it I will neither affirm nor deny; but if there be such, I need address no word to them. To those, however, who really love the Union may I not speak?

Before entering upon so grave a matter as the destruction of our national fabric, with all its benefits, its memories, and its hopes, would it not be wise to ascertain precisely why we do it? Will you hazard so desperate a step while there is any possibility that any portion of the ills you fly from have no real existence? Will you, while the certain ills you fly to are greater than all the real ones you fly from, will you risk the commission of so fearful a mistake?

All profess to be content in the Union if all constitutional rights can be maintained. Is it true, then, that any right plainly written in the Constitution has been denied? I think not. Happily, the human mind is so constituted that no party can reach to the audacity of doing this. Think, if you can, of a single instance in which a plainly written provision of the Constitution has ever been denied. If by the mere force of numbers a majority should deprive a minority of any clearly written constitutional right, it might in a moral point of view justify revolution; certainly would if such right were a vital one. But such is not our case. All the vital rights of minorities and of individuals are so plainly assured to them by affirmations and negations, guaranties and prohibitions, in the Constitution that controversies never arise concerning them. But no organic law can ever be framed with a provision specifically applicable to every question which may occur in practical administration. No foresight can anticipate nor any document of reasonable length contain express provisions for all possible questions. Shall fugitives from labor be surrendered by national or by State authority? The Constitution does not expressly say.

May Congress prohibit slavery in the Territories? The Constitution does not expressly say. Must Congress protect slavery in the Territories? The Constitution does not expressly say.

From questions of this class spring all our constitutional controversies, and we divide upon them into majorities and minorities. If the minority will not acquiesce, the majority must, or the Government must cease. There is no other alternative, for continuing the Government is acquiescence on one side or the other. If a minority in such case will secede rather than acquiesce, they make a precedent which in turn will divide and ruin them, for a minority of their own will secede from them whenever a majority refuses to be controlled by such minority. For instance, why may not any portion of a new confederacy a year or two hence arbitrarily secede again, precisely as portions of the present Union now claim to secede from it? All who cherish disunion sentiments are now being educated to the exact temper of doing this.

.... Plainly the central idea of secession is the essence of anarchy. A majority held in restraint by constitutional checks and limitations, and always changing easily with deliberate changes of popular opinions and sentiments, is the only true sovereign of a free people. Whoever rejects it does of necessity fly to anarchy or to despotism. Unanimity is impossible. The rule of a minority, as a permanent arrangement, is wholly inadmissible; so that, rejecting the majority principle, anarchy or despotism in some form is all that is left.

Reading and Discussion Questions
1.   What does Lincoln say in reference to his views of the union between the states?
2.   Why does Lincoln argue, "secession is the essence of anarchy?" How do Lincoln's comments in this regard square with Rousseau's notions of democracy in the reading from The Social Contract?

22.5   Proclamation of the German Empire

While both Italy and the United States were fighting wars of unification, so too was Germany. The Prussian state at the end of the Congress of Vienna was composed of 39 independent states. Under King Wilhelm I and Prime Minister Otto von Bismarck these states were brought under the control of Prussia. The proclamation of German empire was issued from the palace at Versailles, France, which Prussia had just defeated in the Franco-Prussian War. The official account of the reestablishment of the German empire appeared in Berlin, January 24, 1871.

Source: "Official Account of Proclamation of the German Empire, January 24, 1871." In James Harvey Robinson, ed., Readings in European History, 2 Vols., (Boston: Ginn and Co., 1904-1905), II: 595-597.

In the palace of Louis XIV, in that ancient center of a hostile power which for centuries has striven to divide and humiliate Germany, the solemn proclamation of the German empire was made on January 18, exactly one hundred and seventy years after the assumption of the royal dignity by the Prussian sovereigns at Konigsberg. Though the German people, owing to the necessities of the times, were represented at the ceremony only by the German army, the eyes of the entire nation were gratefully turned to the place where, surrounded by sovereigns, generals, and soldiers, King William announced to the world the assumption by himself and his heirs of a title for the reestablishment of which we have been yearning during the sixty long years it has been in abeyance.

As yet the infatuation of the enemy does not permit us to throw aside the weapons we have taken up in self-defense; and as our unity arose out of the first part of the campaign, so will our empire be strengthened by the remaining feats of arms. By the self-sacrificing devotion of all classes of society, the nation has proved that it still possesses that warlike prowess which distinguished our ancestors. It has recovered its ancient position in Europe; and, neither fearing an adversary nor envying any neighbor, discreet and temperate in its acts and aims, it accepts the destiny prophesied for it in the proclamation of its new emperor. This destiny is to add to its power not by conquest but by promoting culture, liberty, and civilization. As far as the German people are concerned, there will be no more wars in Europe after the determination of the present campaign. . . .

Owing to the unfavorable weather the festive procession which was to conduct his Majesty from the prefecture to the palace did not take place. The crown prince, with Lieutenant-General Blumenthal, his chief of staff, and an escort of Prussians, Würtembergers, Badeners, and Bavarians, drove to the palace to receive his royal father at the eastern portal in front of the Princes' Stairway. In the courtyard of the palace a company of the king's own troops was drawn up as a guard of honor. . . .

At a quarter past twelve his Majesty entered the hall, when a choir consisting of men of the Seventh, Forty Seventh, and Fifty-Eighth regiments intoned the choral, "Let all the world rejoice in the Lord." . . . When the choir ceased, the congregation sang one verse of the choral, "Praise and honor unto the Lord." The ordinary military liturgy was then read by the clergymen and a sermon preached by the Reverend A. Rogge. Alluding to the well-known inscription on the ceiling of the hall, "***Le roi governe par lui-même***," the preacher observed that the kings of Prussia had risen to greatness by adopting a different and more religious motto, namely, "The kings of the earth reign under me, saith the Lord." The *Te Deum laudamus* closed the service.

The king then walked up to where the colors were displayed, and, standing before them, read the document proclaiming the reestablishment of the German empire. Count Bismarck having read the king's proclamation to the German nation, the grand duke of Baden stepped forth and exclaimed, "Long live his Majesty the emperor!" The cheers of the assembly were taken up by the bands playing the national anthem.

Reading and Discussion Questions

1. What do you suppose is the significance of the proclamation being read from the court of the defeated enemy?
2. In what ways does this announcement differ from that of made by Victor Emmanuel to the Sardinian assembly (document 22.6)?
3. Discuss the fact that only German soldiers were present at the announcement in terms both of Enlightenment philosophies, Romanticism, and the announcements call for perpetual peace after the cessation of hostilities.

22.6 Victor Emmanuel and the Catholic Church

Victor Emmanuel (1820–1878) was the first king of a united Italy. The path to this position was not an easy one. Interstate allegiances, foreign wars, and shaky coalitions all aligned to upgrade Italy from Metternich's assertion that it was simply a "geographic expression." In this address to the Sardinian assembly, Emmanuel noted what seemed to him to be the largest check against Italian unification: the Church.

Source: Victor Emmanuel address to the Sardinian parliament, April 2, 1860. James Harvey Robinson, ed., *Readings in European History*, 2 Vols. (Boston: Ginn and Co. 1904–1906), II, 574–575.

Le roi governe par lui-même: the king governs alone

The last time that I opened this parliament, in the midst of the travails of Italy and dangers to the state, faith in divine justice encouraged me to prophesy a happy issue for us. In a very short space of time an invasion has been repelled; Lombardy has been freed, thanks to the glorious exploits of our heroes, and central Italy has been delivered, thanks to the remarkable courage of its inhabitants; and to-day the representatives of right and of the hopes of the nation are assembled about me.

We owe many benefits to a magnanimous ally, to the bravery of his soldiers as well as ours, to the self-abnegation of the volunteers, and to the harmony of the various peoples; and we render thanks to God, for without superhuman aid these enterprises, memorable not only for our own generation but for ages to come, could not have been achieved.

Out of gratitude to France for the services she has rendered to Italy, and in order to consolidate the union of the two nations, which have a community of origin, of principles, and of destiny, some sacrifice was necessary; I have made that one which costs most to my own heart. Subject to the vote of the people and the approbation of the parliament, I have agreed to a treaty providing for the reunion of Savoy and of the district of Nice to France.

We still have many difficulties to overcome, but, sustained by public opinion and by the love of the people, I will not permit any right or liberty to be infringed or diminished.

Although I am as consistent in my respect toward the supreme head of our religion as the Catholic rulers, my ancestors, have always shown themselves, nevertheless, should the ecclesiastical authority resort to spiritual arms in support of its temporal interests, I will, relying upon a pure conscience and the traditions of my forefathers, find strength to maintain civil liberty and my authority, for the exercise of which I owe an account only to God and to my people. . . .

Reading and Discussion Questions

1. Victor Emmanuel makes a clear distinction between the Church and the divine. What is the motive behind this distinction?
2. The King notes that public opinion must be on the nation's side in order for it to succeed. Would a European monarch have had the same concern for public opinion a century earlier?

Industrialization and its Discontents

Chapter 23

1750-1914

Industrialization in Western Europe transformed culture and society. Despite the many problems associated with industrialization, Europeans gained a standard of living never before experienced by such large numbers of people. Europe became the hub of the world.

New technologies such as the steam engine led to wave after wave of innovations. Soon there was a need for steel for railroads and a growing demand for coal to power machinery. The workplace was transformed in response to growing consumer demands. The large population boom also acted as a catalyst for change, placing stress upon pre-industrial social institutions. Modes of transportation and communication were transformed quickening the pace and intensity of European imperialism.

The rapid pace of change led to social strife. New political philosophies based on furthering individual or class liberties prompted people to seek new rights and freedoms. The idea of liberty made an impact on all social classes, generating tension and at times, rebellion, which forced dramatic changes upon European populations.

Living conditions became a prime subject of discussion. Debilitating sickness and premature death were a part of life for those who worked in factories, as they had been when they lived in the countryside. But critics of industrialization popularized their views through pamphlets and books that discussed worker issues and proposed new social and political arrangements to end worker suffering.

23.1 Adam Smith, *Wealth of Nations*

Adam Smith (1723-1790) was a political philosopher who wrote *The Wealth of Nations* (1776) to explain why some countries like Great Britain experienced higher levels of widespread wealth than poor countries. Smith explained that limited government regulation of economic activity and support for creative entrepreneurship allowed populations to flourish amid rising standards of living. He countered an assumption popular for centuries throughout Europe that people willingly sacrificing their self-interests for the common good could only achieve the common good in a society. Influenced by other writers in the Scottish Enlightenment, Smith insisted the pursuit of self-interests contributed to the good of a society. Smith's book, while part of a long line of economic treatise among European intellectuals, is credited for establishing the systematic study of economic activity and thus earned Smith the title of "father of economics." *The Wealth of Nations* widely influenced the rise of liberal regimes in North American and Europe from the late eighteenth century until the present.

Source: Adam Smith, *An Inquiry Into the Nature and Causes of the Wealth of Nations.* Ed. R. H. Campbell and A. S. Skinner, vol. IIof the *Glasgow Edition of the Works and Correspondence of Adam Smith* (Indianapolis: Liberty Fund, 1981), 456.

...every individual necessarily labors to render the annual revenue of society as great he can. He generally, indeed, neither intends to promote the public interest, nor knows how much he is promoting it. By preferring the support of domestic of that of foreign industry, he intends only his own security; and by directing that industry in such a manner as its produce may be of the greatest value, he intends only his own gain, and he is in this, as in many other cases, led by an invisible hand to promote an end which was no part of his intention.

Reading and Discussion Questions

1. Does the "invisible hand" metaphor still apply today compared to 1776 when Smith wrote *The Wealth of Nations*? Why or why not?
2. What does Smith mean by "his own security"?
3. What scale does Smith's "society" include? Global? Country? Community?

23.2 John Stuart Mill, *On Liberty*

John Stuart Mill (1806-1873) was a British philosopher whose writings focused on individual rights and freedoms. He wrote many books and essays in the span of his career and his book *On Liberty* (1869) focused on the idea that individuals should be able to act anyway they choose as long as their actions do not harm others. This famous "do no harm" principle directly impacted the evolution of social values and political principles in the nineteenth century.

Source: John Stuart Mill, *The Collected Works of John Stuart Mill, Volume XVIII - Essays on Politics and Society Part I,* ed. John M. Robson, Introduction by Alexander Brady (Toronto: University of Toronto Press, London: Routledge and Kegan Paul, 1977), 223-224.

That principle is, *that the* sole end *for which* mankind are warranted, individually or collectively, in interfering with *the* liberty of action of *any* of *their* number, is self-protection. *That the only purpose for which power can* be *rightfully exercised over any member* of a *civilized community, against his will,* is to prevent harm to others. *His* own good, either physical or moral, is not a sufficient warrant. He *can*not *rightfully* be compelled to do or *for*bear because it *will* be better *for* him to do so, because it *will* make him happier, because, in *the* opinions of others, to do so would be wise, or even right. *The*se are good reasons *for* remonstrating with him, or reasoning with him, or persuading him, or entreating him, but not *for* compelling him, or visiting him with *any* evil in case he do otherwise. To justify *that, the* conduct from *which* it is desired to deter him, must be calculated to produce evil to someone else. *The only* part of *the* conduct of *any* one, *for which* he is amenable to society, is *that which* concerns others. In *the* part *which* merely concerns himself, *his* independence is, of right, absolute. *Over* himself, *over his* own body and mind, *the* individual is sovereign.

Reading and Discussion Questions

1. Is Mill's idea too simplified to work or is his idea of individual liberty something transmittable to all eras of human existence?
2. How might working class conditions in Britain and the industrial revolution have shaped Mill's principle?
3. While often used in defense of workers and lower classes, how might Mill's "do no harm" principle be equally applied to protect the middle class and the wealthy?

23.3 Frederich Engels, *Condition of the Working Class in England*

The Condition of the Working Class in England in 1844 reflects Friederick Engel's (1820–1895) observations on the state of workers in Manchester, England. Engels was a political philosopher interested in the dynamic of social classes. Engels co-wrote *The Communist Manifesto* (1848) with Karl Marx (1818-1883). Both men focused on the gap between the upper and lower classes. The book focuses on health issues that the working class faced and class division between the wealthy owners and poor workers. This was the precursor to the writing of *The Communist Manifesto*, a book that served as an inspiration for socialist movements across Europe. Which includes issues about the problem with capitalism and class struggle between the rich and the poor. The book gives on a unique direct insight about the workers life and problems during the industrial revolution.

Source: Engels, Frederich, *The Condition of the Working-Class in England in 1844 with a Preface Written in 1892.* Translated by Florence Kelley Wischnewetzky (London: Swan Sonnenschein & Co., 1892), 105.

The result of all these influences is a general enfeeblement of the frame in the working-class. There are few vigorous, well-built, healthy persons among the workers, i.e., among the factory operatives, who are employed in confined rooms, and we are here discussing these only. They are almost all weakly, of angular but not powerful build, lean, pale, and of relaxed fiber, with the exception of the muscles especially exercised in their work. Nearly all suffer from indigestion, and consequently from a more or less hypochondria, melancholy, irritable, nervous condition. Their enfeebled constitutions are unable to rest disease, and are therefore seized by it on every occasion. Hence they are prematurely, and die early. On this point the mortality statistics supply unquestionably testimony.

Reading and Discussion Questions

1. How did Engels's concerns reflect his critique of industrialization?
2. How might his belief in socialism shape his observations of the working class? Would his ideological concerns bias his views toward working conditions?
3. How might descriptions such as Engels's impact political reform movements to improving working conditions?

23.4 Charles Dickens, *David Copperfield*

Charles Dickens (1812-1870) was one of the most prolific writers in the English language, authorizing many great works including *A Tale of Two Cities* and *A Christmas Carol*. He wrote his book *David Copperfield* in 1849, during the height of the industrial revolution in England. The book was partially a self-reflection piece for Dickens, who as a young man worked in a factory. For David Copperfield, the story's protagonist, factory life was difficult. His unkind stepfather had placed him there; he cleaned wine bottles and lived mostly on bread. Through his writing Dickens was able to express his own discontent with the conditions of factory life in Britain.

Source: Dickens, Charles. *David Copperfield* (Philadelphia: T.B. Peterson & Brothers, 1850), 195-96.

Murdstone and Grinby's trade was among a good many kinds of people, but an important branch of it was the supply of wines and spirits to certain packet ships. I forget now where they chiefly went, but I think there were some among them that made voyages both to the East and West Indies. I know that a great many empty bottles were one of the consequences of this traffic, and that certain men and boys were employed to examine them against the light, and reject those that were flawed, and to rinse and wash them. When the empty bottles ran short, there were labels to be pasted on full ones, or corks to be fitted to them, or seals to be put upon the casks. All this work was my work, and of the boys employed upon it I was one. There were three or four of us, counting me. My working place was established in a corner of the warehouse, where Mr. Quinion could see me, when he chose to stand up on the bottom rail of his stool in the counting-house, and look at me through a window above the desk. Hither, on the first morning of my so auspiciously beginning life on my own account, the oldest of the regular boys was summoned to show me my business. His name was Mick Walker, and he wore a ragged apron and a paper cap. He informed me that his father was a bargeman… No words can express the secret agony of my soul as I sunk into this companionship; compared these henceforth everyday associates with those of my happier childhood—not to say with Steerforth, Traddles, and the rest of those boys; an felt my hops of growing up to be a learned and distinguished man, crushed in my bosom. The deep remembrance of the sense I had, of being utterly without hope now; of the shame I felt in my position; of the misery it was to my young heart to believe that day by day what I had learned and thought, and delighted in , and raised my fancy and my emulation up by, would pass away from me, little by little, never to be brought back any more; cannot be written.

Reading and Discussion Questions

1. Why does David Copperfield's character emphasize getting an education?
2. Child labor was a common practice in nineteenth century factories, does Dickens hold a negative or positive view for his characters experience?
3. How do Dickens's true feelings break through his writing and shift the story from fiction to one of polemics?

23.5 Parliamentary Report on English Female Miners, 1842

Great Britain was the first country to undergo an industrial revolution, fueled in large part by the abundant coal deposits of Wales, Yorkshire, and Lancashire. Mining, like textile manufacture, was an occupation that exploited women and children. Not only did women and children work for less, their small bodies and nimble limbs permitted them to crawl the narrow tunnels to mine and haul the coal much more easily than men. Despite the clear economic advantages of using women and children in the English mines, by the 1840s there was a growing concern that the social and moral consequences of this exploitation were ruining the miners' family life. Agitation for reform in the mines compelled Parliament to investigate working conditions there and enact reform legislation to correct abuses. The following parliamentary reports printed in 1842 describe the working conditions for English women miners.

Source: Great Britain, Parliamentary Papers (1842), Vol. XVI, pp. 24, 196.

In England, exclusive of Wales, it is only in some of the colliery districts of Yorkshire and Lancashire that female Children of tender age and young and adult women are allowed to descend into the coal mines and regularly to perform the same kinds of underground work, and to work for the same number of hours, as boys and men; but in the East of Scotland their employment in the pits is general; and in South Wales it is not uncommon. West Riding of Yorkshire: Southern Part - In many of the collieries in this district, as far as relates to the underground employment, there is no distinction of sex, but the labour is distributed indifferently among both sexes, except that it is comparatively rare for the women to hew or get the coals, although there are numerous instances in which they regularly perform even this work. In great numbers of the coalpits in this district the men work in a state of perfect nakedness, and are in this state assisted in their labour by females of all ages, from girls of six years old to women of twenty-one, these females being themselves quite naked down to the waist.

"Girls," says the Sub-Commissioner [J. C. Symons], "regularly perform all the various offices of trapping, hurrying [Yorkshire terms for drawing the loaded coal wagons], filling, riddling, tipping, and occasionally getting, just as they are performed by boys. One of the most disgusting sights I have ever seen was that of young females, dressed like boys in trousers, crawling on all fours, with belts round their waists and chains passing between their legs, at day pits at Hunshelf Bank, and in many small pits near Holmfirth and New Mills: it exists also in several other places. I visited the Hunshelf Colliery on the 18th of January: it is a day pit; that is, there is no shaft or descent; the gate or entrance is at the side of a bank, and nearly horizontal. The gate was not more than a yard high, and in some places not above 2 feet.

"When I arrived at the board or workings of the pit I found at one of the sideboards down a narrow passage a girl of fourteen years of age in boy's clothes, picking down the coal with the regular pick used by the men. She was half sitting half lying at her work, and said she found it tired her very much, and of course she didn't like it.' The place where she was at work was not 2 feet high. Further on were men lying on their sides and getting. No less than six girls out of eighteen men and children are employed in this pit.

"Whilst I was in the pit the Rev. Mr Bruce, of Wadsley, and the Rev. Mr Nelson, of Rotherham, who accompanied me, and remained outside, saw another girl of ten years of age, also dressed in boy's clothes, who was employed in hurrying, and these gentlemen saw her at work. She was a nice-looking little child, but of course as black as a tinker, and with a little necklace round her throat.

"In two other pits in the Huddersfield Union I have seen the same sight. In one near New Mills, the chain, passing high up between the legs of two of these girls, had worn large holes in their trousers; and any sight more disgustingly indecent or revolting can scarcely be imagined than these girls at work - no brothel can beat it.

"On descending Messrs Hopwood's pit at Barnsley, I found assembled round a fire a group of men, boys, and girls, some of whom were of the age of puberty; the girls as well as the boys stark naked down to the waist, their hair bound up with a tight cap, and trousers supported by their hips. (At Silkstone and at Flockton they work in their shifts and trousers.) Their sex was recognizable only by their breasts, and some little difficulty occasionally arose in pointing out to me which were girls and which were boys, and which caused a good deal of laughing and joking. In the Flockton and Thornhill pits the system is even more indecent; for though the girls are clothed, at least three-fourths of the men for whom they "hurry" work stark naked, or with a flannel waistcoat only, and in this state they assist one another to fill the corves 18 or 20 times a day: I have seen this done myself frequently.

"When it is remembered that these girls hurry chiefly for men who are not their parents; that they go from 15 to 20 times a day into a dark chamber (the bank face), which is often 50 yards apart from any one, to a man working naked, or next to naked, it is not to be supposed but that where opportunity thus prevails sexual vices are of common occurrence. Add to this the free intercourse, and the rendezvous at the shaft or bullstake, where the corves are brought, and consider the language to which the young ear is habituated, the absence of religious instruction, and the early age at which contamination begins, and you will have before you, in the coal-pits where females are employed, the picture of a nursery for juvenile vice which you will go far and wide above ground to equal."

TWO WOMEN MINERS

Betty Harris, age 37: I was married at 23, and went into a colliery when I was married. I used to weave when about 12 years old; can neither read nor write. I work for Andrew Knowles, of Little Bolton, and make sometimes 7s a week, sometimes not so much. I am a drawer, and work from 6 in the morning to 6 at night. Stop about an hour at noon to eat my dinner; have bread and butter for dinner; I get no drink. I have two children, but they are too young to work. I worked at drawing when I was in the family way. I know a woman who has gone home and washed herself, taken to her bed, been delivered of a child, and gone to work again under the week.

I have a belt round my waist, and a chain passing between my legs, and I go on my hands and feet. The road is very steep, and we have to hold by a rope; and when there is no rope, by anything we can catch hold of. There are six women and about six boys and girls in the pit I work in; it is very hard work for a woman. The pit is very wet where I work, and the water comes over our clog-tops always, and I have seen it up to my thighs; it rains in at the roof terribly. My clothes are wet through almost all day long. I never was ill in my life, but when I was lying in.

My cousin looks after my children in the day time. I am very tired when I get home at night; I fall asleep sometimes before I get washed. I am not so strong as I was, and cannot stand my work so well as I used to. I have drawn till I have had the skin off me; the belt and chain is worse when we are in the family way. My feller (husband) has beaten me many a time for not being ready. I were not used to it at first, and he had little patience.

I have known many a man beat his drawer. I have known men take liberties with the drawers, and some of the women have bastards.

Patience Kershaw, age 17, Halifax: I go to pit at 5 o'clock in the morning and come out at 5 in the evening; I get my breakfast, porridge and milk, first; I take my dinner with me, a cake, and eat it as I go; I do not stop or rest at any time for the purpose, I get nothing else until I get home, and then have potatoes and meat, not every day meat.

I hurry in the clothes I have now got on - trousers and a ragged jacket; the bald place upon my head is made by thrusting the corves; I hurry the corves a mile and more under ground and back; they weigh 3 cwt. I hurry eleven a day. I wear a belt and chain at the workings to get the corves out. The getters that I work for are naked except their caps; they pull off all their clothes; I see them at work when I go up.

Sometimes they beat me if I am not quick enough, with their hands; they strike me upon my back. The boys take liberties with me sometimes; they pull me about. I am the only girl in the pit; there are about 20 boys and 15 men; all the men are naked. I would rather work in mill than in coal-pit.

Note by Sub-Commissioner Scriven: This girl is an ignorant, filthy, ragged, and deplorable looking object, and such a one as the uncivilized natives of the prairies would be shocked to look upon.

Reading and Discussion Questions

1. Considering the wretched conditions in which they worked, why would so many women work in the mines?
2. What were the psychological, familial, and social stresses the women miners endured?
3. Marx and Engels argued that capitalism and industrialism are inherently exploitive of women. Reading this document, would you agree?

23.6 Friedrich Nietzsche, from *Beyond Good and Evil*

Collectively, Friedrich Nietzsche's (1844-1900) writings are a fierce rejection of Western Civilization. His ideas influenced scientists, intellectuals, authors, and philosophers well into the twentieth century. Raised the son of a Lutheran minister in the Prussian region, as an adult he rejected middle-class Christian morality. He became a professor of classics in his early twenties at the university in Basel, Switzerland in 1869. He also served for a short time as a medical orderly during the Franco-Prussian War (1870-1871). Throughout his life, he suffered from mental and physical frailty, and his illnesses forced him to resign his post at the university in 1879. After this early retirement from his professional duties, he became interested in philosophy and natural sciences. For the next two years, he wrote scathing critiques of traditional approaches to philosophy and the study of the human psyche. He published this work, Beyond Good and Evil, in German, in1886. Nietzsche had a breakdown in 1889, and retreated for a year to a mental institution. He never fully recovered and spent the rest of his life being taken care of by his mother and sister.

Source: *Beyond Good and Evil*, trans. Helen Zimmern (Edinburgh: Darien Press, 1907), 5-12.

1.   The Will to Truth, which is to tempt us to many a hazardous enterprise, the famous Truthfulness of which all philosophers have hitherto spoken with respect, what questions has this Will to Truth not laid before us! What strange, perplexing, questionable questions! It is already a long story; yet it seems as if it were hardly commenced. Is it any wonder if we at last grow distrustful, lose patience, and turn impatiently away? That this Sphinx teaches us at last to ask questions ourselves? Who is it really that puts questions to us here? What really is this "Will to Truth" in us? In fact we made a long halt at the question as to the origin of this Will - until at last we came to an absolute standstill before a yet more fundamental question. We inquired about the value of this Will. Granted that we want the truth: why not rather untruth? And uncertainty?Even ignorance? The problem of the value of truth presented itself before us - or was it we who presented our-selves before the problem? Which of us is the Oedipus here? Which the Sphinx? It would seem to be a rendezvous of questions and notes of interrogation. And could it be believed that it at last seems to us as if the problem had never been propounded before, as if we were the first to discern it, get a sight of it, and risk raising it. For there is risk in raising it, perhaps there is no greater risk.

2.   "How could anything originate out of its opposite? For example, truth out of error?or the Will to Truth out of the will to deception? or the generous deed out of selfishness? or the pure sun-bright vision of the wise man out of covetousness? Such genesis is impossible; whoever dreams of it is a fool, nay, worse than a fool; things of the highest value must have a different origin, an origin of their own - in this transitory, seductive, illusory, paltry world, in this turmoil of delusion and cupidity, they cannot have their source. But rather in the lap of Being, in the intransitory, in the concealed God, in the 'Thing-in-itself' - there must be their source, and nowhere else!" - This mode of reasoning discloses the typical prejudice by which metaphysicians of all times can be recognized, this mode of valuation is at the back of all their logical procedure; through this "belief" of theirs, they exert themselves for their "knowledge," for something that is in the end solemnly christened "the Truth." The fundamental belief of metaphysicians is the belief in antitheses of values. It never occurred even to the wariest of them to doubt here on the very threshold (where doubt, however, was most necessary); though they had made a solemn vow, "de omnibus dubitandum." For it may be doubted, firstly, whether antitheses exist at all; and secondly, whether the popular valuations and antitheses of value upon which metaphysicians have set their seal, are not perhaps merely superficial estimates, merely provisional perspectives, besides being probably made from some corner, perhaps from below - "frog perspectives," as it were, to borrow an expression current among painters. In spite of all the value which may belong to the true, the positive, and the unselfish, it might be possible that a higher and more fundamental value for life generally should be assigned to pretence, to the will to delusion, to selfishness, and cupidity. It might even be possible that what constitutes the value of those good and respected things, consists precisely in their being insidiously related, knotted, and crocheted to these evil and apparently opposed things - perhaps even in being essentially identical with them. Perhaps! But who wishes to concern himself with such dangerous "Perhapses"! For that investigation one must await the advent of a new order of philosophers, such as will have other tastes and inclinations, the reverse of those

hitherto prevalent - philosophers of the dangerous "Perhaps" in every sense of the term. And to speak in all seriousness, I see such new philosophers beginning to appear.

3.   Having kept a sharp eye on philosophers, and having read between their lines long enough, I now say to myself that the greater part of conscious thinking must be counted amongst the instinctive functions, and it is so even in the case of philosophical thinking; one has here to learn anew, as one learned anew about heredity and "ineptness." As little as the act of birth comes into consideration in the whole process and continuation of heredity, just as little is "being-conscious" opposed to the instinctive in any decisive sense; the greater part of the conscious thinking of a philosopher is secretly influenced by his instincts, and forced into definite channels. And behind all logic and its seeming sovereignty of movement, there are valuations, or to speak more plainly, physiological demands, for the maintenance of a definite mode of life....

4.   The falseness of an opinion is not for us any objection to it: it is here, perhaps, that our new language sounds most strangely. The question is, how far an opinion is life-furthering, life-preserving, species-preserving, perhaps species-rearing; and we are fundamentally inclined to maintain that the falsest opinions (to which the synthetic judgments a priori belong), are the most indispensable to us; that without a recognition of logical fictions, without a comparison of reality with the purely imagined world of the absolute and immutable, without a constant counterfeiting of the world by means of numbers, man could not live - that the renunciation of false opinions would be a renunciation of life, a negation of life. To recognize untruth as a condition of life: that is certainly to impugn the traditional ideas of value in a dangerous manner, and a philosophy which ventures to do so, has thereby alone placed itself beyond good and evil.

5.   That which causes philosophers to be regarded half-distrustfully and half-mockingly, is not the oft-repeated discover how innocent they are - how often and easily they make mistakes and lose their way, in short, how childish and childlike they are, - but that there is not enough honest dealing with them, whereas they all raise a loud and virtuous outcry when the problem of truthfulness is even hinted at in the remotest manner. They all pose as though their real opinions had been discovered and attained through the self-evolving of a cold, pure, divinely indifferent dialectic (in contrast to all sorts of mystics, who, fairer and foolisher, talk of "inspiration"); whereas, in fact, a prejudiced proposition, idea, or "suggestion," which is generally their heart's desire abstracted and refined, is defended by them with arguments sought out after the event. They are all advocates who do not wish to be regarded as such, generally astute defenders, also, of their prejudices, which they dub "truths," - and very far from having the conscience' which bravely admits this to itself; very far from having the good taste or the courage which goes so far as to let this be understood, perhaps to warn friend or foe, or in cheerful confidence and self-ridicule. The spectacle of the Tartuffery of old Kant, equally stiff and decent, with which he entices us into the dialectic by-ways that lead (more correctly mislead) to his "categorical imperative" - makes us fastidious ones smile, we who find no small amusement in spying out the subtle tricks of old moralists and ethical preachers. Or, stiff more so, the hocus-pocus of mathematical form, by means of which Spinoza has as it were clad his philosophy in mail and mask - in fact, the "love of his wisdom," to translate the term fairly and squarely - in order thereby to strike terror at once into the heart of the assailant who should dare to cast a glance on that invincible maiden, that Pallas Athene: - how much of personal timidity and vulnerability does this masquerade of a sickly recluse betray!

6.   It has gradually become clear to me what every great philosophy up till now has consisted of - namely, the confession of its originator, and a species of involuntary and unconscious autobiography: and moreover that the moral (or immoral) purpose in every philosophy has constituted the true vital germ out of which the entire plant has always grown. Indeed, to understand how the abstrusest metaphysical assertions of a philosopher have been arrived at, it is always well (and wise) to first ask oneself: "What morality do they (or does he) aim

at?" Accordingly, I do not believe that an "impulse to knowledge" is the father of philosophy; but that another impulse, here as elsewhere, has only made use of knowledge (and mistaken knowledge!) as an instrument. But whoever considers the fundamental impulses of man with a view to determining how far they may have here acted as inspiring genii (or as demons and cobolds), will find that they have all practiced philosophy at one time or another, and that each one of them would have been only too glad to look upon itself as the ultimate end of existence and the legitimate lord over all the other impulses. For every impulse is imperious, and as such, attempts to philosophize. To be sure, in the case of scholars, in the case of really scientific men, it may be otherwise - better," if you will; there may really be such a thing as an "impulse to knowledge," some kind of small, independent clockwork, which, when well wound up, works away industriously to that end, without the rest of the scholarly impulses taking any material part therein. The actual "interests" of the scholar, therefore, are generally in quite another direction - in the family, perhaps, or in money-making, or in politics; it is, in fact, almost indifferent at what point of research his little machine is placed, and whether the hopeful young worker becomes a good philologist, a mushroom specialist, or a chemist; he is not characterized by becoming this or that. In the philosopher, on the contrary, there is absolutely nothing impersonal; and above all, his morality furnishes a decided and decisive testimony as to who he is, - that is to say, in what order the deepest impulses of his nature stand to each other….

Reading and Discussion Questions
1. What ideas and beliefs does Nietzsche attack?
2. What ideas does Nietzsche propound?
3. Why were Nietzsche's views considered so dangerous?

23.7 Advertisement for a Vitascope, 1896

The Vitascope was an early film projector, first demonstrated in 1894 in Richmond Indiana by Charles Francis Jenkins and Thomas Armat. Thomas A. Edison later had a business interest as well. This advertisement is from 1896.

Reading and Discussion Questions
1. Which sector of society is being targeted by this advertisement?
2. The poster shows the Vitascope projecting a ballet performance, accompanied by an orchestra. How does the new technology of the Vitascope show a modern adaptation of traditional forms of cultural expression?

Source: Library of Congress

The Challenge of Modernity: East Asia

Chapter 24

1750-1910

The impact of Great Britain, France, the United States, and later Germany and Russia forced both China and Japan into defensive postures. Both countries had sought to keep out what they considered subversive foreign influences after an earlier period of exposure to Western traders and missionaries. China had created a tightly controlled system of overseas trade based in Guangzhou (Canton); Japan allowed only the Dutch to trade with them. But the expansion of trade in both legitimate goods and opium and the need of the British for regularization of diplomatic practices pushed Britain and China into a cycle of war and "unequal treaties" under which China was at an increasing disadvantage. Japan, suddenly thrust into international commerce and diplomacy by the young United States, now sought to protect its borders without pushing the Western powers into seizing any of its territory.

Historians have long debated the relative weight that should be assigned to cultural and material reasons for the differing paths of China and Japan. China's long history as the region's cultural leader, some have argued, made it difficult for the empire to remake itself to face the Western challenge; Japan, on the other hand, has a long history of cultural borrowing and, thus, found it easier to borrow from the Euro-American world. Some historians have argued that China's earlier experience with imperialism stunted the modernizing tendencies within the empire and kept it from responding; they argue that Japan had the advantage of being "opened" later and so could respond more effectively. Others have argued that Japan's tradition of military prowess played a role, still others that China's more complete incorporation into the modern "world system" crippled its ability to respond more independently.

24.1 The Nanjing Treaty

The First Opium War (1839-1842) between Great Britain and China over trade disputes ended with the signing of the Nanjing Treaty in 1842. British victory over China showcased the industrialized power of the British Navy and the vulnerability of China to outside powers.

Source: Sir Edward Hertslet. *Treaties &c., between Great Britain and China.* (London: Harrison & Sons, 1896).

HER Majesty the Queen of the United Kingdom of Great Britain and Ireland, and His Majesty the Emperor of China, being desirous of putting an end to the misunderstandings and consequent hostilities which have arisen between the two countries, have resolved to conclude a Treaty for that purpose, and have therefore named as their Plenipotentiaries, that is to say:—

Her Majesty the Queen of Great Britain and Ireland, Sir Henry Pottinger, Bart., a Major-General in the service of the East India Company, &c.;

And His Imperial Majesty the Emperor of China, the High Commissioners Keying, a Member of the Imperial House, a guardian of the Crown Prince, and General of the garrison of Canton; and Elepoo, of the Imperial Kindred, graciously permitted to wear the insignia of the first rank, and the distinction of a peacock's feather, lately Minister and Governor-General, &c., and now Lieutenant-General Commanding at Ohapoo.

Who, after having communicated to each other their respective full powers, and found them to be in good and due form, have agreed upon and concluded the following Articles:—

ARTICLE I.

There shall henceforward be peace and friendship between Her Majesty the Queen of the United Kingdom of Great Britain and Ireland and His Majesty the Emperor of China, and between their respective subjects, who shall enjoy full security and protection for their persons and property within the dominions of the other.

ARTICLE II.

His Majesty the Emperor of China agrees, that British subjects, with their families and establishments, shall be allowed to reside, for the purpose of carrying on their mercantile pursuit, without molestation or restraint, at the cities and towns of Canton, Amoy, Foochowfoo, Ningpo, and Shanghai.

ARTICLE III.

Cession of Island of Hong Kong to Great Britain.

ARTICLE IV.

Indemnity. Payment by China of 6,000,000 dollars for value of Opium delivered up as a Hansom for British Subjects.

ARTICLE V.

Abolition of Privileges of Hong Merchants at Ports of residence of British Merchants.Payment by China of 3,000,000 dollars for Debts due to British Subjects by certain Hong Merchants.

ARTICLE VI.

Indemnity.Payment by China of 12,000,000 dollars for Expenses of British Expedition to demand Redress. Deduction of ransom received by British Forces for Chinese towns

ARTICLE VII.

Periods for payment to be made by China of Indemnities of 21,000,000 dollars.

ARTICLE VIII.

All British Subjects (European and Indian) confined in China to be released.

ARTICLE IX

Amnesty. Release and Indemnity to Chinese formerly in British employ.

ARTICLE X.

Tariff to be issued of Import, Export, and Transit Duties.

Done at Nanking, and signed and sealed by the Plenipotentiaries on board Her Britannic Majesty's ship "Cornwallis," this 29th day of August, 1842; corresponding with the Chinese date, 24th day of the 7th month, in the 22nd year of Taoukwang.

(L.S.) HENRY POTTINGER,

Reading and Discussion Questions

1. Compare the terms of this treaty with Document 21.4, Qianlong Emperor's letter to King George III.   What has changed in the 49 years that separate these documents?
2. What were the consequences for China of British subjects being allowed to reside on Chinese soil for "the purpose of their mercantile pursuits without molestation and restraint"

24.2 A Chinese Traveler on the Marvels of Western Technology

Li Gui (1842-1903) was one of the first civilian Chinese to travel abroad. Little is known about his life except that he was born in 1842 near Nanjing to a wealthy family where he received a good education steeped in the Confucian classics. The Taiping Rebellion (1851-1864) interrupted his studies, however, and he eventually found employment with the Maritime Customs Service, which gave him an appreciation of the complex interrelationships among trade, commerce, technology, and society that increasingly characterized the nineteenth century. The diary Li kept of his 1876 journey to the United States, *A New Account of a Trip Around the Globe*, includes detailed observations of the Philadelphia Centennial Exhibition, including a description of the Machinery Hall in the excerpt included here.

Source: Desnoyers, Charles, *A Journey to the East* (Ann Arbor: University of Michigan Press, 2004), p. 118

The display of machinery was immense, with machines for digging coal, pumping water, forging and smelting, land cultivation, dredging [another fifteen kinds of machines are listed]...every kind of machine—so many that it was impossible to count. There is now probably nothing done without the aid of machines. That which creates the machines is a machine; that which drives the machines is also a machine. To this one much now proclaim the state of the cosmos to be that of one vast machine. Moreover, improvements are constantly springing from the minds of the ingenious, and these advances stimulate still more innovation. No sooner is a machine developed than it is copied, and the competition continues without letup. From sun up to sun down, and again from sun down to the new day, how wondrous is this business of mechanical innovation! We Chinese have a saying: "Where there are dealings, there are sure to be ingenious minds; the ancients, therefore, did not encourage them." However, this is certainly not a maxim for us to follow today! If we were to employ those with such "ingenuity" solely as tools for the benefit of the country and people, then they would not scheme to profit themselves and their relatives. In that case, why not try to use them? As for the proper use of machines, we must not speak of citing the ancients' well sweeps and generalize about the use of such devices as inappropriate, but instead, buy all those without exception that might benefit people.

Reading and Discussion Questions
1. What best describes Li Gui's reaction to the machines he saw on display?
2. Do Li's observations suggest that he advocated that China adopt Western technology?
3. How does Li reconcile the clash between technological innovation and tradition?

24.3 Jesuits in China

In his *Jesuits in China* (1894), Robert C. Jenkins discussed the influence of the Jesuit missionaries in China. As a priest, Jenkins had knowledge of Church laws and access to the records of the missionary works. While historically and predominantly a Confucian society, the Chinese entertained for a time the beliefs of Christianity. Commercial trade with the West allowed Jesuits missionaries into China, where they enjoyed success until Christianity grew large enough to threaten traditional Chinese religious beliefs. Issues arose when Christians commenced challenging the Chinese tradition of worshiping their emperor, thereby attacking his authority and power.

Source: Robert Jenkins. *The Jesuits in China and the Legation of Cardinal de Tournon: An Examination of Conflicting Evidence and an Attempt at an Impartial Judgment.* (London: David Nutt, 1894).

"On the Law of God;" a work which had been the chief means by which so many Chinese in the earlier days of the mission had been converted to Christianity. "There are two different points," observed a Mandarin to the Bishop, "to be decided in the present dispute -- one relates to your Supreme Pontiffs; but the other, which involves the meaning of Chinese words, and our own opinion regarding our ceremonies, this belongs to our great Epaperor." [letter of Father Thomas to Card, de Tournon, "Lo stato presente," p. 122.]

i.The Bishop proceeds to recapitulate the heads of difference and to adjudicate upon them.

In regard to the name of the Deity he decides that the form *Tien Chu*, the Lord of Heaven, is to be universally adopted, to the exclusion of *Tien*, Heaven, and *Xang-Ti*, Supreme Emperor.

ii. He prohibits the tablets which were placed in many of the churches, inscribed "Worship Heaven" (*King-Tien*).

iii. He alleges that the questions proposed to Pope Alexander VII. were not truthful, and therefore that the supposed permission given in regard to the worship of Confucius and of ancestors was not to be relied on.

iv. He prohibits the missionaries from being present at the festivals or sacrifices connected with this worship.

v. He directs that on the tablets in honor of the dead there should only be inscribed the name of the dead person, and in private houses there should be added the true doctrine of the Church in regard to the honour due to the departed.

vi. He condemns the following propositions:
1. That the Chinese Philosophy, properly understood, has not in it anything contrary to the Christian Law.
2. That the ancients designed by the name *Tay Kie*, to declare God as the first Cause of all things.
3. That the worship which Confucius assigned to spirits was rather a civil than a religious rite.
4. That the book which the Chinese call *Te King*, is a sum of sound doctrine, both moral and physical.

vii. He warns the missionaries against allowing Chinese books to be read in their schools, inasmuch as 'they contain atheistic and superstitious matter.

Reading and Discussion Questions

1. How did religious tensions contribute to the Chinese resistance to foreign intervention?
2. Besides questioning the worship of the Emperor, were these reforms radical in trying to win souls to Christianity?

24.4 The "Opening" of Japan

In 1852, Commodore Matthew C. Perry (1794-1858) was dispatched to Japan by U.S. President Millard Fillmore (1800-1874). Perry's squadron set anchor in the harbor near the Tokugawa capital of Edo, on July 8, 1853. As expressed in the following letter from President Fillmore to the Japanese Emperor, delivered by Perry to the worried Tokugawa officials who greeted him, the United States was eager to break Japan's seclusion policy, sign diplomatic and commercial treaties, and thus "open" the nation to the West. For the Japanese, who had carefully regulated overseas contacts for over 200 years and whose technology could not compare to that displayed by the American squadron, Perry's arrival and President Fillmore's letter were unwelcome and ominous. Commodore Perry stayed in Japan for fewer than ten days in 1853. As he promised in his letter of July 14, 1853, however, he returned to Japan about six months later with a much larger and more intimidating fleet, comprising six ships with more than 100 mounted cannon. In March of 1854, the Tokugawa shogunate capitulated to all the American demands, signing the Treaty of Kanagawa with Perry.

Source: Narrative of the Expedition of an American Squadron to China and Japan, performed in the years 1852,1853, and 1854, under the Command of Commodore M. C. Perry United States Navy, by Order of the Government of the United States, compiled by Francis L. Hawks, vol. I (Washington, D.C., A.O.P. Nicholson, Printer, 1856), 256-259.

From Millard Fillmore, President of the United States of America, to His Imperial Majesty, the Emperor of Japan

November 13, 1852

GREAT and Good Friend: I send you this public letter by Commodore Matthew C. Perry, an officer of the highest rank in the navy of the United States, and commander of the squadron now visiting your imperial majesty's dominions. I have directed Commodore Perry to assure your imperial majesty that I entertain the kindest feelings towards your majesty's person and government, and that I have no other object in sending him to Japan but to propose to your imperial majesty that the United States and Japan should live in friendship and have commercial intercourse with each other.

The Constitution and laws of the United States forbid all interference with the religious or political concerns of other nations. I have particularly charged Commodore Perry to abstain from every act which could possibly disturb the tranquility of your imperial majesty's dominions.

The United States of America reach from ocean to ocean, and our Territory of Oregon and State of California lie directly opposite to the dominions of your imperial majesty. Our steamships can go from California to Japan in eighteen days.

Our great State of California produces about sixty millions of dollars in gold every year, besides silver, quicksilver, precious stones, and many other valuable articles. Japan is also a rich and fertile country, and produces many very valuable articles. Your imperial majesty's subjects are skilled in many of the arts. I am desirous that our two countries should trade with each other, for the benefit both of Japan and the United States.

We know that the ancient laws of your imperial majesty's government do not allow of foreign trade, except with the Chinese and the Dutch; but as the state of the world changes and new governments are formed, it seems to be wise, from time to time, to make new laws. There was a time when the ancient laws of your imperial majesty's government were first made.

About the same time America, which is sometimes called the New World, was first discovered and settled by the Europeans. For a long time there were but a few people, and they were poor. They have now become quite numerous; their commerce is very extensive; and they think that if your imperial majesty were so far to change the ancient laws as to allow a free trade between the two countries it would be extremely beneficial to both.

If your imperial majesty is not satisfied that it would be safe altogether to abrogate the ancient laws which forbid foreign trade, they might be suspended for five or ten years, so as to try the experiment. If it does not prove as beneficial as was hoped, the ancient laws can be restored. The United States often limit their treaties with foreign states to a few years, and then renew them or not, as they please.

I have directed Commodore Perry to mention another thing to your imperial majesty. Many of our ships pass every year from California to China, and great numbers of our people pursue the whale fishery near the shores of Japan. It sometimes happens, in stormy weather, that one of our ships is wrecked on your imperial majesty's shores. In all such cases we ask, and expect, that our unfortunate people should be treated with kindness, and that their property should be protected, till we can send a vessel and bring them away. We are very much in earnest in this.

Commodore Perry is also directed by me to represent to your imperial majesty that we understand there is a great abundance of coal and provisions in the Empire of Japan. Our steamships, in crossing the great ocean, burn a great deal of coal, and it is not convenient to bring it all the way from America. We wish that our steam-ships and other vessels should be allowed to stop in Japan and supply themselves with coal, provisions, and water. They will pay for them in money, or anything else your imperial majesty's subjects may prefer; and we request your imperial majesty to appoint a convenient port, in the southern part of the empire, where our vessels may stop for this purpose. We are very desirous of this.

These are the only objects for which I have sent Commodore Perry, with a powerful squadron, to pay a visit to your imperial majesty's renowned city of Edo: friendship, commerce, a supply of coal and provisions, and protection for our shipwrecked people.

We have directed Commodore Perry to beg your imperial majesty's acceptance of a few presents. They are of no great value in themselves; but some of them may serve as specimens of the articles manufactured in the United States, and they are intended as tokens of our sincere and respectful friendship.

May the Almighty have your imperial majesty in His great and holy keeping!

In witness whereof, I have caused the great seal of the United States to be hereunto affixed, and have subscribed the same with my name, at the city of Washington, in America, the seat of my government, on the thirteenth day of the month of November, in the year one thousand eight hundred and fifty-two.

Your good friend,

Millard Fillmore

By the President:

Edward Everett, Secretary of State

Reading and Discussion Questions

1. How would you describe the attitude toward Japan as expressed in President Fillmore's letter?
2. Why does the President indicate that he has dispatched Perry "with a powerful squadron"?
3. How do you think the emperor of Japan responded to this letter?

24.5   The King of Siam to President Buchanan

In, 1861, Mongkut (1804-1868), the King of Siam (now Thailand) wrote to President James Buchanan, hoping to send the President a gift of elephants. As a young ruler and throughout his life, Mongkut employed tutors from the United States who influenced his ideas. The King wished to modernize Thailand and wished to build friendship with the United States to further his goals for Thailand. As a token of his willingness to expand trade with the United States, Mongkut wished to give a special gift to the country. Elephants were important to Thailand because they were used as beasts of burden, and Mongkut believed the United States still had need for such animals, especially in its western territories. King Mongkut wrote a letter that inquired about the suitability of the environment of America to support elephants. His letter made it to the United States, but it did not make to President Buchanan Before he was replaced by Abraham Lincoln, who kindly refused the gift from King Mongkut.

Source: Letter from King of Siam to President Buchanan, February 14, 1861 - Smithsonian Institute, Washington, D.C.

Somdetch Phra Paramendr Maha Mongkut

By the blessing of the highest Superagency of the whole Universe. The King of Siam-the Sovereign of all interior Tributary Countries adjacent and around in every direction-viz.-

To

His Most Respected Excellent Presidency

The President of United States of America who having been chosen by the Citizens of the United States as most distinguished, was made President and Chief Magistrate in the affairs of the Nation for an appointed time of office viz.-

On this occasion, occurred in February Christian Era 1861 corresponding to the lunar time being in connection of the Siamese month of Magh and Phagun, the 3rd and 4th month from the commencement of the cold Season in the Year of Monkey, second decade Siamese Astronomical Era 1222-a ship of War, a sailing vessel of the United States' Navy, the "John Adams" arrived. . . . Captain Berrien with the officers of the ship of war came up to pay a friendly visit to the Country, and has had an interview with ourselves, hence, to him we have entrusted our Royal Letter in separate envelope which accompanies this and the presents specified in that letter.

Having heard this it has occurred to us that, if on the continent of America there should be several pairs of young male and female elephants turned loose in forests where there was abundance of water and grass in any region under the Sun's declination both North and South called by the English the Torrid Zone-and all were forbidden to molest them; to attempt to raise them would be well and if the climate there should prove favorable to elephants, we are of opinion that after a while they will increase till there be large herds as there are here on the Continent of Asia until the inhabitants of America will be able to catch them and tame and use them as beasts of burden making them of benefit to the country. Since Elephants being animals of great size and strength can bear burdens, and travel through uncleared woods and matted jungles where no carriage and cart roads have yet been made. . .

On this account we desire to procure and send elephants to be let loose in increase and multiply in the continent of America. It is desirable that the president of the United States and Congress give us their views in reference to this matter at as early a day as possible.

If the president and Congress approve of this matter and should provide a vessel to come for the elephants, if that vessel should arrive in Siam in any month of any year after March and April as above mentioned, let notice be sent on two or three months previous to those months of that year, in order that the elephants may be caught and tamed.

Given at our Royal Audience Hall Anant Samagome in the Grand Palace . . .

[ileg.]from the worthy & good friend of [ileg.] United States of America & her Government

Mongkut

Major Rex

Reading and Discussion Questions

1. King Mongkut was influenced by his American tutors to improve material and social conditions in Thailand; so the King sent elephants to help finish the modernization of America. Was Mongku giving the animals so that Thailand could have a hand in the making of America or was it a gift from one ruler to another?
2. Why might Mongkut request that a ship from the United States come first to Thailand before providing the elephants?
3. Although commerce and trade opened up lines of communications, what limitations continued to exist in the broader culture awareness between the different parts of the world?

Chapter 25 Adaptation and Resistance: the Ottoman and Russian Empires

1683-1908

Understanding the challenges faced by the Ottoman and Russian Empires in the modern period involves discovering how both empires reacted to important developments in Western Europe, notably the Enlightenment, modernization, industrialization, and the development of constitutional government.

In 1836, Pyotr Ya Chaadaev (1794-1856), a Russian philosopher, published his *Philosophical Letters*, describing the state of affairs in Russia. He found Russia a "peculiar civilization," of neither eastern nor western culture, poorly educated, grappling with the realties of modernization and competition associated with enlightenment. Upon publication, Chaadaev was immediately arrested and declared insane. He spent eighteen months in prison for his comments. His words did not reappear in print in Russian until 1935, after a period in which Russians came to fully realize the economic importance of western modernization.

Similarly in 1799, Sir William Eton, Esq., a writer and traveler of the Ottoman Empire, provided eye-witness accounts of events from his travels in his book, *A Survey of the Turkish Empire* (1799). He found, "It is undeniable that the power of the Turks was once formidable to their neighbors, not by their numbers only, but by their military and civil institutions, far surpassing those of their opponents." The Ottoman and Russian Empires competed for territory and influence, sometimes leading to open warfare. After the Russo-Turkish War of 1787-92, the military rapidly declined in power. Eton suggested, "The present reigning Sultan, Selim III (1761-1808), has made an attempt to introduce the European discipline into the Turkish army." However, Eton noted the Turkish military's disloyalty and their disdain for any type of reform. He found "The cavalry is as much afraid of their own infantry as of the enemy; for in a defeat they fire at them to get their horses to escape more quickly; In short, it is a mob assembled rather than an army levied." Eton described a chaotic and unstable military power not interested in western influence. This instability and mindset did not create an environment for economic development and growth within the Ottoman Empire.

The Gulhane decree is a list of reforms set down by Mustafa Resid Pasa, the Foreign Minister of the Ottoman Empire in 1839. The Ottomans economically lagged behind the Western world and wanted to modernize their empires with reforms based on emulating the West. The Gulhane decree was an important first step which eventually led the Ottomans to adopt a constitutional form of government in1876, including a parliament to represent the people of the empire.

As late as 1913 Russia only produced 6.4percent of total worldwide manufacturing production, while possessing at least 53,234 kilometers of railroad track to ship goods to market. The Ottoman Empire, known as the "Sick Man of Europe," faired worse. Both empires lagged behind the West economically up to the eve of World War I, and both sat poised for fundamental long-lasting change in its wake.

25.1 Decree on Western Dress

The *Decree on Western Dress* (1701)by Peter the Great were reforms developed and set down to modernize and westernize the Russian Empire in the eighteenth-century. It was one among over 3000 such decrees and edicts issued by Peter during his vigorous campaign to transform Russia into a serious contender for European power. From his childhood, Peter remained fascinated with western European advances and what he often considered superior ways of life. Many of his reforms resulted from Russian military defeat in the initial years of the Great Northern War (1700-1721), in which Russia's alliance ultimately defeated Sweden for control of northern Europe.

The passage below was written by Jean Rousset de Missy, a French historical writer of the time. In the passage, de Missy describes the reforms in dress enforced by Peter the Great.

Source: Jean Rousset de Missy, in *Readings in European History: A Collection of Extracts from the Sources Chosen with the Purpose of Illustrating the Progress of Culture in Western Europe since the German Invasions*, by James Harvey Robinson. Abridged Edition in One Volume (Boston: Ginn and Company, 1906), pp. 390-391.

The tsar labored at the reform of fashions, or, more properly speaking, of dress. Until that time the Russians had always worn long beards, which they cherished and preserved with much care, allowing them to hang down on their bosoms, without even cutting the moustache. With these long beards they wore the hair very short, except the ecclesiastics, who, to distinguish themselves, wore it very long. The tsar, in order to reform that custom, ordered that gentlemen, merchants, and other subjects, except priests and peasants, should each pay a tax of one hundred rubles a year if they wished to keep their beards; the commoners had to pay one kopeck each. Officials were stationed at the gates of the towns to collect that tax, which the Russians regarded as an enormous sin on the part of the tsar and as a thing which tended to the abolition of their religion.

These insinuations, which came from the priests, occasioned the publication of many pamphlets in Moscow, where for that reason alone the tsar was regarded as a tyrant and a pagan; and there were many old Russians who, after having their beards shaved off, saved them preciously, in order to have them placed in their coffins, fearing that they would not be allowed to enter heaven without their beards. As for the young men, they followed the new custom with the more readiness as it made them appear more agreeable to the fair sex.

From the reform in beards we may pass to that of clothes. Their garments, like those of the Orientals, were very long, reaching to the heel. The tsar issued an ordinance abolishing that costume, commanding all the boyars (nobles) and all those who had positions at the court to dress after the French fashion, and likewise to adorn their clothes with gold or silver according to their means.

As for the rest of the people, the following method was employed. A suit of clothes cut according to the new fashion was hung at the gate of the city, with a decree enjoining upon all except peasants to have their clothes made on this model, under penalty of being forced to kneel and have all that part of their garments which fell below the knees cut off, or pay two grivas every time they entered the town with clothes in the old style. Since the guards at the gates executed their duty in curtailing the garments in a sportive spirit, the people were amused and readily abandoned their old dress, especially in Moscow and its environs, and in the towns which the tsar oftenest visited.

The dress of the women was changed, too. English hairdressing was substituted for the caps and bonnets hitherto worn; bodices, stays, and skirts, for the former undergarment.....

The same ordinance-also provided that in the future women, as well as men, should be invited to entertainments, such as weddings, banquets, and the like, where both sexes should mingle in the same hall, as in Holland and England. It was likewise added that these entertainments should conclude with concerts and dances, but that only those should be admitted who were dressed in English costumes. His Majesty set the example in all these changes.

Reading and Discussion Questions

1.   Why would geopolitical conditions prompt Peter the Great to institute reforms of personal dress?
2.   What insight does the decree on dress shed upon the character of Peter the Great?
3.   Why would the clergy and peasants be exempted from the decree?

25.2   Russia and the West

Petyr Chaadaev (1794-1856) was associated with literary intellectuals of Moscow in the mid-nineteenth century. He spent some time in western Europe during the Napoleonic Wars and later traveled through Europe in the 1820s. His observations of European society starkly contrasted with his own impressions of Russia, which he believed sorely lagged behind the scientific and political advancements of western Europe. His harsh words, found in a series of "Philosophical Letters" published in France reflected Chaadaev's insistence that Russians must turn their focus to the West and away from the East.

Source: Chaadaev, P. I. A., and Mary-Barbara Zeldin. *Philosophical Letters, & Apology of a Madman.* (Knoxville: University of Tennessee Press, 1969).

One of the worst features of our peculiar civilization is that we have not yet discovered truths that have elsewhere become truisms, even among nations that in many respects are far less advanced than we are. It is a result of never having walked hand in hand with other nations; we belong to none of the great families of mankind; we are neither of the West nor of the East, and we possess the traditions of neither. Somehow divorced from time and space, the universal education of mankind has not touched upon us.

At first brutal barbarism, then crude superstition, the cruel and humiliating foreign domination, the spirit of which was later inherited by our national rulers—such is the sad history of our youth….Our first years, spent in immobile brutishness, have left no traces of our minds, we have nothing that is ours on which to base our thinking; moreover, isolated by a fate unknown to the universal development of humanity, we have absorbed none of mankind's ideas of traditional transmission.

What were we doing at the time when, from the midst of the struggle between the energetic barbarism of the northern peoples and the high idea of Christianity, the edifice of modern civilization was being built up? Obedient to our doom, we turned to miserable, despised Byzantium for a moral code which was to become the basis of our education.

We belong to that number of nations which does not seem to make up an integral part of the human race, but which exists only to teach the world some great lesson.

Reading and Discussion Questions

1.   How does Chaadaev's harsh tone reflect growing disdain for Russian culture and politics on behalf of its intellectuals?
2.   While obviously an overblown depiction of Russian society, in what manner did Enlightenment thinking directly affect Chaadaev's view of Russia?
3.   Why would Chaadaev attribute the "backward" state of Russian society to ancient Byzantium?

25.3 "Mr. Sansonov"

The writer Roy Bainton (1920-2012) traveled to Russia in 2000 to collect firsthand accounts of the Russian Revolution. He interviewed the elderly about their childhoods, and took their stories to provide a detailed account of conditions in Russia during the period. Bainton provides a glimpse into the lives of what life was like for people during the early twentieth century in Russia. In the passage below, a person remembers a certain Mr. Sansonov, who was a police official before the Revolution.

Source: Bainton, Roy, *1917: Russia's Year of Revolution* (Constable & Robinson, 2005), 49-50.

My best friend was Nadewsha Sansonov. Her dad was Narva's chief of police. The Sansonovs had an old aunt living with them. She was dumb. She had her tongue cut out whilst still young for bearing false witness. I began to realize that for the poor, life was very cheap. For them, cruelty and beating were a way of life. On more than one occasion I saw prisoners stripped naked in the snow and tied to a post to be whipped whilst big guard dogs snapped at them. Mr Sansonov didn't think he was being cruel, just "firm" – which everybody seemed to accept. Everyone seemed to live in fear of being sent to Siberia. One night the servants were screaming in our kitchen. My father rushed in and found a demented working man brandishing a knife - he wanted to kill Father. A furious fight followed and Dad overpowered him. The man's name was Baraban, and he seemed to imagine that Father was responsible for his son being exiled to Siberia for committing some crime at the mill. Once Father had explained in detail that he had nothing to do with this, the man flung himself at his knees, sobbing and begging for mercy. Father never reported the incident, but we gave the man a warm meal and sent him on his way.

Reading and Discussion Questions
1. In your opinion, do you think that all Russian officials truly believed that the harsh punishment they inflicted was the right thing to do? Why or why not?
2. What evidence is there that the Bolshevik Revolution changed the treatment of the lower classes in Russia?
3. How might the process of industrialization in Russia have shaped a different response to its benefits and problems than what was experienced in Western Europe?

25.4 The Turkish Army

In these excerpts from the British diplomat Sir William Eton's 1798 book, *A Survey of the Turkish Empire,* he describes the once powerful and expanding Turkish Empire and its commanding army. He then provides the latest observation of the Turkish military situation. He found the military leadership incapable of introducing any modernization or reforms. Eton notes the disorganization of the troops, their inferior weapons, and their inability to tactically face an enemy. Although not included in the passages below, Eton goes on to detail the attempts of Sultan Selim III to introduce Western military traditions and organization, including the creation of a new army of officers and men armed, trained and drilled on a European model.

Source: Eton, William. *A Survey of the Turkish Empire. In Which Are Considered I. Its Government ... Ii. The State of the Provinces ... Iii. The Causes of the Decline of Turkey ... Iv. The British Commerce with Turkey ... With Many Other Important Particulars.* London, 1798, 61, 71, 73-74.

It is undeniable that the power of the 'Turks was once formidable to their neighbor not by their numbers only, but by their military and civil institutions, far surpassing those of their opponents, who were never united in a rational system; governed often by courtiers, priests, or women; possessing no rational system of finance, no great resources in cases of exigency, no system of war even comparable to the Turks, a feudal government, internal dissentions, no wise or solid alliances amongst each other; and yet they all trembled at the name of the Turks, who, with a confidence procured by their constant successes, held the Christians no less in contempt as warriors than they did on account of their religion. Proud and vain-glorious, conquest was to them a passion, a gratification, and even a mean of salvation, a sure way of immediately attaining a delicious paradise. Hence their zeal for the extension of their empire, or rather a wild enthusiasm, even beyond the pure patriotism of the heroes of antiquity; hence their profound respect for the military profession, and their glory even in being obedient and submissive to discipline.

. . .

Besides that the Turks refuse all melioration, they are seditious and mutinous; their armies are encumbered with immense baggage, and their camp has all the conveniences of a town, shops, &c. for such was their ancient custom when they wandered with their hordes. When their sudden fury is abated, which is at the least obstinate resistance, they are seized with a panic, and have no rallying as formerly…. The cavalry (which is the only part of their army that deserves the name of troops) is as much afraid of their own foot as of the enemy; for in a defeat they fire at them to get their horses to escape quicker. In short, it is a mob assembled rather than an army levied. None of those numerous details of a well-organized body, necessary to give quickness, strength, and regularity to its actions, to avoid confusion, to repair damages, to apply every part to some use; … no systematic attack, defense, or retreat; no accident foreseen, or provided for.

. . .

The artillery they have, and which is chiefly brass, comprehends many find pieces of cannon; but notwithstanding the reiterated instruction of so many French engineers, they are profoundly ignorant of its management. Their musket-barrels are much esteemed; but they are too heavy; nor do they possess any quality superior to common iron barrels, which have been much hammered, and are very soft Swedish iron.

Reading and Discussion Questions
1. What attitude does Eton take in his description of the Ottoman Empire?
2. To what degree did the instability within the military affect the economy of the Ottoman Empire?
3. Why did the military disdain western influence and modernization?

25.5 The Gulhane Decree

The Ottomans and the Russians throughout the period covered in this chapter did make attempts to modernize and westernize their empires to adapt to the western challenge. Starting in 1699, Peter the Great issued edicts and decrees such as *Creating a New Russia,* an attempt to westernize Russian dress, or his 1723 *Statute for a College of Manufactures,* which called for the creation of factories throughout the empire. Likewise, in 1839, the Ottomans set down the Gulhane decrees, guaranteeing each subject's security of person and property, tax reform, and equality in conscription for military service.

Source: Mustafa Resid Pasa. "The Guhane Degree and the Beginning of the Tanzimat Reform Era in the Ottoman Empire, 1839. From Gülhane Hatt-I Hümayunu, Originally issued 3 November 1839, from the English translation of the Gülhane Edict adapted and revised by Ahmet Ersoy, based on the text provided by J. C. Hurewitz in *Diplomacy in the Near and Middle East* (Princeton: Van Nostrand, 1956)

From the very first day of our accession to the throne, our thoughts have been devoted exclusively to the development of the empire and the promotion of the prosperity of the people. Therefore, if the geographical position of the Ottoman provinces, the fertility of the soil, and the aptitude and intelligence of the inhabitants are considered, it is manifest that, by striving to find appropriate means, the desired results will, with the aid of God, be realized within five or ten years. Thus, full of confidence in the help of the Most High and certain of the support of our Prophet, we deem it necessary and important from now on to introduce new legislation to achieve effective administration of the Ottoman Government and Provinces. Thus the principles of the requisite legislation are three:

1. The guarantees promising to our subjects perfect security for life, honor, and property.
2. A regular system of assessing taxes
3. An equally regular system for the conscription of requisite troops and the duration of their service.

Indeed there is nothing more precious in this world than life and honor. What man, however much his character may be against violence, can prevent himself from having recourse to it, and thereby injure the government and the country, if his life and honor are endangered? If, on the contrary, he enjoys perfect security, it is clear that he will not depart from ways of loyalty and all his actions will contribute to the welfare of the government and of the people.

Reading and Discussion Questions

1. In what ways is the influence of Islam evident in the decree?
2. What outside influences may have caused the need for these reform decrees?
3. How might the decrees have led to an introduction of constitutionalism and representative government in the Ottoman Empire?

25.6 The Iranian and Turkish Constitutional Revolutions of 1906 and 1908

On August 5, 1906, Mozzafar ud-din Shah of the Qajar dynasty issued the decree for the first constitution in West Asia following ten years of the increasingly popular demands of the Iranian upper and nascent middle classes for a national assembly. On August 18, 1906, the first legislative assembly was formed in Tehran to prepare the drafting of an electoral law (September 9, 1906) and then inauguration of the National Consultative Assembly (October 7, 1906). On December 30, 1906, the Fundamental (Mashrutehl) Laws of Iran were promulgated and approved by Mozaffar ud-Din Shah. In a little over five months, Iran had moved from an autocratic monarchy to a constitutional republic based on the representation of six classes: princes and the Qajar tribe, doctors of divinity and students, nobles and notables, merchants, landed proprietors and peasants, and trade guilds.

On July 24, 1908, the Young Turks forced the Ottoman Sultan, Abdul Majid II to restore the December 23, 1876 Ottoman Constitution (Dusturiyyah) that he had dissolved earlier in February of 1878. In that year, Abdul Majid II had to deal mainly with the skills of the Ottoman reformer, statesman, and Grand Vezir, Midhat Pasha, who was dismissed twice and sentenced to death before finally being expelled to the Saudi city of Taif. The Young Turks and the internal Ottoman social and political complexities thirty years later, however, were tougher opponents, better organized and more daring. The Young Turks had widespread popular and military support to challenge Ottoman autocracy. The constitutional revolutions in Persia and Turkey mirrored other constitutional movements in Meiji Japan (1889), in Czarist Russia (1905), in Ming China (1911) and in Mexico (1911-17).

Source: Edward G. Browne, *The Persian Revolution of 1905-1909*, (London: Franck Cass & Co. Ltd, 1910), 363-65

THE FUNDAMENTAL LAWS OF PERSIA, DECEMBER 30, 1906 (51 ARTICLES)

The Fundamental Laws of Persia, promulgated in the reign of the late Muzaffar'd-Din Shah, and ratified by him on Dhu'l Qa'da 14 A.H. 1324 [December 30, 1906].

In the Name of God, the Merciful, the Forgiving

WHEREAS in accordance with the Imperial **farman** dated the fourteenth of Jumada the Second, A.H. 1324 [August 5, 1906], a command was issued for the establishment of a National Council to promote the progress and happiness of our Kingdom and people, strengthen the foundations of our government, and give effect to the enactments of the Sacred Law of His Holiness the Prophet.

AND WHEREAS, by virtue of the fundamental principle [therein laid down], we have conferred on each individual of the people of our realm, for the amending and superintending of the affairs of the commonwealth, according to their degrees, the right to participate in choosing and appointing the Members of this Assembly by popular election,

THEREFORE the National Consultative Assembly is now opened, in accordance with our Sacred Command; and we do define as follows the principles and articles of the Fundamental Law regulating the aforesaid National Council, which Law comprises the duties and functions of the above-mentioned Assembly, its limitations, and its relations with the various departments of the State. On the Constitution of the Assembly:

ART. 1. The National Consultative Assembly is founded and established in conformity with the farman, founded on justice, dated the fourteenth of the Second Jumada, A.H. 1324 (= Aug. 5, 1906).

ART. 2. The National Consultative Assembly represents the whole of the people of Persia, who [thus] participate in the economic and political affairs of the country.

ART. 3. The National Consultative Assembly shall consist of the Members elected in Tehran and the provinces, and shall be held in Tehran.

ART.15. The National Consultative Assembly has the right in all questions to propose any measure which it regards as conducive to the well-being of the Government and the People, after due discussion and deliberation thereof in all sincerity and truth; and having due regard to the majority of votes, to submit such measure, in complete confidence and security, after it has received the approval of the Senate, by means of the First Minister of the State, so that it may receive the Royal Approval and be duly carried out.

ART.16. All laws necessary to strengthen the foundations of the State and Throne and to set in order the affairs of the Realm and the establishment of the Ministries must be submitted for approval to the National Consultative Assembly.

ART.18. The regulation of all financial matters, the construction and regulation of the Budget, all changes in fiscal arrangements, the acceptance or rejection of all incidental and subordinate expenditure, as also the new Inspectorships [of Finance] which will be founded by the Government, shall be subject to the approval of the Assembly.

Farman: an imperial order

PROCLAMATION OF THE OTTOMAN CONSTITUTION OF 1908 BY THE YOUNG TURKS

1. The basis for the Constitution will be respect for the predominance of the national will. One of the consequences of this principle will be to require without delay the Responsibility of the minister before the Chamber, and consequently, to consider the Minister as having resigned, when he does not have a majority of the votes of the Chamber.

2. Provided that the number of senators does not exceed one-third the number of deputies , the Senate will be named as follows: one-third by the Sultan and two-thirds by the nation, and the term of senators will be of limited duration.

3. It will be demanded that all Ottoman subjects, having completed their twentieth year, regardless of whether they possess property or fortune, shall have the right to vote. Those who have lost their civil rights will naturally be deprived of this right.

4. It will be demanded that the right freely to constitute political groups be inserted in a precise fashion in the constitutional charter, in order that Article 1 of the Constitution of 1293 A.H [= 1876] be respected.

7. The Turkish tongue will remain the official state language. Official correspondence and discussion will take place in Turkish.

8. Every citizen will enjoy complete liberty and equality, regardless of nationality or religion, and be submitted to the same obligations. All Ottomans, being equal before the law as regards rights and duties relative to the State, are eligible for government posts, according to their individual capacity and their education. Non-Muslims will be equally liable to the military law.

9. The free exercise of the religious privileges which have been accorded to different nationalities will remain intact.

10. The reorganization and distribution of the State forces, on land as well as on sea, will be undertaken in accordance with the political and geographical situation of the country, taking into account the integrity of the other European powers.

14. Provided that the property rights of landholders are not infringed upon (for such rights must be respected and must remain intact, according to law), it will be proposed that peasants be permitted to acquire land, and they will be accorded means to borrow money at moderate rate.

15. Education will be free. Every Ottoman citizen, within the limits of the prescriptions of the Constitution, may operate a private school in accordance with the special laws.

16. All schools will operate under the surveillance of the state. In order to obtain for Ottoman citizens an education of a homogeneous and uniform character, the official schools will be open, their instruction will be open, their instruction will be free, and all nationalities will be admitted. Instruction in Turkish will be obligatory in public schools. In official schools, public instruction will be free. Secondary and higher education will be given in the public and official schools indicated above: it will use the Turkish tongue. Schools of commerce, agriculture, and industry will be opened with the goal of developing the resources of the country.

18. Steps shall also be taken for the formation of roads and railways and canals to increase the facilities of communication and increase the sources of the wealth of the country. Everything that can impede commerce or agriculture shall be abolished.

Reading and Discussion Questions

1. What are the similarities between the Ottoman and Persian documents?   What are the differences?   In which country are legislative and constitutional reforms more far reaching?

2. In which document do we more clearly see the influence of the constitutional revolutions that had transformed Western societies in the eighteenth and nineteenth centuries?

Chapter 26   The New Imperialism in the Nineteenth Century

Two patterns characterize the evolution of imperialism–colonialism in the period 1750–1900. The first was a shift from coastal trade forts under chartered companies—the old imperialism on the cheap—to government takeover, territorial conquest, and colonialism. Great Britain pioneered this "new imperialism" in India but also prevented the other European countries for a century from following in its footsteps.

The second pattern was the rise of direct territorial imperialism–colonialism by European countries in the course of the disintegration of the Ottoman Empire, under assault by Russia since the end of the eighteenth century and, in the course of the nineteenth century, in Asia and Africa. The Europeans first protected the Ottomans from Russia, only later to help themselves to Ottoman provinces, beginning with the capture of Algeria by France.

26.1   The Benefits of British Rule

Under the implications of "Civilizing mission" Europeans implied that the native indigenous population were uncivilized and became the justification for colonization. Natives were referred to as uncivilized, primitive, and savages and Europeans saw it as their duty to rescue the people of India. Europeans defined themselves as civilized, advanced, and scientifically superior to the native populations. Dadabhai Naoroji, was an earlier Indian political leader who brought into light the benefits and disadvantages brought under British rule. In the end, Dadabhai Naoroji (1825–1917)concludes that benefits outweigh the disadvantages.

Source: Dadabhai Naoroji, *Essays, Speeches, Addresses and Writings* (Bombay: Caxton Printing Works, 1887), 131-136.

The Benefits of British Rule for India:

In the Cause of Humanity: Abolition of suttee and infanticide. Destruction of Dacoits, Thugs, Pindarees, and other such pests of Indian society.Allowing remarriage of Hindu widows, and charitable aid in time of famine. Glorious work all this, of which any nation may well be proud, and such as has not fallen to the lot of any people in the history of mankind.

In the Cause of Civilization: Education, both male and female. Though yet only partial, an inestimable blessing as far as it has gone, and leading gradually to the destruction of superstition, and many moral and social evils. Resuscitation of India's own noble literature, modified and refined by the enlightenment of the West.

Politically: Peace and order. Freedom of speech and liberty of the press.Higher political knowledge and aspirations.Improvement of government in the native states.Security of life and property.Freedom from oppression caused by the caprice or greed of despotic rulers, and from devastation by war.Equal justice between man and man (sometimes vitiated by partiality to Europeans).Services of highly educated administrators, who have achieved the above-mentioned results.

Materially: Loans for railways and irrigation. Development of a few valuable products, such as indigo, tea, coffee, silk, etc. Increase of exports. Telegraphs.

Generally: A slowly growing desire of late to treat India equitably, and as a country held in trust. Good intentions. No nation on the face of the earth has ever had the opportunity of achieving such a glorious work as this. I hope in the credit side of the account I have done no injustice, and if I have omitted any item which anyone may think of importance, I shall have the greatest pleasure in inserting it. I appreciate, and so do my countrymen, what England has done for India, and I know that it is only in British hands that her regeneration can be accomplished. Now for the debit side.

The Detriments of British Rule:

In the Cause of Humanity: Nothing. Everything, therefore, is in your favor under this heading.

In the Cause of Civilization: As I have said already, there has been a failure to do as much as might have been done, but I put nothing to the debit. Much has been done, though.

Politically: Repeated breach of pledges to give the natives a fair and reasonable share in the higher administration of their own country, which has much shaken confidence in the good faith of the British word. Political aspirations and the legitimate claim to have a reasonable voice in the legislation and the imposition and disbursement of taxes, met to a very slight degree, thus treating the natives of India not as British subjects, in whom representation is a birthright. Consequent on the above, an utter disregard of the feelings and views of the natives. The great moral evil of the drain of wisdom and practical administration, leaving none to guide the rising generation.

Financially: All attention is engrossed in devising new modes of taxation, without any adequate effort to increase the means of the people to pay; and the consequent vexation and oppressiveness of the taxes imposed, imperial and local. Inequitable financial relations between England and India, i.e., the political debt of 100,000,000 clapped on India's shoulders, and all home charges also, though the British Exchequer contributes nearly 3,000,000 to the expense of the colonies.

Materially: The political drain, up to this time, from India to England, of above 500,000,000, at the lowest computation, in principal alone, which with interest would be some thousands of millions. The further continuation of this drain at the rate, at present, of above 12,000,000 per annum, with a tendency to increase. The consequent continuous impoverishment and exhaustion of the country, except so far as it has been very partially relieved and replenished by the railway and irrigation loans, and the windfall of the consequences of the American war, since 1850. Even with this relief, the material condition of India is such that the great mass of the poor have hardly tuppence a day and a few rags, or a scanty subsistence. The famines that were in their power to prevent, if they had done their duty, as a good and intelligent government. The policy adopted during the last fifteen years of building railways, irrigation works, etc., is hopeful, has already resulted in much good to your credit, and if persevered in, gratitude and contentment will follow. An increase of exports without adequate compensation; loss of manufacturing industry and skill. Here I end the debit side.

Summary: To sum up the whole, the British rule has been: morally, a great blessing; politically, peace and order on one hand, blunders on the other; materially, impoverishment, relieved as far as the railway and other loans go. The natives call the British system "Sakar ki Churi," the knife of sugar. That is to say, there is no oppression, it is all smooth and sweet, but it is the knife, notwithstanding. I mention this that you should know these feelings. Our great misfortune is that you do not know our wants. When you will know our real wishes, I have not the least doubt that you would do justice. The genius and spirit of the British people is fair play and justice.

Reading and Discussion Questions

1. Why would Dadabhai Naoroji, a native Indian, conclude that the benefits of British rule outweigh the disadvantages?
2. Although Dadabhai Naoroji concludes that benefits of British rule outweigh its disadvantages, why would he come to this conclusion if he describes political, financial, and material corruption within the British government against the Indian people?
3. Given the political structure of British rule in India, would you conclude that Dadabhai Naoroji was a native elite or a revolutionary?

26.2 The Diamond Fields of South Africa, 1870

European colonization exploited the resources Africa had to offer. When diamonds were discovered in South Africa in 1867 and gold in 1884 in the interior, an economic growth and immigration of Europeans settled in Africa. This intensified the relationship between European and the indigenous people. The struggle to control these important economic resources was a factor in relations between Europeans and the indigenous population. The discovery of precious metals also led to the Boers and the British wars.

Source: Eva March Tappan, ed., *The World's Story: A History of the World in Story, Song and Art* (Boston: Houghton Mifflin, 1914), Vol. III: Egypt, Africa, and Arabia, pp. 437-457.

The worker was washing the dirt in a rough cradle, separating the stones from the dust, and the owner, as each sieveful was brought to him, threw out the stones on his table and sorted them through with the eternal bit of slate or iron formed into the shape of a trowel. For the chance of a sieveful one of our party offered him half a crown,—which he took. I was glad to see it all inspected without a diamond, as had there been anything good the poor fellow's disappointment must have been great. That halfcrown was probably all that he would earn during the week,—all that he would earn perhaps for a month. Then there might come three or four stones in one day. I should think that the tedious despair of the vacant days could hardly be compensated by the triumph of the lucky minute. These "river" diggers have this in their favor,—that the stones found near the river are more likely to be white and pure than those which are extracted from the mines. The Vaal itself in the neighborhood of Barkly is pretty, —with rocks in its bed and islands and trees on its banks. But the country around, and from thence to Kimberley, which is twenty-four miles distant, is as ugly as flatness, barrenness, and sand together can make the face of the earth.

The commencement of diamond-digging as a settled industry was in 1872. It was then that dry-digging was commenced, which consists of the regulated removal of ground found to be diamondiferous and of the washing and examination of every fraction of the soil. The district which we as yet know to be so specially gifted extends up and down the Vaal River from the confluence of the Modder to Hebron, about seventy-five miles, and includes a small district on the cast side of the river. Here, within twelve miles of the river, and within a circle, of which the diameter is about two and a half miles, are contained all the mines,—or dry diggings,—from which have come the real wealth of the country. I should have said that the most precious diamond yet produced, one of 288 carats, was found close to the river about twelve miles from Barkly. This prize was made in 1872.

It is of the dry diggings that the future student of the Diamond Fields of South Africa will have to take chief account. The river diggings were only the prospecting work which led up to the real mining operations,—as the washing of the gullies in Australia led to the crushing of quartz and to the sinking of deep mines in search of alluvial gold. Of these dry diggings there are now four, Du Toit's Pan, Bultfontein, Old De Beers,—and Colesberg

Kopje, or the great Kimberley mine, which though last in the Field has thrown all the other diamond mines into the shade. The first working at the three first of these was so nearly simultaneous, that they may almost be said to have been commenced at once. I believe, however, that they were in fact opened in the order I have given.

Reading and Discussion Questions

1. How did the discovery of diamond mines contribute to the "Scramble for Africa" in the late nineteenth century?
2. How did the discovery of diamonds change the relationship between Afrikaners, Europeans, and Africans?
3. Did the discovery of minerals in South Africa change the relationship between Afrikaners and the British government? If so, how?

26.3 Rudyard Kipling, "The White Man's Burden"

This poem, by Rudyard Kipling (1865-1936), is one of the most famous apologies for the New Imperialism in Africa and Asia. Kipling assumes that the colonizing powers did the natives a favor by bringing "civilization" to them.

Source: Rudyard Kipling, Rudyard Kipling's Verse (1885–1918), Garden City, NY: Doubleday, Page & Co. (1919).

THE WHITE MAN'S BURDEN (1899)

Take up the White Man's burden—
Send forth the best ye breed—
Go bind your sons to exile
To serve your captives' need;
To wait in heavy harness,
On fluttered folk and wild—
Your new-caught, sullen peoples,
Half-devil and half-child.

Take up the White Man's Burden—
In patience to abide,
To veil the threat of terror
And check the show of pride;
By open speech and simple,
An hundred times made plain,
To seek another's profit,
And work another's gain.

Take up the White Man's burden—
The savage wars of peace—
Fill full the mouth of Famine
And bid the sickness cease;
And when your goal is nearest
The end for others sought,
Watch Sloth and heathen Folly
Bring all your hope to nought.

Take up the White Man's burden—
No tawdry rule of kings,
But toil of serf and sweeper—
The tale of common things.
The ports ye shall not enter,
The roads ye shall not tread,
Go make them with your living,
And mark them with your dead.
Take up the White Man's burden—
And reap his old reward:
The blame of those ye better,
The hate of those ye guard—
The cry of hosts ye humour
(Ah, slowly!)toward the light:—
"Why brought ye us from bondage,
Our loved Egyptian night?"
Take up the White Man's burden—
Ye dare not stoop to less
Nor call too loud on Freedom
To cloak your weariness;
By all ye cry or whisper,
By all ye leave or do,
The silent, sullen peoples
Shall weight your Gods and you.
Take up the White Man's burden—
Have done with childish days—
The lightly proffered laurel,
The easy, ungrudged praise.
Comes now, to search your manhood
Through all the thankless years,
Cold, edged with dear-bought wisdom,
The judgment of your peers!

Reading and Discussion Questions

1. What is the "white man's burden"?
2. What imagery does Kipling use to describe the "natives"?

26.4 Edward D. Morel, *The Black Man's Burden*

Edward Morel (1873-1924) was a British journalist who was interested in the economic and social impact of imperialism on Africa. The Black Man's Burden was a direct response to Rudyard Kipling's "The White Man's Burden".

Source: Edward D. Morel, *The Black Man's Burden* (London: The National Labor Press, 1920), 7-11.

It is with the peoples of Africa, then, that our inquiry is concerned. It is they who carry the "Black man's" burden. They have not withered away before the white man's occupation. Indeed, if the scope of this volume permitted, there would be no difficulty in showing that Africa has ultimately absorbed within itself every Caucasian and, for that matter, every Semitic invader too. In hewing out for himself a fixed abode in Africa, the white man has massacred the African in heaps. The African has survived, and it is well for the white settlers that he has.

In the process of imposing his political dominion over the African, the white man has carved broad and bloody avenues from one end of Africa to the other. The African has resisted, and persisted.

For three centuries the white man seized end enslaved millions of Africans and transported them, with every circumstance of ferocious cruelty, across the seas. Still the African survived and, in his land of exile, multiplied exceedingly.

But what the partial occupation of his soil by the white man has failed to do; what the mapping out of European political "spheres of influence" has failed to do; what the maxim and the rifle; the slave gang, labor in the bowels of the earth and the lash, have failed to do; what imported measles, smallpox and syphilis have failed to do; what even the oversea slave trade failed to do, the flower of modern capitalistic exploitation, assisted by modern engines of destruction, may yet succeed in accomplishing.

For from the evils of the latter, scientifically applied and enforced, there is no escape for the African. Its destructive effects are not spasmodic: they are permanent. In its permanence resides its fatal consequences. It kills not the body merely, but the soul. It breaks the spirit. It attacks the African at every turn, from every point of vantage. It wrecks his polity, uproots him from the land, invades his family life, destroys his natural pursuits and occupations, claims his whole time, enslaves him in his own home.

Economic bondage and wage slavery, the grinding pressure of a life of toil, the incessant demands of industrial capitalism - these things a landless European proletariat physically endures, though hardly. [...] The recuperative forces of a temperate climate are there to arrest the ravages, which alleviating influences in the shape of prophylactic and curative remedies will still further circumscribe. But in Africa, especially in tropical Africa, which a capitalistic imperialism threatens and has, in part, already devastated, man is incapable of reacting against unnatural conditions. In those regions man is engaged in a perpetual struggle against disease and an exhausting climate, which tells heavily on child-bearing; and there is no scientific machinery for salving the weaker members of the community. The African of the tropics is system of monotonous, uninterrupted labour, with its long and regular hours, involving, moreover, as it frequently does, severance from natural surroundings and nostalgia, the condition of melancholy resulting from separation from home, a malady to which the African is prone. Climatic conditions forbid it. When the system is forced upon him, the tropical African droops and dies.

Nor is violent physical opposition to abuse and injustice henceforth possible for the African in any part of Africa. His chances of effective resistance have been steadily dwindling with the increasing perfectibility in the killing power of modern armament. Gunpowder broke the effectiveness of his resistance to the slave trade, although he continued to struggle. He has forced and, on rare occasions and in exceptional circumstances ̶h̶o̶o̶t̶o̶n̶,̶ ̶i̶n̶ ̶f̶r̶o̶m̶ ̶t̶h̶e̶ ̶o̶l̶d̶-̶f̶a̶s̶h̶i̶o̶n̶e̶d̶ ̶m̶u̶s̶k̶e̶t̶,̶ ̶t̶h̶e̶ ̶e̶l̶e̶p̶h̶a̶n̶t̶ gun, the seven-pounder, and even the repeating rifle and the gatling gun. He has been known to charge right down repeatedly, foot and horse, upon the square, swept on all sides with the pitiless and continuous hail of maxims. But against the latest inventions, physical bravery, though associated with a perfect knowledge of the country, can do nothing. The African cannot face the high-explosive shell and the bomb-dropping aeroplane. He has inflicted sanguinary reverses upon picked European troops, hampered by the climate and by commissariat difficulties. He cannot successfully oppose members of his own race free from these impediments, employed by his white adversaries, and trained in all the diabolical devices of scientific massacre. And although the conscripting of African armies for use in Europe or in Africa as agencies for the liquidation of white man's quarrels must bring in its train evils from which the white man will be the first to suffer, both in Africa and in Europe; the African himself must eventually disappear in the process. Winter in Europe, or even in Northern Africa, is fatal to the tropical or subtropical African, while in the very nature of the case anything approaching real European control of Africa, of hordes of African soldiery armed with weapons of precisions is not a feasible proposition. The Black man converted by the European into a scientifically-equipped machine for the slaughter of his kind, is certainly not more merciful than the white man similarly equipped for like purposes in dealing with unarmed communities. And the experiences of the civilian population of Belgium, East Prussia, Galicia and Poland [First World War] is indicative of the sort of visitation involved for peaceable and powerless African communities if the white man determines to add to his appalling catalogue of past misdeeds toward the African, the crowning wickedness of once again, as in the day of the slave trade, supplying him with the means of encompassing his own destruction.

Thus the African is really helpless against the material gods of the white man, as embodied in the trinity of imperialism, capitalistic-exploitation, and militarism. If the white man retains these goes [sic] and if he insists upon making the African worship them as assiduously as he has done himself, the African will go the way of the Red Indian, the Amerindian, the Carib, the Guanche, the aboriginal Australian, and many more. And this would be at once a crime of enormous magnitude, and a world disaster

An endeavor will now be made to describe the nature, and the changing form, which the burden inflicted by the white man in modern times upon the black has assumed. It can only be sketched here in the broadest outline, but in such a way as will, it is hoped, explain the differing causes and motives which have inspired white activities in Africa and illustrate, by specific and notable examples, their resultant effects upon African peoples. It is important that these differing causes and motives should be understood, and that we should distinguish between them in order that we may hew our way later on through the jungle of error which impedes the pathway to reform. Diffused generalities and sweeping judgments generate confusion of thought and hamper the evolution of a constructive policy based upon clear apprehension of the problem to be solved.

The history of contact between the white and black peoples in modern times is divisible into two distinct and separate periods: the period of the slave trade and the period of invasion, political control, capitalistic exploitation, and, the latest development, militarism. Following the slave trade period and preceding the period of invasion, occurs the trade interlude which, indeed, has priority of both periods, as when the Carthagenians bartered salt and iron implements for gold dust on the West Coast. But this interlude concerns our investigations only when we pass from destructive exposure to constructive demonstration.

The first period needs recalling, in order to impress once more upon our memories the full extent of the African's claim upon us, the white imperial peoples, for tardy justice, for considerate and honest conduct.

Our examination of the second period will call for sectional treatment. The history of contact and is consequences during this period may be roughly sub-divided thus:

- The struggle for supremacy between the European invading Settlers and the resident African peoples in those portions of Africa where the climate and other circumstances permit of European rearing families of white children.
- Political action by European Governments aimed at the assertion of sovereign rights over particular areas of African territory.
- Administrative policy, sanctioned by European Governments, and applied by their local representatives in particular areas, subsequent to the successful assertion of sovereign rights.

These sub-divisions are, perhaps, somewhat arbitrary. The distinctiveness here given to them cannot be absolutely preserved. There is, for instance, a natural tendency for both a and b to merge into c as, though efflux of time, the originating cause and motive of contact is obscured by developments to which contact has given rise.

Thus racial contention for actual possession of the soil, and political action often resulting in so-called treaties of Protectorate thoroughly unintelligible to the African signees, are both landmarks upon the road leading to eventual administrative policy: i.e., to direct government of the black man by the white.

Reading and Discussion Questions

1. How does Morel rebut Kipling?
2. What role does Morel assign to technology and the environment in the exploitation of Africa by Western powers?

26.5 *Letters of a Javanese Princess*

Dutch colonization of the island of Java (now a part of Indonesia), began in the late sixteenth century. Raden Ayu Kartini (1879-1904), a Javanese aristocrat, grew up exposed to both Javanese Muslim traditions as well as European cultural influences. Her father served as a regent (regional governor) working with the Dutch colonial government in the city of Japara, and spoke Dutch fluently. Kartini received a primary education based on Javanese and Western intellectual traditions. She then secured a scholarship to continue her education in Holland, but her parents opposed the plan. During this period, in 1899, Kartini started writing letters to several different correspondents in Europe. The exchange of letters eased her sense of isolation, as in Javanese culture, it was improper for her, as an upper-class single woman, to venture out alone in public. She wrote regularly to Rosa Abendanon-Maudri, the wife of a high level Dutch colonial official who had been Kartini's tutor and mentor while she and her husband were stationed in Japara. Kartini also wrote to Stella Zeehandelaar, a Dutch feminist and reformer, whom Kartini found through an announcement, advertising for a "pen-pal" that she placed in a Dutch newspaper. By 1903, Kartini decided to abandon her plans to study in Holland and to stay in Java. She agreed to a marriage, which according to tradition her parents arranged, with a Javanese man who was the regent in Rembang. As a married woman, she was allowed more freedom to pursue many of her goals, including founding a vocational school for Javanese girls. Kartini died prematurely in 1904, from complications during childbirth. Her letters, which spanned from 1899 to 1904, were first published in Europe, in Dutch, in 1911. In 1920, a new, expanded English language edition was published in London, with the title Letters of a Javanese Princess. The following is an excerpt from Kartini's letter, dated January, 12 1900, to Stella Zeehandelaar.

Source: Raden Ajeng Kartini, *Letters of a Javanese Princess*, trans. Agnes Louise Symmers (New York: Alfred A. Knopf, 1920), 39-
44

I shall relate to you the history of a girl of intelligent and cultivated Javanese. The boy had passed his examinations, and was number one in one of three principal high schools of Java. Both at Semarang, where he went to school, and at Batavia, where he stood his examinations, time doors of the best houses were open to the amiable schoolboy, with his agreeable and cultivated manners and great modesty.

Every one spoke Dutch to him, and he could express himself in that language with distinction. Fresh from this environment, he went back to the house of his parents. He thought it would be proper to pay his respects to the authorities of the place and he found himself in the presence of the Resident who had heard of him, and here it was that my friend made a mistake. He dared to address the great man in Dutch.

The following morning notice of an appointment as clerk to a comptroller in the mountains was sent to him.

There the young man must remain to think over his "misdeeds" and forget all that he had learned at the schools. After some years a new comptroller or possibly assistant comptroller came; then the measure of his misfortunes was made to overflow. The new chief was a former school-fellow, one who had never shone through his abilities. The young man who had led his classes in everything must now creep upon the ground before the onetime dunce, and speak always high Javanese to him, while he himself was answered in bad Malay. Can you understand the misery of a proud and independent spirit so humbled? And how much strength of character it must have taken to endure that petty and annoying oppression?

But at last he could stand it no longer, he betook himself to Batavia and asked his excellency the Governor General for an audience; it was granted him. The result was that he was sent to Preanger, with a commission to make a study of the rice culture there. He made himself of service through the translation of a pamphlet on the cultivation of water crops from Dutch into Javanese and Sudanese. The government presented him in acknowledgement with several hundred guilders. In the comptroller's school at Batavia, a teacher's place was vacant—a teacher of the Javanese language be it understood—and his friends (among the Javanese) did all in their power to secure this position for him, but without result. It was an absurd idea for a Native to have European pupils who later might become ruling government officials. Perish the thought! I should like to ask who could teach Javanese better than a born Javanese?

The young man went back to his dwelling place; in the meantime another Resident had come, and the talented son of the brown race might at last become an assistant wedono.* Not for nothing had he been banished for years to that distant place. He had learned wisdom there; namely, that one cannot serve a European official better than by creeping in the dust before him, and by never speaking a single word of Dutch in his presence.

Others have now come into power, and lately when the position of translator of the Javanese language became vacant it was offered to our friend (truly opportunely) now that he does not stand in any one's way!

Stella, I know an Assistant Resident, who speaks Malay with a Regent, although he knows that the latter speaks good Dutch. Every one else converses confidentially with this native ruler but the Assistant Resident—never.

My brothers speak in high Javanese to their superiors, who answer them in Dutch or in Malay. Those who speak Dutch to them are our personal friends; several of whom have asked my brothers to speak to them in the Dutch language, but they prefer not to do it, and Father also never does. The boys and Father know all too well why they must hold to the general usage.

There is too much idle talk about the word "prestige," through the imaginary dignity of the under officials. I do not bother about prestige. I am only amused at the manner in which they preserve their prestige over us Javanese.

Sometimes I cannot suppress a smile. It is distinctly diverting to see the great men try to inspire us with awe. I had to bite my lips to keep from laughing outright when I was on a journey not long ago, and saw an Assistant Resident go from his office to his house under the shade of a gold umbrella, which a servant held spread above his noble head. It was such a ridiculous spectacle! Heavens! If he only knew how the humble crowds who respectfully retreated to one side before the glittering sunshade, immediately his back was turned, burst out laughing.

There are many, yes very many Government officials, who allow the native rulers to kiss their feet, and their knees. Kissing the foot is the highest token of respect that we Javanese can show to our parents, or elderly blood relatives, and to our own rulers. We do not find it pleasant to do this for strangers; no, the European makes himself ridiculous in our eyes whenever he demands from us those tokens of respect to which our own rulers alone have the right.

It is a matter of indifference when Residents and Assistant Residents allow themselves to be called "Kandjeng," but when overseers, railroad engineers (and perhaps tomorrow, station-masters too) allow themselves to be thus addressed by their servants, it is absurdly funny. Do these people really know what Kandjeng means? It is a title that the natives give to their hereditary rulers. I used to think that it was only natural for the stupid Javanese to love all this flim-flam, but now I see that the civilized, enlightened Westerner is not averse to it, that he is daft about it.

I never allow women older than I to show all the prescribed ceremonies to me, even though I know they would gladly, for though I am so young, I am a scion of what they consider an ancient, noble and honoured house; for which in the past, they have poured out both blood and gold in large measure. It is strange how attached inferiors are to those above them. But to me, it goes against the grain when people older than I creep in the dust before me. With heavy hearts, many Europeans here see how the Javanese, whom, they regard as their inferiors, are slowly awakening, but at every turn a brown man comes up, who shows that he has just as good brains in his head, and a just as good heart in his body, as the white man.

But we are going forward, and they cannot hold back the current of time. I love the Hollanders very, very much, and I am grateful for everything that we have gained through them. Many of them are among our best friends, but there are also others who dislike us, for no other reason than we are bold enough to emulate them in education and culture.

In many subtle ways they make us feel their dislike. "I am a European, you are a Javanese," they seem to say, or "I am the master, you the governed." Not once, but many times, they speak to us in broken Malay; although they know very well that we understand the Dutch language. It would be a matter of indifference to me in what language they addressed us, if the tone were only polite. Not long ago, a Raden Ajoe was talking to a gentleman, and impulsively she said, "Sir, excuse me, but may I make a friendly request, please, speak to me in your own language. I understand and speak Malay very well, but alas, only high Malay. I do not understand this passer-Malay." How our gentleman hung his head! Why do many Hollanders find it unpleasant to converse with us in their own language? Oh yes, now I understand; Dutch is too beautiful to be spoken by a brown mouth.

A few days ago we paid a visit to Totokkers (Europeans who are new-comers in Java). Their domestics were old servants of ours, and we knew that they could speak and understand Dutch very well. I told the host this, and what answer did I receive from my gentleman? "No, they must not speak Dutch." "No, why?" I asked.

"Because natives ought not to know Dutch." I looked at him in amazement, and a satirical smile quivered at the corners of my mouth. The gentleman grew fiery red, mumbled something into his beard, and discovered something interesting in his boots, at least he devoted all of his attention to them.

Reading and Discussion Questions

1. What does this passage tell us about the relationship between education and imperialism? About language and imperialism?
2. What ideas and perspectives inform Kartini's views? How does her background affect her perceptions of colonial society in Java?
3. What does Kartini tell us about Dutch relations with and views of the Javanese, and about colonial societies in general?

26.6 Tea Pickers, Northern India

This photograph, from the early 20th century, shows laborers picking tea on a steep hillside in the foothills of the Himalayas in northern India.   Tea was an important export crop in British India.   In much of the industrializing world it became a widely consumed beverage among all classes.

Reading and Discussion Questions

1. Examine the tea pickers.   How would you characterize their work?   Why are all the workers, except the foreman, women?
2. How does the great popularity of tea in the 19th century demonstrate the global economy of this period?

Source: Library of Congress

Creoles and Caudillos: Latin America in the Nineteenth Century

Chapter 27

The Spanish Empire in the Americas developed during the colonial era, 1500-1800, when Spanish soldiers along with missionaries embarked to convert and conquer the native population of the Americas. This marked the development of mercantilist trading relations, imperial bureaucracies, new religious institutions, and race-based social hierarchies in Latin America. The sources in this chapter demonstrate the changes that took place during the movement for independence and the post-independence nation-building that occurred from 1820s through 1870s.

Many Latin American leaders came from elite groups due to their racial positions under the Spanish and Portuguese class systems. The Europeans born in Europe were referred to as *chapetones* or *gachupines* while the decendants of Europeans born in the Americas were referred to as *criollos*. The native indigenous populations were at the bottom of the hierarchal system along with African slaves. In the political systems of colonial Latin America, the chapetones or gachupines held positions of power in imperial bureaucracies. The criollos owned the local land and formed the nobility and ruled the rest of the remaining Indian population.

The European conflicts that developed during the Napoleonic wars created political instability in the Americas as in Europe. The criollos advocated independence largely due to the inspiration of the French and American revolutions as well as enlightened ideas about liberty and equality. This created an opportunity for independence and replacing the social division that existed among the criollos and the Indians whom had grown tired of the imperial bureaucracy. Selections in this chapter were chosen to demonstrate the conditions in which the Latin American colonists found themselves.

By the middle of the nineteenth century, Latin America countries focused on creating and consolidating political power within their respective boundaries. The challenge of creating a national identity along with nation building was a formidable task that gave rise to oligarchs, dictatorships, and anarchy among the newly independent nation along with examples of political and economic progress. This gave rise to political figures, mainly criollos, and intellectuals who championed to nationalism and liberalism and implement them into their national identities. As political struggles were fought, Latin American leaders composed their respective constitutions that defined and legitimized their sovereignty even though most were modeled on European or American examples. Selective sources in this chapter demonstrate a few key figures who were essential to the process of nation building in Latin America.

By the end of the nineteenth century, most Latin American countries achieved stability and economic progress. As the Industrial Revolution expanded, European nations invested into Latin American countries for their resources and as consumers of European products. The economic growth experienced among Latin American countries allowed them to enter into the global economy by the end of the twentieth century.

27.1   Alexander Von Humboldt on New Spain

During his expedition through Latin America from 1799 to 1804, Alexander von Humboldt (1769-1859), a naturalist and explorer, left a detailed description of the social, political, and economic conditions of the Spanish colonies. Because Spanish law prohibited entry into New Spain to anyone who was not Spanish, Humboldt's perspective was unique among other Europeans. His description of the inequality among the inhabitants gave a specific description of the social stratification in which the people of Latin America were categorized by the purity of their European heritage. Although Humboldt was unaware of the political change about to take place, he was able to describe the tensions between the inhabitants of New Spain that leads to the revolutions of the early nineteenth century.

Source: Alexander von Humboldt, *Political Essay on the Kingdom of New Spain*, trans. John Black (London: Longman, Hurst, Rees, Orme, and Brown, 1811), Volume I, Book II, Chapter VII.

Amongst the inhabitants of pure origin the whites would occupy the second place, considering them only in the relation of number. They are divided into whites born in Europe, and descendants of Europeans born in the Spanish colonies of America or in the Asiatic islands. The former bear the name of Chapetones or Gachupines, and the second that of Criollos. The natives of the Canary islands, who go under the general denomination of Islenos (islanders), and who are the gerans of the plantations, are considered as Europeans. The Spanish laws allow the same rights to all whites; but those who have the execution of the laws endeavour to destroy an equality which shocks the European pride. The government, suspicious of the Creoles, bestows the great places exclusively on the natives of Old Spain. For some years back they have disposed at Madrid even of the most trifling employments in the administration of the customs and the tobacco revenue. At an epoch when every thing tended to a uniform relaxation in the springs of the state, the system of venality made an alarming progress. For the most part it was by no means a suspicious and distrustful policy; it was pecuniary interest alone which bestowed all employments on Europeans. The result has been a jealous and perpetual hatred between the Chapetons and the Creoles. The most miserable European, without education, and without intellectual cultivation, thinks himself superior to the whites born in the new continent. He knows that, protected by his countrymen, and favored by chances common enough in a country where fortunes are as rapidly acquired as they are lost, he may one day reach places to which the access is almost interdicted to the natives, even to those of men distinguished for their talents, knowledge and moral qualities. The natives prefer the denomination of Americans to that of Creoles. Since the peace of Versailles, and, in particular, since the year 1789, we frequently hear proudly declared, "I am not a Spaniard, I am an American!" words which betray the workings of a long resentment. In the eye of law every white Creole is a Spaniard; but the abuse of the laws, the false measures of the colonial government, the example of the United States of America, and the influence of the opinions of the age, have relaxed the ties which formerly united more closely the Spanish Creoles to the European Spaniards. A wise administration may reestablish harmony, calm their passions and resentments, and yet preserve for a long time the union among the members of one and the same great family scattered over Europe and America, from the Patagonian coast to the north of California. . .

Reading and Discussion Questions

1. Why would the Spanish have such complex social, economical, and political stratification among its inhabitants?
2. What are the long term effects of imposing such a system on the inhabitants?

27.2   Simón de Bolívar, Message to the Congress of Angostura

During the nineteenth century, most Latin American leaders came from the elite of their respective societies. Simon de Bolivar (1783-1830) served as president to Gran Columbia from 1813 to 1832. Angostura, present day Bolivar city, was the place where Bolivar summoned delegates that represented Venezuela and Columbia to discuss the independence wars against the Spanish in the early 1800s'; however, creating a national identity, while also creating new political institutions, proved especially troubling to many Latin American countries. Plagued by regime uncertainly and political unrest. Latin American leaders often failed to harmonize nationalism with political liberalism and thus left unfulfilled Bolivar's goal of creating free, self-governing institutions.

Source: Simón Bolívar, "An Address of Bolivar at the Congress of Angostura," February 15, 1819. (Washington, D.C.: Press of B. S. Adams, 1919).

Nothing in our fundamental laws would have to be altered were we to adopt a legislative power similar to that held by the British Parliament. Like the North Americans, we have divided national representation into two chambers: that of Representatives and the Senate. The first is very wisely constituted. It enjoys all its proper functions, and it requires no essential revision, because the Constitution, in creating it, gave it the form and powers which the people deemed necessary in order that they might be legally and properly represented. If the Senate were hereditary rather than elective, it would, in my opinion, be the basis, the tie, the very soul of our republic. In political storms this body would arrest the thunderbolts of the government and would repel any violent popular reaction. Devoted to the government because of a natural interest in its own preservation, a hereditary senate would always oppose any attempt on the part of the people to infringe upon the jurisdiction and authority of their magistrates. . .The creation of a hereditary senate would in no way be a violation of political equality. I do not solicit the establishment of a nobility, for as a celebrated republican has said, that would simultaneously destroy equality and liberty. What I propose is an office for which the candidates must prepare themselves, an office that demands great knowledge and the ability to acquire such knowledge. All should not be left to chance and the outcome of elections. The people are more easily deceived than is Nature perfected by art; and although these senators, it is true, would not be bred in an environment that is all virtue, it is equally true that they would be raised in an atmosphere of enlightened education. The hereditary senate will also serve as a counterweight to both government and people; and as a neutral power it will weaken the mutual attacks of these two eternally rival powers.

The British executive power possesses all the authority properly appertaining to a sovereign, but he is surrounded by a triple line of dams, barriers, and stockades. He is the head of government, but his ministers and subordinates rely more upon law than upon his authority, as they are personally responsible; and not even decrees of royal authority can exempt them from this responsibility. The executive is commander in chief of the army and navy; he makes peace and declares war; but Parliament annually determines what sums are to be paid to these military forces. While the courts and judges are dependent on the executive power, the laws originate in and are made by Parliament. Give Venezuela such an executive power in the person of a president chosen by the people or their representatives, and you will have taken a great step toward national happiness. No matter what citizen occupies this office, he will be aided by the Constitution, and therein being authorized to do good, he can do no harm, because his ministers will cooperate with him only insofar as he abides by the law. If he attempts to infringe upon the law, his own ministers will desert him, thereby isolating him from the Republic, and they will even bring charges against him in the Senate. The ministers, being responsible for any transgressions committed, will actually govern, since they must account for their actions.

Reading and Discussion Questions

1. Why did Bolivar insist that he had no plans to establish a national nobility modeled upon European aristocracy?
2. How might the absence of such an elite hamper efforts to create stable political institutions?

27.3 Pope Leo XIII, *In Plurimis*

Slavery played a major role in the New World from the early days of colonization. In the 15th and 16th centuries, the Portuguese pioneered the slave trade by establishing trading posts along the coast of Africa. To establish economic progress without forced labor was a significant task. By the time of its independence from Portugal the majority of Brazil's populations were enslaved, and the Brazilian economy was based on intensive production of goods such as mining, cotton, and sugar. Not until the late 19th century and the expansion of industrialization did labor saving machines become widely available, thereby rendering slavery economically unnecessary. In Plurimis, Pope Leo XIII (1810-1903) provided a brief history of slavery up to 1888, by which time all of Latin American countries had abolished slavery with the exception of Brazil.

Source: *In Plurimis:* Encyclical of Pope Leo XIII on the Abolition of Slavery (1888)

To the Bishops of Brazil,

. . .

21. And now, venerable brethren, Our thoughts and letters desire to turn to you that We may again announce to you and again share with you the exceeding joy which We feel on account of the determinations which have been publicly entered into in that empire with regard to slavery. If, indeed, it seemed to Us a good, happy, and propitious event, that it was provided and insisted upon by law that whoever were still in the condition of slaves ought to be admitted to the status and rights of free men, so also it conforms and increases Our hope of future acts which will be the cause of joy, both in civil and religious matters. Thus the name of the Empire of Brazil will be justly held in honor and praise among the most civilized nations, and the name of its august emperor will likewise be esteemed, whose excellent speech is on record, that he desired nothing more ardently than that every vestige of slavery should be speedily obliterated from his territories. But, truly, until those precepts of the laws are carried into effect, earnestly endeavor, We beseech you, by all means, and press on as much as possible the accomplishment of this affair, which no light difficulties hinder. Through your means let it be brought to pass that masters and slaves may mutually agree with the highest goodwill and best good faith, nor let there be any transgression of clemency or justice, but, whatever things have to be carried out, let all be done lawfully, temperately, and in a Christian manner. Is is, however, chiefly to be wished that this may be prosperously accomplished, which all desire, that slavery may be banished and blotted out without any injury to divine or human rights, with no political agitation, and so with the solid benefit of the slaves themselves, for whose sake it is undertaken.

22. To each one of these, whether they have already been made free or are about to become so, We address with a pastoral intention and fatherly mind a few salutary cautions culled from the words of the great Apostle of the Gentiles. Let them, then, endeavor piously and constantly to retain grateful memory and feeling towards those by whose council and exertion they were set at liberty. Let them never show themselves unworthy of so great a gift nor ever confound liberty with licence; but let them use it as becomes well ordered citizens for the industry of an active life, for the benefit and advantage both of their family and of the State. To respect and

increase the dignity of their princes, to obey the magistrates, to be obedient to the laws, these and similar duties let them diligently fulfill, under the influence, not so much of fear as of religion; let them also restrain and keep in subjection envy of another's wealth or position, which unfortunately daily distresses so many of those in inferior positions, and present so many incitements of rebellion against security of order and peace. Content with their state and lot, let them think nothing dearer, let them desire nothing more ardently than the good things of the heavenly kingdom by whose grace they have been brought to the light and redeemed by Christ; let them feel piously towards God who is their Lord and Liberator; let them love Him, with all their power; let them keep His commandments with all their might; let them rejoice in being sons of His spouse, the Holy Church; let them labor to be as good as possible, and as much as they can let them carefully return His love. Do you also, Venerable Brethren, be constant in showing and urging on the freedmen these same doctrines; that, that which is Our chief prayer, and at the same time ought to be yours and that of all good people, religion, amongst the first, may ever feel that she has gained the most ample fruits of that liberty which has been obtained wherever that empire extends.

. . .

Given at St. Peter's, in Rome, the fifth day of May, 1888, the eleventh of Our pontificate,
LEO XIII.

Reading and Discussion Questions

1. Why is Leo XII giving his speech to the Bishops of Brazil and not the leaders of Brazil's new government?
2. Why are the bishops responsible for ensuring that order, civil obedience, and the distribution of wealth remain in the hand of the elite Brazilians?

27.4 Jose Martí, "Our America"

The great champion of Cuban freedom, José Martí (1853-1895), founded the Cuban Revolutionary Party in 1892 to struggle for independence from Spain. Living in exile in the United States, he warned Cubans in this 1891 essay not to emulate foreign solutions to their problems but to look to their own creativity.

Source: "Nuestra America," El Partido Liberal (Mexico City), January 30, 1891, p. 4.

To govern well requires an understanding and appreciation of local realities. Anyone who would govern well in the Americas does not need to know how the Germans or the French govern themselves, but rather needs to possess a basic knowledge of his own country, its resources, advantages, and problems and how to utilize them for the benefit of the nation, and needs to know local customs and institutions. The goal is to reach that happy state in which everyone can enjoy the abundance Nature has bestowed so generously on the Americas. Each must work for that enjoyment and be prepared to defend that abundance with his life. Good government arises from the conditions and needs of each nation. The very spirit infusing government must reflect local realities. Good government is nothing more and nothing less than a balance of local needs and resources.

The person who knows his own environment is far superior to anyone dependent on imported books for knowledge. Such a natural person has more to contribute to society than someone versed in artificial knowledge. The native of mixed ancestry is superior to the white person born here but attracted to foreign ideas. No struggle exists between civilization and barbarism but rather between false erudition and natural knowledge. Natural people are good; they respect and reward wisdom as long as it is not used to degrade, humiliate, or belittle them. They are ready to defend themselves and to demand respect from anyone wounding their pride or threatening their well-being. Tyrants have risen to power by conforming to these natural elements; they also have fallen by betraying them. Our republics have paid through tyranny for their inability to understand the true national reality, to derive from it the best form of government, and to govern accordingly. In a new nation, to govern is to create.

In nations inhabited by both the educated and the uneducated, the uneducated will govern because it is their nature to confront and resolve problems with their hands, while the educated dither over which formula to import, a futile means to resolve local problems. The uneducated people are lazy and timid in matters related to intelligence and seek to be governed well, but if they perceive the government to be injurious to their interests they will overthrow it to govern themselves. How can our universities prepare men to govern when not one of them teaches anything either about the art of government or the local conditions? The young emerge from our universities indoctrinated with Yankee or French ideas, aspiring to govern a people they do not understand. Those without a rudimentary knowledge of political reality should be barred from a public career. Prizes should be awarded not for the best poetry but for the best essays on national reality. Journalists, professors, and academicians ought to be promoting the study of national reality. Who are we, where have we been, which direction should we go? It is essential to ask such basic questions in our search for truth. To fail to ask the right questions or to fail to answer them truthfully dooms us. We must know the problems in order to respond to them, and we must know our potentials in order to realistically frame our responses. Strong and indignant natural people resent the imposition of foreign solutions, the insidious result of sterile book learning, because they have little or nothing to do with local conditions and realities. To know those realities is to possess the potential to resolve problems. To know our counters and to govern them in accordance with that knowledge is the only way to liberate ourselves from tyranny. Europeanized education here must give way to American education. The history of the Americas, from the Incas to the present, must be taught in detail even if we forego the courses on ancient Greece. Our own Greece is much more preferable to the Greece which is not ours. It is more important and meaningful to us. Statesmen with a nationalist view must replace politicians whose heads are in Europe even thought their feet remain in the Americas. Graft the world onto our nations if you will, but the trunk itself must be us. Silence the pedant who thrives on foreign inspiration.

There are no lands in which a person can take a greater pride than in our own long-suffering American republics. The Americas began to suffer, and still suffer, from the effort of trying to reconcile the discordant and hostile elements which they inherited from a despotic and greedy colonizer. Imported ideas and institutions with scant relationship to local realities have retarded the development of logical and useful governments. Our continent, disoriented for three centuries by governance that denied people the right to exercise reason, began in independence by ignoring the humble who had contributed so much in the effort to redeem it. At least in theory, reason was to reign in all things and for everyone, not just scholastic reason at the expense of the simpler reason of the majority. But the problem with our independence is that we changed political formulas without altering our colonial spirit.

The privileged made common cause with the oppressed to terminate a system which they found opposed to their own best interests. The colonies continue to survive in the guise of republics. Our America struggles to save itself from the monstrous errors of the past - its haughty capital cities, the blind triumph over the disdained masses, the excessive reliance on foreign ideas, and unjust, impolitic hatred of the native races - and relies on innate virtues and sacrifices to replace our colonial mentality with that of free peoples.

With our chest of an athlete, our hands of a gentleman, and our brain of a child, we presented quite a sight. We masqueraded in English breeches, a French vest, a Yankee jacket, and a Spanish hat. The silent Indians hovered near us but took their children into the mountains to orient them. The Afro-Americans, isolated in this continent, gave expression to thought and sorrow through song. The peasants, the real creators, viewed with indignation the haughty cities. And we the intellectuals wore our fancy caps and gowns in countries where the population dressed in headbands and sandals. Our genius will be in the ability to combine headband and cap, to amalgamate the cultures of the European, Indian, and Afro-American, and to ensure that all who fought for liberty enjoy it. Our colonial past left us with judges, generals, scholars, and bureaucrats. The idealistic young have been frustrated in efforts to bring change. The people have been unable to translate triumph into benefits. The European and Yankee books hold no answers for our problems and our future. Our problems grow. Frustrations mount. Exhausted by these problems and frustrations, by the struggles between the intellectual and the military, between reason and superstition, between the city and the countryside, and by the contentious urban politicians who abuse the natural nation, tempestuous or inert by turns, we turn now to a new compassion and understanding.

The new nations look about, acknowledging each other. They ask, "Who and what are we?" We suggest tentative answers. When a local problem arises, we are less likely to seek the answer in London or Paris. Our styles may all still originate in France but our thought is becoming more American. The new generation rolls up its sleeves, gets its hands dirty, and sweats. It is getting results. Our youth now understands that we are too prone to imitate and that our salvation lies in creativity. "Creativity" is the password of this new generation. The wine is from the plantain, and even if it is bitter, it is our wine! They understand that the form a government takes in a given country must reflect the realities of that country. Fixed ideas must become relative in order for them to work. Freedom to experiment must be honest and complete. If these republics do not include all their populations and benefit all of them, then they will fail.

The new American peoples have arisen; they look about; they greet each other. A new leadership emerges which understands local realities. New leaders read and study in order to apply their new knowledge, to adapt it to local realities, not to imitate. Economists study problems with an historical context. Orators eschew flamboyance for sober reality. Playwrights people the stages with local characters. Academicians eschew scholastic theories to discuss pressing problems. Poets eschew marble temples and Gothic cathedrals in favor of local scenes. Prose offers ideas and solutions. In those nations with large Indian populations, the Presidents are learning to speak Indian languages.

The greatest need of Our America is to unite in spirit. The scorn of our strong neighbor the United States is the greatest present danger to Our America. The United States now pays greater attention to us. It is imperative that this formidable neighbor get to know us in order to dissipate its scorn. Through ignorance, it might even invade and occupy us. Greater knowledge of us will increase our neighbor's understanding and diminish that threat.

A new generation reshapes our continent. This new generation recreates Our America. It sows the seeds of a New America from the Río Grande to the Straits of Magellan. The hopes of Our America lie in the originality of the new generation.

Reading and Discussion Questions

1. What is "natural knowledge" according to Martí? Why for Martí is the struggle not so much between civilization and barbarism, but between false erudition and natural knowledge?
2. What does Martí mean when he says "to govern is to create?"
3. What is Martí's view of history and Western Civilization?   How does he regard the United States?

27.5   United States Recognition of Cuban Independence

During the early nineteenth century, Cuba remained a part of the Spanish Empire while the rest of Latin America rebelled against Spanish and Portuguese rule. In 1898, the U.S. sent the battle ship *Maine* to protect American interests in Cuba during the revolt against the Spanish. Although the explosion of the battleship remains controversial, American press blamed Spanish authorities and called for military intervention. The Teller Amendment, an amendment name after Henry M. Teller (1830-1914) proposed that the U.S. not establish permanent control over Cuba after their cessation with Spain and, demanded that the government of Spain relinquished its authority and government over the island.

Source: United States Congress, Senate Subcommittee on Foreign Relations, US Recognition of Cuban Independence, 1898. 62nd Congress, 2nd Session, Teller Amendment, (Washington, D.C.: Government Printing Office, 1913).

Whereas, the abhorrent conditions which have existed for more than three years in the Island of Cuba, so near our own borders, have shocked the moral sense of the people of the United States, have been a disgrace to Christian civilization, culminating, as they have, in the destruction of a United States battleship, with two hundred and sixty-six of its officers and crew, while on a friendly visit in the harbor of Havana, and can not longer be endured, as has been set forth by the President of the United States in his message to Congress of April eleventh, eighteen hundred and ninety-eight, upon which the action of Congress was invited: Therefore, Resolved, by the Senate and House of Representatives of the United States of America in Congress assembled, First. That the people of the Island of Cuba are, and of right ought to be, free and independent. Second. That it is the duty of the United States to demand, and the Government of the United States does hereby demand, that the Government of Spain at once relinquish its authority and government in the Island of Cuba, and withdraw its land and naval forces from Cuba and Cuban waters. Third. That the President of the United States be, and he hereby is, directed and empowered to use the entire land and naval forces of the United States, and to call into the actual service of the United States, the militia of the several States, to such extent as may be necessary to carry these resolutions into effect. Fourth. That the United States hereby disclaims any disposition or intention to exercise sovereignty, jurisdiction, or control over said Islands except for the pacification thereof, and asserts its determination, when that is accomplished, to leave the government and control of the Island to its people. Approved, April 20, 1898.

Reading and Discussion Questions

1. What kind of relationship existed between the United States and most Latin American countries, particularly with regard to their European mother countries?
2. What sorts of special relationships or hurdles did less powerful, Latin countries like Cuba face with regard to the United States? If Jose Martí were still alive, what would have been his reaction to the Teller Amendment?
3. What advantage might closer relations with the United States offer to newly independent colonies like Cuba?

World War and Competing Visions of Modernity to 1945

Chapter 28

Few periods of world history involved as much change, heightened violence, and social disarray as the first half of the twentieth century. The watershed event of World War I witnessed the passing away of the old European aristocracy, which controlled much of the continent since the collapse of the Roman Empire. New technology and production brought rising standards of living but also equipped modern armies with destructive capacities never before witnessed. The interdependence of global financial institutions rapidly spread economic depression from one part of the world to the next. It was a period that began with the assassination of an aristocratic heir to an empire and ended with the dropping of two atomic bombs.

Ironically, the violence of the early 20th century coincided with political empowerment of countless millions of people. Mass political movements spawned progressive reform in Great Britain and the United States, the Bolshevik Revolution in Russia, and the rise of facism in Germany, Italy, and Japan. Each ideological movement grew from efforts to deal with the profound economic and social changes of the nineteenth century, particularly the shift from agrarian and commercial communities to industrial, urban centers.

How countries reacted to these changes depended on a variety of factors. Some societies aggressively pursued a policy of territorial expansion, fueled by industrial war machines. Italy, Germany, and Japan sought to catch up to the older empires of Great Britain and France and used every means necessary to achieve their goals. Russia quickly expanded as well by consolidating power over its neighbors and turning them into the satellite states of the Soviet Union. Other countries like Great Britain, France, and the United States forged military alliances to resist the expansion of the others. For a brief time in the 1930s, intellectuals and political leaders believed there were only two alternatives: socialism or fascism. Gone was the old liberalism of the nineteenth century. It was discredited by uneven economic progress and the alliance system that ignited World War I. Faith in progress—the hallmark of the modern era—collapsed in the presence of global, total war.

In some ways, total war was preceded by mass politics as people began taking seriously the political affirmation of their worth as human beings. In turn, politics came to be seen as a solution to economic distress and cultural disunity. As dedication to political institutions rose, so too did power as the modern state reached the zenith of its legitimacy. With unbridled power, those who control politics unleashed waves of attacks upon anyone not meeting their national ideological demands. Millions were thus murdered by their own governments.

The following documents illustrate the depths of brutality by illustrating both the ideas that brought about the revolutions and wars of the twentieth century and the unprecedented consequences of those ideas.

28.1 Theodore Roosevelt, "War for Righteousness"

Otherwise peaceful, democratic societies waged war as vigorously as totalitarian regimes, sometimes with a capacity for brutality unmatched by less democratic countries. The United States in World War I provides a case in point.

Americans came late to the "Great War," but did with just as much enthusiasm and fervent spirit as any of the major European countries who started the conflict. One reason for American involvement depended upon a religious impulse deeply embedded in American intellectual life. President Theodore Roosevelt (1858-1919), well known for his support of American entry into World War I and influenced by Christian liberalism, illustrates how religious rhetoric was used to justify warlike hostility.

Source: Theodore Roosevelt, *Fear God and Take Your Own Part* (George H. Doran, 1914), 65-67.

The first thing to do is to make these citizens understand that war and militarism are terms whose values depend wholly upon the sense in which they are used. The second thing is to make them understand that there is a real analogy between the use of force in international and the use of force in intra-national or civil matters; although of course this analogy must not be pushed too far.

In the first place, we are dealing with a matter of definition. A war can be defined as violence between nations, as the use of force between nations. It is analogous to violence between individuals within a nation—using violence in a large sense as equivalent to the use of force. When this fact is clearly grasped, the average citizen will be spared the mental confusion he now suffers because he thinks of war as in itself wrong. War, like peace, is properly a means to an end—righteousness. Neither war nor peace is in itself righteous, and neither should be treated as of itself the end to be aimed at. Righteousness is the end. Righteousness when triumphant brings peace; but peace may not bring righteousness. Whether war is right or wrong depends purely upon the purpose for which, and the spirit in which, it is waged. Here the analogy with what takes place in civil life is perfect. The exertion of force or violence by which one man masters another may be illustrated by the case of a black-hander who kidnaps a child, knocking down the nurse or guardian; and it may also be illustrated by the case of the guardian who by violence withstands and thwarts the black-hander in his efforts to kidnap the child, or by the case of the policeman who by force arrests the black-hander or white-slaver or whoever it is and takes his victim away from him. There are, of course, persons who believe that all force is immoral, that it is always immoral to resist wrongdoing by force. I have never taken much interest in the individuals who profess this kind of twisted morality; and I do not know the extent to which they practically apply it. But if they are right in their theory, then it is wrong for a man to endeavor by force to save his wife or sister or daughter from rape or other abuse, or to save his children from abduction and torture. It is a waste of time to discuss with any man a position of such folly, wickedness, and poltroonery. But unless a man is willing to take this position, he cannot honestly condemn the use of force or violence in war—for the policeman who risks and perhaps loses or takes life in dealing with an anarchist or white-slaver or black-hander or burglar or highwayman must be justified or condemned on precisely the same principles which require us to differentiate among wars and to condemn y certain nations in certain wars and equally without stint to praise other nations in certain other wars.

If the man who objects to war also objects to the use of force in civil life as above outlined, his position is logical, although both absurd and wicked. If the college presidents, politicians, automobile manufacturers, and the like, who during the past year or two have preached pacifism in its most ignoble and degrading form are willing to think out the subject and are both sincere and fairly intelligent, they must necessarily condemn a police force or a ***posse comitatus*** just as much as they condemn armies; and they must regard the activities of the sheriff and the constable as being essentially militaristic and therefore to be abolished.

---

posse comitatus: "law of the country"

Reading and Discussion Questions

1. How does Roosevelt define "righteousness"? How does this idea prove foundational for his support for warfare?
2. In what ways does Roosevelt offer a "military" solution to the social problems plaguing early twentieth century America?

28.2 Liquidating the Kulaks

Joseph Stalin (1878-1953) served as the leader of the Soviet Union from the late 1920s when he consolidated his power over the country's Communist party until his death in 1953. His rise to power left behind a trail of brutality unparalleled in world history, beginning with the Bolshevik Revolution of 1917, which he helped orchestrate, to the mass slaughter of innocent Russians who opposed his socialist policies. After consolidating his political power in the 1920s, Stalin commenced collectivizing the Soviet economy whereby central planners determined the allocation of all economic resources. Agriculture remained a key focus of Stalin's efforts even though he also pressed for aggressive industrialization. Stalin's central planners proved incapable of controlling agricultural production, and Stalin forced millions of peasant farmers into large, mechanized farmers where labor could be best controlled. When agricultural production inevitably failed to meet his goals, Stalin blames the *kulaks*, a small group of relatively affluent farmers who resisted collectivization. Hundreds of thousands of kulaks were captured, shot, deported, or transferred to labor camps. Soviet agricultural production subsequently collapsed in key areas thus fostering a devastating famine and food shortages, which resulted in the deaths of hundreds of thousands of additional people. Altogether, Stalin's agricultural campaigns and forced collectivization during the 1930s costs the lives of millions.

Source: Joseph Stalin, "Speech at a conference of Marxist students on the agrarian question." December 27, 1929.

. . . The so-called theory of the "equilibrium" between the sectors of our national economy is still current among Communists. This theory has, of course, nothing in common with Marxism. Nevertheless, this theory is advocated by a number of people in the camp of the Right deviators.

This theory is based on the assumption that to begin with we have a socialist sector-which is one compartment, as it were-and that in addition we also have a non-socialist or, if you like, capitalist sector-which is another compartment. These two "compartments" move on different rails and glide peacefully forward, without touching each other. Geometry teaches that parallel lines do not meet. But the authors of this remarkable theory believe that these parallel lines will meet eventually, and that when they do, we will have socialism. This theory overlooks the fact that behind these so-called "compartments" there are classes, and that these compartments move as a result of a fierce class struggle, a life-and-death struggle, a struggle on the principle of "who will win?"

It is not difficult to see that this theory has nothing in common with Leninism. It is not difficult to see that, objectively, the purpose of this theory is to defend the position of individual peasant farming, to arm the kulak elements with a "new" theoretical weapon in their struggle against the collective farms, and to destroy confidence in the collective farms...

. . . Can we advance our socialized industry at an accelerated rate as long as we have an agricultural base, such as is provided by small peasant farming, which is incapable of expanded reproduction, and which, in addition, is the predominant force in our national economy?

No, we cannot. Can Soviet power and the work of socialist construction rest for any length of time on two different foundations: on the most large-scale and concentrated socialist industry, and the most scattered and backward, small-commodity peasant farming? No, they cannot.

Can Soviet power and the work of socialist construction rest for any length of time on two different foundations: on the most large-scale and concentrated socialist industry, and the most scattered and backward, small-commodity peasant farming? No, they cannot. Sooner or later this would be bound to end in the complete collapse of the whole national economy.

What, then, is the solution? The solution lies in enlarging the agricultural units, in making agriculture capable of accumulation, of expanded reproduction, and in thus transforming the agricultural bases of our national economy.

But how are the agricultural units to be enlarged?

There are two ways of doing this. There is the capitalist way, which is to enlarge the agricultural units by introducing capitalism in agricultureaway which leads to the impoverishment of the peasantry and to the development of capitalist enterprises in agriculture. We reject this way as incompatible with the Soviet economic system.

There is a second way: the socialist way, which is to introduce collective farms and state farms in agriculture, the way which leads to the amalgamation of the small-peasant farms into large collective farms, employing machinery and scientific methods of farming, and capable of developing further, for such agricultural enterprises can achieve expanded reproduction. And so, the question stands as follows: either one way or the other either back -to capitalism, or forward-to socialism. There is no third way, nor can there be.

Reading and Discussion Questions
1.   How does Stalin dismiss the arguments of those who called for restraint and moderation?
2.   To what degree does Stalin's position illustrate the compatibility between socialism and industrialization?

28.3   Critics of Modernity: The Southern Agrarians

The Industrial Revolution prompted intellectual response from a wide array of observers. Supporters of industrialization pointed to increased standards of living eventually obtained by workers, increased productivity that reduced prices within reach of the masses, and the empowerment of individual and groups of consumers. For critics of industrialization, most attention is given to socialists, fascists, or others who largely approved of the shift from pre-industrial, agrarian communities to metropolitan, factory work. Socialists often lent support to industrialization as a means of progress. They simply thought the benefits were not equally shared between owners and workers. But industrialization also had conservative critiques who believed the process undermined traditional institutions and the social order they sustained. Conservative critics defended agrarian values and communities and often argued industrialization proceeded at a rapid pace thanks to the impetus and encouragement of political classes, not a free market. The Southern Agrarians, a group of poets, writers, and scholars centered at Vanderbilt University in Tennessee in the interwar period, challenged the industrialization of the American South. They argued it undermined tradition and consolidated their society into a homogenized culture where money was the master of all things.

Source: Twelve Southerners, *I'll Take My Stand* (LSU Press, 1930).

Industrialism is the economic organization of the collective American society. It means the decision of society to invest its economic resources in the applied sciences. But the word science has acquired a certain sanctitude. It is out of order to quarrel with science in the abstract, or even with the applied sciences when their applications are made subject to criticism and intelligence. The capitalization of the applied sciences has now become extravagant and uncritical; it has enslaved our human energies to a degree now clearly felt to be burdensome. The apologists of industrialism do not like to meet this charge directly; so they often take refuge in saying that they are devoted simply to science! They are really devoted to the applied sciences and to practical production. Therefore it is necessary to employ a certain skepticism even at the expense of the Cult of Science, and to say, It is an Americanism, which looks innocent and disinterested, but really is not either.

The contribution that science can make to a labor is to render it easier by the help of a tool or a process, and to assure the laborer of his perfect economic security while he is engaged upon it. Then it can be performed with leisure and enjoyment. But the modern laborer has not exactly received this benefit under the industrial regime. His labor is hard, its tempo is fierce, and his employment is insecure. The first principle of a good labor is that it must be effective, but the second principle is that it must be enjoyed. Labor is one of the largest items in the human career; it is a modest demand to ask that it may partake of happiness.

The regular act of applied science is to introduce into labor a labor-saving device or a machine. Whether this is a benefit depends on how far it is advisable to save the labor The philosophy of applied science is generally quite sure that the saving of labor is a pure gain, and that the more of it the better. This is to assume that labor is an evil, that only the end of labor or the material product is good. On this assumption labor becomes mercenary and servile, and it is no wonder if many forms of modern labor are accepted without resentment though they are evidently brutalizing. The act of labor as one of the happy functions of human life has been in effect abandoned, and is practiced solely for its rewards.

Even the apologists of industrialism have been obliged to admit that some economic evils follow in the wake of the machines. These are such as overproduction, unemployment, and a growing inequality in the distribution of wealth. But the remedies proposed by the apologists are always homeopathic. They expect the evils to disappear when we have bigger and better machines, and more of them. Their remedial programs, therefore, look forward to more industrialism. Sometimes they see the system righting itself spontaneously and without direction: they are Optimists. Sometimes they rely on the benevolence of capital, or the militancy of labor, to bring about a fairer division of the spoils: they are Cooperationists or Socialists. And sometimes they expect to find super-engineers, in the shape of Boards of Control, who will adapt production to consumption and regulate prices and guarantee business against fluctuations: they are Sovietists. With respect to these last it must be insisted that the true Sovietists or Communists-if the term may be used here in the European sense-are the Industrialists themselves. They would have the government set up an economic super-organization, which in turn would become the government. We therefore look upon the Communist menace as a menace indeed, but not as a Red one; because it is simply according to the blind drift of our industrial development to expect in America at last much the same economic system as that imposed by violence upon Russia in 1917.

Turning to consumption, as the grand end which justifies the evil of modern labor, we find that we have been deceived. We have more time in which to consume, and many more products to be consumed. But the tempo of our labors communicates itself to our satisfactions, and these also become brutal and hurried. The constitution of the natural man probably does not permit him to shorten his labor-time and enlarge his consuming-time indefinitely. He has to pay the penalty in satiety and aimlessness. The modern man has lost his sense of vocation.

Reading and Discussion Questions

1. Why would the Agrarians depict applied science as the quintessential end of industrialism?
2. Did the Agrarians recognize any compatability between conserving their traditional communities and enjoying the material benefits of capitalism? How might they have reconciled the two in light of the modern state?

28.4 Mohandas Gandhi and the Quit India Movement

The British Raj (Hindi for "reign") over India ended in 1947 due largely to Mohandas Gandhi (1869-1948), whose non-violent protests inspired civil rights movements throughout the world. Born to an affluent family, Gandhi studied law in London, then moved to South Africa, where he advocated civil rights for Indians living in Africa. He returned to Indian in 1915 to champion the cause of India's lower castes, women, peasants, farmers, and the ostracized "untouchables." Gandhi relied upon a strategy of non-violence and civil disobedience, which he learned while studying in London. Jailed many times for his opposition to British colonial rule, Gandhi became leader of the Indian National Congress and organized a series of peaceful protests against British taxation, which gradually coalesced into an independence movement by World War II. Spawned by speeches delivered to the Indian National Congress, Gandhi's "Quit India" movement clashed with British demands for Indian cooperation in the war against Germany. The movement inspired both violent and non-violent protests, mass arrests, and thousands of deaths; however, British will to retain control over India quickly dissolved.

Source: Mohandas Gandhi, "Quit India Speeches," to the All India Congress Committee, August 8, 1942, Bombay.

Ours is not a drive for power, but purely a non-violent fight for India's independence. In a violent struggle, a successful general has been often known to effect a military coup and to set up a dictatorship. But under the Congress scheme of things, essentially non-violent as it is, there can be no room for dictatorship. A non-violent soldier of freedom will covet nothing for himself, he fights only for the freedom of his country. The Congress is unconcerned as to who will rule, when freedom is attained. The power, when it comes, will belong to the people of India, and it will be for them to decide to whom it placed in the entrusted. May be that the reins will be placed in the hands of the Parsis, for instance-as I would love to see happen-or they may be handed to some others whose names are not heard in the Congress today. It will not be for you then to object saying, "This community is microscopic. That party did not play its due part in the freedom's struggle; why should it have all the power?" Ever since its inception the Congress has kept itself meticulously free of the communal taint. It has thought always in terms of the whole nation and has acted accordingly...

. . .

The Congress has no sanction but the moral one for enforcing its decisions. It believes that true democracy can only be the outcome of non-violence. The structure of a world federation can be raised only on a foundation of non-violence, and violence will have to be totally abjured from world affairs. If this is true, the solution of Hindu-Muslim question, too, cannot be achieved by a resort to violence. If the Hindus tyrannize over the Mussalman, with what face will they talk of a world federation? It is for the same reason that I do not believe in the possibility of establishing world peace through violence as the English and American statesmen propose to do. ...

I, therefore, want freedom immediately, this very night, before dawn, if it can be had. Freedom cannot now wait for the realization of communal unity. If that unity is not achieved, sacrifices necessary for it will have to be much greater than would have otherwise sufficed. But the Congress must win freedom or be wiped out in the effort. And forget not that the freedom which the Congress is struggling to achieve will not be for the Congressmen alone but for all the forty cores of the Indian people. Congressmen must for ever remain humble servants of the people. …

Here is a mantra, a short one, that I give you. You may imprint it on your hearts and let every breath of yours give expression to it. The mantra is: 'Do or Die'. We shall either free India or die in the attempt; we shall not live to see the perpetuation of our slavery. Every true Congressman or woman will join the struggle with an inflexible determination not to remain alive to see the country in bondage and slavery. Let that be your pledge. Keep jails out of your consideration. … Take a pledge, with God and your own conscience as witness, that you will no longer rest till freedom is achieved and will be prepared to lay down your lives in the attempt to achieve it. He who loses his life will gain it; he who will seek to save it shall lose it. Freedom is not for the coward or the faint-hearted.

Reading and Discussion Questions

1. How did Gandhi deflect accusations that he was absorbed by a personal quest for power?
2. What tensions exist in Gandhi's speech between a commitment to nonviolence and a desire to end British colonial rule at all cost?
3. Why was Gandhi unwilling to endorse gradual process of decolonizing India?

28.5 Mussolini Repudiates Political Liberalism, 1923

Italian Fascists repudiated democratic capitalism and disregarded the liberal belief in the rule of law and the consent of the governed. Benito Mussolini (1883-1945) was perhaps fascism's most articulate spokesman. He was born the son of a blacksmith and worked as a school teacher and day laborer before becoming editor of a Socialist newspaper prior to World War I. He supported Italy's entry into the war and was wounded in the conflict. In 1919, he was one of many small-time candidates trying to make a mark in Italian politics. A powerful orator and opportunist, Mussolini presented a message of order and action that won him the support of working and middle-class Italians who had been hit hard by the inflation that plagued Europe after the war. In 1923 Mussolini explained why the Fascists so hated and repudiated liberal principles.

Source: From Benito Mussolini, "Force and Consent" (1923), as trans. in Jonathan F. Scott and Alexander Baltzly, eds., Readings in European History Since 1814 (New York: F. S. Crofts, 1931),680-682.

Liberalism is not the last word, nor does it represent the definitive formula on the subject of the art of government. Liberalism is the product and the technique of the nineteenth century. It does not follow that the Liberal scheme of government, good for the nineteenth century, for a century, that is, dominated by two such phenomena as the growth of capitalism and the strengthening of the sentiment of nationalism, should be adapted to the twentieth century, which announces itself already with characteristics sufficiently different from those that marked the preceding century. I challenge Liberal gentlemen to tell if ever in history there has been a government that was based solely on popular consent and that renounced all use of force whatsoever. A government so constructed there has never been and never will be. Consent is an ever-changing thing like the shifting sand on the sea coast, it can never be permanent: It can never be complete. If it be accepted as an axiom that any system of government whatever creates malcontents, how are you going to prevent this discontent from overflowing and constituting a menace to the stability of the State? You will prevent it by force. By the assembling of the greatest force possible. By the inexorable use of this force whenever it is necessary. Take away from any government whatsoever force - and by force is meant physical, armed force - and leave it only its immortal principles, and that government will be at the mercy of the first organized group that decides to overthrow it. Fascism now throws these lifeless theories out to rot.) The truth evident now to all who are not warped by [liberal] dogmatism is that men have tired of liberty. They have made an orgy of it. Liberty is today no longer the chaste and austere virgin for whom the generations of the first half of the last century fought and died. For the gallant, restless and bitter youth who face the dawn of a new history there are other words that exercise a far greater fascination, and those words are: order, hierarchy, discipline...

Know then, once and for all, that Fascism knows no idols and worships no fetishes. It has already stepped over, and if it be necessary it will turn tranquilly and step again over, the more or less putrescent corpse of the Goddess of Liberty.

Reading and Discussion Questions

1. How does Mussolini interpret the political history of the nineteenth century?
2. Why does Mussolini feel that men have tired of liberty?
3. For Mussolini, what role does force play in society?

28.6 Adolf Hitler: German Economic Goals and the Jewish Question

Antisemitism was central to Hitler's political vision and strategy. In this document, an unsigned memorandum on the Four Year Plan of 1936—a plan that was to strengthen the German economy and military preparedness—Hitler presented the ideological rationale of this plan as the "apocalyptic" struggle against Bolshevism and world Jewry.

Source: Unsigned Memorandum on the Four Year Plan, August 1936, Documents on German Foreign Policy, 1918–1945, Series C (1933–37) (Washington, D.C., n.d.), vol. 5, 853–62.

Politics are the conduct and the course of the historical struggle for life of the peoples. The aim of these struggles is the assertion of existence. Even the idealistic ideological struggles have their ultimate cause and are most deeply motivated by nationally determined purposes and aims of life. Religions and ideologies are, however, always able to impart particular harshness to struggles of this kind, and therefore are also able to give them great historical impressiveness. They leave their imprint on the content of centuries. In such cases it is not possible for people and States living within the sphere of such ideological or religious conflicts to dissociate or exclude themselves from these events. . . .

Since the outbreak of the French Revolution, the world has been moving with ever increasing speed towards a new conflict, the most extreme solution of which is called Bolshevism, whose essence and aim, however, is solely the elimination of those strata of mankind which have hitherto provided the leadership and their replacement by worldwide Jewry.

No State will be able to withdraw or even remain at a distance from this historical conflict. Since Marxism, through its victory in Russia, has established one of the greatest empires in the world as a forward base for its future operations, this question has become a menacing one. . . .Germany.

Germany will, as always, have to be regarded as the focal point of the Western world in face of the Bolshevist attacks. I do not regard this as an agreeable mission but rather as a handicap and encumbrance upon our national life regrettably resulting from our position in Europe. We cannot, however, escape this destiny. . . .

It is not the aim of this memorandum to prophesy the time when the untenable situation in Europe will become an open crisis. I only want in these lines, to set down my conviction that this crisis cannot and will not fail to arrive and that it is Germany's duty to secure her own existence by every means in the face of this catastrophe, and to protect herself against it, and that from this compulsion there arises a series of conclusions relating to the most important tasks to which our people have ever been set. For a victory of Bolshevism over Germany would not lead to a Versailles Treaty but the final destruction, indeed to the annihilation of the German people.

The extent of such a catastrophe cannot be foreseen. How, indeed, would the whole of densely populated Western Europe (including Germany) after a collapse into Bolshevism live through probably the most gruesome catastrophe for the people which has been visited upon mankind since the downfall of the States of antiquity?

In face of the necessity of defense against this danger, all other considerations must recede into the background as being completely irrelevant. . . .

I consider it necessary for the Reichstag to pass the following two laws: (1) A law providing the death penalty for economic sabotage, and (2) A law making the whole of Jewry liable for all damage inflicted by individual specimens of this community of criminals upon the German economy, and thus upon the German people. . . .

Reading and Discussion Questions

1. What is the conflict that Hitler sees the world moving toward in 1936?
2. How and why does Hitler conflate Bolshevism with world Jewry?

28.7   Korean "Comfort Girls"

Wars typically reduce, or eliminate, customs and traditional institutions that restrain human violence throughout a society, not just on the battlefield. The recipient population of an atrocity often inflicts similar acts upon their enemy as a means of striking revenge. A vicious cycle then develops with civilian populations and prisoners of war suffering the worst casualties. The issue of Korean "Comfort Girls" illustrates not only a cruel consequence of World War II in Asia, it also highlights longstanding cultural conflict between the countries of Korea and Japan. Koreans insisted that young girls were kidnapped to be sex slaves or lured into such activities by the false promises of Japanese soldiers. The report below provides a description of daily life for the "Comfort Girls." It also shows the lengths to which the Japanese military went to organize sexual activity between their soldiers and the women.

Source: United States Office of War Information, Psychological Warfare Team Attached to U.S. Army Forces India-Burma Theater APO 689. Report NO. 49, October 1, 1944

Early in May of 1942 Japanese agents arrived in Korea for the purpose of enlisting Korean girls for "comfort service" in newly conquered Japanese territories in Southeast Asia. The nature of this "service" was not specified but it was assumed to be work connected with visiting the wounded in hospitals, rolling bandages, and generally making the soldiers happy. The inducement used by these agents was plenty of money, an opportunity to pay off the family debt, easy work, and the prospect of a new life in a new land, Singapore. On the basis of these false representations many girls enlisted for overseas duty and were rewarded with an advance of a few hundred yen.

The majority of the girls were ignorant and uneducated, although a few had been connected with "oldest profession on earth" before. The contract they signed bound them to Army regulations and to war for the "house master" for a period of from six months to a year depending on the family debt for which they were advanced

. . . .

Approximately 800 of these girls were recruited in this manner and they landed with their Japanese "house master" at Rangoon around August 20th, 1942. They came in groups of from eight to twenty-two. From here they were distributed to various parts of Burma, usually to fair sized towns near Japanese Army camps. ...

In Myitkyina the girls were usually quartered in a large two story house (usually a school building) with a separate room for each girl. There each girl lived, slept, and transacted business. In Myitkina their food was prepared by and purchased from the "house master" as they received no regular ration from the Japanese Army. They lived in near-luxury in Burma in comparison to other places. This was especially true of their second year in Burma. They lived well because their food and material was not heavily rationed and they had plenty of money with which to purchase desired articles. They were able to buy cloth, shoes, cigarettes, and cosmetics to supplement the many gifts given to them by soldiers who had received "comfort bags" from home. ...

PRIORITY SYSTEM

The conditions under which they transacted business were regulated by the Army, and in congested areas regulations were strictly enforced. The Army found it necessary in congested areas to install a system of prices, priorities, and schedules for the various units operating in a particular area. According to interrogations the average system was as follows:

1.   Soldiers 10AM to 5PM   1.50 yen 20 to 30 minutes
2.   NCOs   5PM to 9PM   3.00 yen 30 to 40 minutes
3.   Officers 9PM to 12PM   5.00 yen 30 to 40 minutes

These were average prices in Central Burma. Officers were allowed to stay overnight for twenty yen. In Myitkyina Col. Maruyama slashed the prices to almost one-half of the average price.

SCHEDULES

The soldiers often complained about congestion in the houses. In many situations they were not served and had to leave as the army was very strict about overstaying. In order to overcome this problem the Army set aside certain days for certain units. Usually two men from the unit for the day were stationed at the house to identify soldiers. A roving MP was also on hand to keep order. Following is the schedule used by the "Kyoei" house for the various units of the 18th Division while at Naymyo.

Sunday	18th Div. Hdqs. Staff
Monday	Cavalry
Tuesday	Engineers
Wednesday	Day off and weekly physical exam
Thursday	Medics
Friday	Mountain artillery
Saturday	Transport

Officers were allowed to come seven nights a week. The girls complained that even with the schedule congestion was so great that they could not care for all guests, thus causing ill feeling among many of the soldiers.

Soldiers would come to the house, pay the price and get tickets of cardboard about two inches square with the prior on the left side and the name of the house on the other side. Each soldier's identity or rank was then established after which he "took his turn in line". The girls were allowed the prerogative of refusing a customer. This was often done if the person were too drunk.

Reading and Discussion Questions

1. How did World War II intensify long term cultural tensions between Japan and Korea?
2. What aspects of the intelligence report illustrate how the Korean women were treated as machines rather than as human beings?

Chapter 29   Reconstruction, the Cold War, and Decolonization

1945-1962

Almost 50 million people lost their lives in World War II with over half being civilians. The economic destruction of the war devastated some of the world's most powerful economies. Great Britain and France, which ushered in the Industrial Revolution, lost much of their manufacturing capacity and found reliance upon their colonies to be increasingly difficult. Germany, perhaps one of the most advanced economies in the world in the early 20th century, was politically divided and economically devastated. Japan, once the economic and political leader of Asia, stood virtually helpless in the wake of the war's aftermath. The Soviet Union, which lost more people than any other during the war, continued down a dangerous path of forced industrialization and economic collectivization. China would soon undergo its own communist revolution and follow a similar path to the Soviets. The rest of Europe and Asia struggled with equal unrest and economic catastrophe as economic exchange broke down across both continents prompting widespread unemployment, famine, disease, and starvation. The global situation appeared bleak with one exception—the United States, the world's largest economy and the only major one to come out of the war relatively unscathed.

Political and business leaders in the United States feared a return of global depression. One solution involved boosting the American export sector, particularly regarding agriculture and machinery such as automobiles. Without a global economic recovery, however, opportunities for expanding global trading networks remained a slim possibility at best. Complicating financial concerns, many American leaders worried about the rise of communist parties throughout the world. Communists and fascists had a long history of mutual hatred; indeed, one reason for the spread of fascism is the 1930s was in response to the rise of violence dispensed by communist groups. But communists refused to submit to fascist governments in Italy, France, Germany, and other parts of Europe. They became leaders of the underground resistance movements and seen by many in Europe as heroically defending their communities from fascists. Communists also promised financial relief, full employment, and economic prosperity. American leaders believed continued global economic turmoil would also fuel communist aggression, which at the most would cause a third world war and at the least stall economic recovery.

United States congressional leaders and Secretary of State, George Marshall, proposed a multi-billion dollar aid package, called the Marshall Plan, to rebuild war torn areas of Europe and Asia under certain stipulations. It was expected that reconstructed governments would join and support newly created international organizations such as United Nations, the Breton Woods Agreement that placed international trade on a dollar-gold standard and the General Agreement on Tariffs and Trade, an effort to lower barriers to global trade. European governments were also expected to distribute Marshall Plan aid through a common international organization that would serve as the foundation for further economic integration. As a result, several European governments formed the Organization for European Economic Cooperation, which became the forerunner of the European Economic Community and European Union.

The Soviet Union, under the control of Joseph Stalin, threatened to offset any gains made by American-lead reconstruction of Europe. The Soviets swiftly moved to consolidate their control over eastern portions of Germany as well as areas of Eastern Europe, including Poland, Hungary, and their own neighboring satellite countries.

Russian technicians dismantled German machinery, even entire factories, to be reassembled in the Soviet Union as part of Stalin's efforts to further modernize the Soviet economy. Coupled with an aggressive tone and what appeared to be an ideological commitment to export communism to other parts of the world, American leaders pledged to support any government or peoples from being taken over by communists. The conflict between the United States and the Soviet Union soon plunged the world into a new state of hostilities as each country sought to undermine the other through a series of proxy wars fought by their allies.

But the Cold War between the two "superpowers" did come dangerously close to igniting full-scale military conflict. The invention of nuclear weapons and the strategy of "mutually assured destruction" if attacked fostered tense relations for nearly forty years. Military buildups, overseas proxy wars, propaganda campaigns, fear of internal enemies, and ideological clashes peppered world history from the late 1940s until 1991, when the Soviet Union dissolved.

29.1   The Marshall Plan

The economic devastation caused by World War II reached catastrophic proportions by 1946. Allied occupation forces could not stem growing starvation, famine, and disease in Western Europe, and Soviet forces commenced "relocating" eastern European factory machinery and natural resources to the Soviet Union. Fearing global economic collapse, leaders of the United States Congress pressed for immediate aid as well as a concerted effort to rebuild Europe before economic plight drove its populations to extreme measures. The United States Secretary of State, George C. Marshall, delivered the commencement address at Harvard University on June 5, 1947, where he summarized American assistance in restoring the economic infrastructure of Europe. No other country in the world was capable at the time of facilitating economic assistance, and the subsequent European Recovery Program, also known as the Marshall Plan, solidified American leadership in global financial policy. To disseminate reconstruction efforts and aid payments, American leaders insisted that European governments work together to lower trade barriers and further economic integration. As a result, several western European countries, including western Germany and France, formed the Organization for European Economic Co-operation, an early institutional move toward uniting Europe into a single economy. For his efforts, George Marshall received the Nobel Peace prize.

Source: George C. Marshall, "Commencement Address," Harvard University, June 5, 1947. http://www.usaid.gov/multimedia/video/marshall/marshallspeech.html

I need not tell you, gentlemen, that the world situation is very serious. That must be apparent to all intelligent people. I think one difficulty is that the problem is one of such enormous complexity that the very mass of facts presented to the public by press and radio make it exceedingly difficult for the man in the street to reach a clear appraisement of the situation. Furthermore, the people of this country are distant from the troubled areas of the earth and it is hard for them to comprehend the plight and consequent reactions of the long suffering peoples, and the effect of those reactions on their governments in connection with our efforts to promote peace in the world.

In considering the requirements for the rehabilitation of Europe, the physical loss of life, the visible destruction of cities, factories, mines and railroads was correctly estimated but it has become obvious during recent months that this visible destruction was probably less serious than the dislocation of the entire fabric of European economy. For the past 10 years conditions have been highly abnormal. The feverish preparation for war and the more feverish maintenance of the war effort engulfed all aspects of national economies. Machinery has fallen into disrepair or is entirely obsolete. Under the arbitrary and destructive Nazi rule, virtually every possible enterprise was geared into the German war machine. Long-standing commercial ties, private institutions, banks, insurance companies, and shipping companies disappeared, through loss of capital, absorption through nationalization, or by simple destruction. In many countries, confidence in the local currency has been severely shaken. The breakdown of the business structure of Europe during the war was complete. Recovery has been seriously retarded by the fact that two years after the close of hostilities a peace settlement with Germany and Austria has not been agreed upon. But even given a more prompt solution of these difficult problems the rehabilitation of the economic structure of Europe quite evidently will require a much longer time and greater effort than had been foreseen.

There is a phase of this matter which is both interesting and serious. The farmer has always produced the foodstuffs to exchange with the city dweller for the other necessities of life. This division of labor is the basis of modern civilization. At the present time it is threatened with breakdown. The town and city industries are not producing adequate goods to exchange with the food producing farmer. Raw materials and fuel are in short supply. Machinery is lacking or worn out. The farmer or the peasant cannot find the goods for sale which he desires to purchase. So the sale of his farm produce for money which he cannot use seems to him an unprofitable transaction. He, therefore, has withdrawn many fields from crop cultivation and is using them for grazing. He feeds more grain to stock and finds for himself and his family an ample supply of food, however short he may be on clothing and the other ordinary gadgets of civilization. Meanwhile people in the cities are short of food and fuel. So the governments are forced to use their foreign money and credits to procure these necessities abroad. This process exhausts funds which are urgently needed for reconstruction. Thus a very serious situation is rapidly developing which bodes no good for the world. The modern system of the division of labor upon which the exchange of products is based is in danger of breaking down.

The truth of the matter is that Europe's requirements for the next three or four years of foreign food and other essential products - principally from America - are so much greater than her present ability to pay that she must have substantial additional help or face economic, social, and political deterioration of a very grave character.

The remedy lies in breaking the vicious circle and restoring the confidence of the European people in the economic future of their own countries and of Europe as a whole. The manufacturer and the farmer throughout wide areas must be able and willing to exchange their products for currencies the continuing value of which is not open to question.

Aside from the demoralizing effect on the world at large and the possibilities of disturbances arising as a result of the desperation of the people concerned, the consequences to the economy of the United States should be apparent to all. It is logical that the United States should do whatever it is able to do to assist in the return of normal economic health in the world, without which there can be no political stability and no assured peace. Our policy is directed not against any country or doctrine but against hunger, poverty, desperation and chaos. Its purpose should be the revival of a working economy in the world so as to permit the emergence of political and social conditions in which free institutions can exist. Such assistance, I am convinced, must not be on a piecemeal basis as various crises develop. Any assistance that this Government may render in the future should provide a cure rather than a mere palliative. Any government that is willing to assist in the task of recovery will find full co-operation I am sure, on the part of the United States Government. Any government which maneuvers to block the recovery of other countries cannot expect help from us. Furthermore, governments, political parties, or groups which seek to perpetuate human misery in order to profit therefrom politically or otherwise will encounter the opposition of the United States.

It is already evident that, before the United States Government can proceed much further in its efforts to alleviate the situation and help start the European world on its way to recovery, there must be some agreement among the countries of Europe as to the requirements of the situation and the part those countries themselves will take in order to give proper effect to whatever action might be undertaken by this Government. It would be neither fitting nor efficacious for this Government to undertake to draw up unilaterally a program designed to place Europe on its feet economically. This is the business of the Europeans. The initiative, I think, must come from Europe. The role of this country should consist of friendly aid in the drafting of a European program and of later support of such a program so far as it may be practical for us to do so. The program should be a joint one, agreed to by a number, if not all European nations.

An essential part of any successful action on the part of the United States is an understanding on the part of the people of America of the character of the problem and the remedies to be applied. Political passion and prejudice should have no part. With foresight, and a willingness on the part of our people to face up to the vast responsibility which history has clearly placed upon our country, the difficulties I have outlined can and will be overcome.

Reading and Discussion Questions

1. According to Marshall, how serious was the problem of wartime devastation in Europe?
2. What could the United States do to offset the problems that Marshall described and why was it so important to them?
3. Why would Marshall insist that Europeans together agree on a common economic recovery program?

29.2 The Suez Crisis

In July 1956, Egyptian president, Gamal Abdel Nasser (1918 – 1970), nationalized the Suez Canal linking the Mediterranean Sea with the Red Sea. Nasser, a promoter of pan-Arabism and closer ties with communist governments in the Soviet Union and China, threatened to escalate Cold War tensions already inflamed by Chinese actions involving Taiwan, Soviet influence in the Middle East, and developing popular movements in Eastern Europe. In October 1956, Israel launched an attack upon Egypt with Great Britain and France quickly joining in the hopes of regaining control over the canal and ousting Nasser from power. While military victory came quickly for the three countries, they failed politically to maintain the legitimacy of their attack. Both the United States and the Soviet Union worked through the United Nations to achieve a cease-fire with subsequent withdrawal of foreign forces from the area. Just before the attacks, U.S. President Dwight Eisenhower outlined his concerns about using military action in the area to British Prime Minister Anthony Eden, who later blamed Eisenhower for Britain's failure to take the canal.

Source: Eisenhower, Dwight D. Top secret To Robert Anthony Eden, 31 July 1956. In The Papers of Dwight David Eisenhower, ed. L. Galambos and D. van Ee, doc. 1935. World Wide Web facsimile by The Dwight D. Eisenhower Memorial Commission of the print edition: Baltimore, MD: The Johns Hopkins University Press, 1996, http://www.eisenhowermemorial.org/presidential-papers/first-term/documents/1935.cfm

From the moment that Nasser announced nationalization of the Suez Canal Company, my thoughts have been constantly with you. Grave problems are placed before both our governments, although for each of us they naturally differ in type and character. Until this morning, I was happy to feel that we were approaching decisions as to applicable procedures somewhat along parallel lines, even though there were, as would be expected, important differences as to detail. But early this morning I received the message, communicated to me through Murphy from you and Harold Macmillan, telling me on a most secret basis of your decision to employ force without delay or attempting any intermediate and less drastic steps.

We recognize the transcendent worth of the Canal to the free world and the possibility that eventually the use of force might become necessary in order to protect international rights. But we have been hopeful that through a Conference in which would be represented the signatories to the Convention of 1888, as well as other maritime nations, there would be brought about such pressures on the Egyptian Government that the efficient operation of the Canal could be assured for the future.

For my part, I cannot over-emphasize the strength of my conviction that some such method must be attempted before action such as you contemplate should be undertaken. If unfortunately the situation can finally be resolved only by drastic means, there should be no grounds for belief anywhere that corrective measures were undertaken merely to protect national or individual investors, or the legal rights of a sovereign nation were ruthlessly flouted. A conference, at the very least, should have a great education effort throughout the world. Public opinion here, and I am convinced, in most of the world, would be outraged should there be a failure to make such efforts. Moreover, initial military successes might be easy, but the eventual price might become far too heavy.

I have given you my own personal conviction, as well as that of my associates, as to the unwisdom even of contemplating the use of military force at this moment. Assuming, however, that the whole situation continued to deteriorate to the point where such action would seem the only recourse, there are certain political facts to remember. As you realize, employment of United States forces is possible only through positive action on the part of the Congress, which is now adjourned but can be reconvened on my call for special reasons. If those reasons should involve the issue of employing United States military strength abroad, there would have to be a showing that every peaceful means of resolving the difficulty had previously been exhausted. Without such a showing, there would be a reaction that could very seriously affect our peoples' feeling toward our Western Allies. I do not want to exaggerate, but I assure you that this could grow to such intensity as to have the most far-reaching consequences.

Reading and Discussion Questions

1. Why did President Eisenhower fear the Suez crisis would jeopardize American relations with the Soviet Union?
2. Why is Eisenhower so concerned that British and French actions might be construed to only protect business interests and investments in the Suez Canal?
3. When Eisenhower writes of an "eventual price" that must be paid for British actions, what kind of long-term repercussions did he have in mind?

29.3 Cuban Missile Crisis

The Cuban Missile Crisis marked a turning point in the Cold War, particularly in terms of global public opinion concerning the dangers of Soviet and American nuclear policies. In 1959, Cuban revolutionary, Fidel Castro, overthrew the U.S.-friendly, Fulgencio Batista, and then sought to strengthen relations with the Soviet Union. President John Kennedy unsuccessfully attempted to remove Castro from power by supporting the Cuban opposition, supplying military advisers, and initiating the failed Bay of Pigs invasion in 1961. Soviet leaders, including Premier Nikita Khrushchev, convinced Castro to accept Soviet nuclear missiles and bombers to stop another invasion. In October 1962, a U-2 spy plane secretly photographed missile sites being constructed in Cuba, and President Kennedy decided to prevent the installation of nuclear missiles through a naval blockade rather than through direct military confrontation. For thirteen days, tensions heightened between the Soviets and the Americans before the Soviets agreed to cease missile deployment in Cuba in exchange for a public promise that the United States would not attempt to overthrow the Castro regime and to secretly remove nuclear missiles being deployed in Turkey and parts of Europe. President Kennedy's brother and chief adviser, Robert, met with the Soviet ambassador Anatoly Dobrynin to work out a final resolution agreeable to both sides.

United States Source: Robert F. Kennedy, *Thirteen Days: A Memoir of the Cuban Missile Crisis* (New York: New American Library, 1969), 107-109.

Soviet Union Source: Russian Foreign Ministry archives, translation from copy provided by NHK, in Richard Ned Lebow and Janice Gross Stein, We All Lost the Cold War (Princeton, NJ: Princeton University Press, 1994), appendix, pp. 523-526, with minor revisions.

United States

Robert F. Kennedy's (edited) Description

I telephoned Ambassador Dobrynin about 7:15 P.M. and asked him to come to the Department of Justice. We met in my office at 7:45. I told him first that we knew that work was continuing on the missile bases in Cuba and that in the last few days it had been expedited. I said that in the last few hours we had learned that our reconnaissance planes flying over Cuba had been fired upon and that one of our U-2s had been shot down and the pilot killed. That for us was a most serious turn of events.

President Kennedy did not want a military conflict. He had done everything possible to avoid a military engagement with Cuba and with the Soviet Union, but now they had forced our hand. Because of the deception of the Soviet Union, our photographic reconnaissance planes would have to continue to fly over Cuba, and if the Cubans or Soviets shot at these planes, then we would have to shoot back. This would inevitably lead to further incidents and to escalation of the conflict, the implications of which were very grave indeed.

He said the Cubans resented the fact that we were violating Cuban air space. I replied that if we had not violated Cuban air space, we would still be believing what Khrushchev had said— that there would be no missiles placed in Cuba. In any case, I said, this matter was far more serious than the air space of Cuba—it involved the peoples of both of our countries and, in fact, people all over the globe.

The Soviet Union had secretly established missile bases in Cuba while at the same time proclaiming privately and publicly that this would never be done. We had to have a commitment by tomorrow that those bases would be removed. I was not giving them an ultimatum but a statement of fact. He should understand that if they did not remove those bases, we would remove them. President Kennedy had great respect for the Ambassador's country and the courage of its people. Perhaps his country might feel it necessary to take retaliatory action; but before that was over, there would be not only dead Americans but dead Russians as well.

He asked me what offer the United States was making, and I told him of the letter that President Kennedy had just transmitted to Khrushchev. He raised the question of our removing the missiles from Turkey. I said that there could be no quid pro quo or any arrangement made under this kind of threat or pressure and that in the last analysis this was a decision that would have to be made by NATO. However, I said, President Kennedy had been anxious to remove those missiles from Italy and Turkey for a long period of time. He had ordered their removal some time ago, and it was our judgment that, within a short time after this crisis was over, those missiles would be gone.

Soviet Union

Anatoly Dobrynin's Cable to the Soviet Foreign Ministry, 27 October 1962:

TOP SECRET Making Copies Prohibited Copy No. I

CIPHERED TELEGRAM

Late tonight R. Kennedy invited me to come see him. We talked alone.

The Cuban crisis, R. Kennedy began, continues to quickly worsen. We have just received a report that an unarmed American plane was shot down while carrying out a reconnaissance flight over Cuba. The military is demanding that the President arm such planes and respond to fire with fire. The USA government will have to do this.

I interrupted R. Kennedy and asked him, what right American planes had to fly over Cuba at all, crudely violating its sovereignty and accepted international norms? How would the USA have reacted if foreign planes appeared over its territory?

"We have a resolution of the Organization of American states that gives us the right to such overflights," R. Kennedy quickly replied.

I told him that the Soviet Union, like all peace-loving countries, resolutely rejects such a "right" or, to be more exact, this kind of true lawlessness, when people who don't like the social-political situation in a country try to impose their will on it—a small state where the people themselves established and maintained [their system]. "The OAS resolution is a direct violation of the UN Charter," I added, "and you, as the Attorney General of the USA, the highest American legal entity, should certainly know that."

R. Kennedy said that he realized that we had different approaches to these problems and it was not likely that we could convince each other. But now the matter is not in these differences, since time is of the essence. "I want," R. Kennedy stressed, "to lay out the current alarming situation the way the president sees it. He wants N.S. Khrushchev to know this. This is the thrust of the situation now."

… The USA government is determined to get rid of those bases—up to in the extreme case, of bombing them, since, I repeat, they pose a great threat to the security of the USA. But in response to the bombing of these bases, in the course of which Soviet specialists might suffer, the Soviet government will undoubtedly respond with the same against us, somewhere in Europe. A real war will begin, in which millions of Americans and Russians will die. We want to avoid that any way we can, I'm sure that the government of the USSR has the same wish…."

"In this regard," R. Kennedy said,' the president considers that a suitable basis for regulating the entire Cuban conflict might be the letter N.S. Khrushchev sent on October.26 and the letter in response from the President. which was sent off today to N.S. Khrushchev through the US Embassy in Moscow. The most important thing for us,' R. Kennedy stressed, "is to get as soon as possible the agreement of the Soviet government to halt further work on the construction of the missile bases in Cuba and take measures under international control that would make it impossible to use these weapons. In exchange the government of the USA is ready, in addition to repealing all measures on the "quarantine," to give the assurances that there will not be any invasion of Cuba and that other countries of the Western Hemisphere are ready to give the same assurances—the US government is certain of this."

"And what about Turkey?" I asked R. Kennedy.

"If that is the only obstacle to achieving the regulation I mentioned earlier, then the president doesn't see any unsurmountable difficulties in resolving this issue," replied R. Kennedy. "The greatest difficulty for the president is the public discussion of the issue of Turkey. Formally the deployment of missile bases in Turkey was done by a special decision of the NATO Council. To announce now a unilateral decision by the president of the USA to withdraw missile bases from Turkey—this would damage the entire structure of NATO and the US position as the leader of NATO, where, as the Soviet government knows very well, there are many arguments. In short.if such a decision were announced now it would seriously tear apart NATO."

27/X-62 A. DOBRYNIN

Reading and Discussion Questions

1. How does Dobrynin's account of the meeting with Robert Kennedy differ from Kennedy's?
2. What strategic goals were most important for Dobrynin and the Soviet government? What did they hope to gain from the crisis?
3. To what degree did the interests of Fidel Castro and the Cuban government play in the discussions between Robert Kennedy and Anatoly Dobrynin?
4. How did President Kennedy learn about the construction of missile bases in Cuba? What role then did technological innovation play in the tense moments of the Cold War?
5. Explain how Robert Kennedy's attitude toward Khrushchev affect the diplomacy between the two countries?
6. What deal was struck between Kennedy and Dobrynin to end the missile crisis?

29.4 Jawaharlal Nehru, "Why India is Non-Aligned"

Jawaharlal Nehru (1889-1964) was a leader of the Indian National Congress and the first prime minister of India after independence from Great Britain in 1947. In this television and radio address, delivered in Washington, D.C. in 1956, Nehru discusses India's position on several political issues, including why they were non-aligned. The non-aligned movement began in the 1950s, as a reaction against the Cold War and to address issues tied to decolonization. Countries who were a part of this movement as non-aligned nations refused to ally with either of the two superpowers: the USSR and the US. The non-aligned nations, many of them newly independent from Western colonization, hoped to assert some influence on peace and security in the face of the growing tensions of the Cold War. They also addressed issues of colonialism and self-determination, disarmament, the role of the UN in world politics, and unequal economic development.

Source: Jawaharlal Nehru, "Why India is Non-Aligned." Television and radio address, Washington, D.C., 18 December 1956

I speak of India because it is my country, and I have some right to speak for her. But many other countries in Asia tell the same story, for Asia today is resurgent, and these countries, which long lay under foreign yoke, have won back their independence and are fired by a new spirit and strive toward new ideals. To them, as to us, independence is as vital as the breath they take to sustain life, and colonialism in any form, or anywhere, is abhorrent.

The vast strides that technology has made have brought a new age, of which the United States of America is the leader. Today, the whole world is our neighbour and the old divisions of continents and countries matter less and less. Peace and freedom have become indivisible, and the world cannot continue for long partly free and partly subject. In this atomic age, peace has also become a test of human survival. Recently, we have witnessed two tragedies which have powerfully affected men and women all over the world. These are the tragedies in Egypt and Hungary. Our deeply felt sympathies must go out to those who have suffered or are suffering, and all of us must do our utmost to help them and to assist in solving these problems in a peaceful and constructive way. But even these tragedies have one hopeful aspect, for they have demonstrated that the most powerful countries cannot revert to old colonial methods, or impose their domination over weak countries. World opinion has shown that it can organize itself to resist such outrages. Perhaps, as an outcome of these tragedies, freedom will be enlarged and will have a more assured basis.

The preservation of peace forms the central aim of India's policy. It is in the pursuit of this policy that we have chosen the path of non-alignment in any military or like pact or alliance. Non-alignment does not mean passivity of mind or action, lack of faith or conviction. It does not mean submission to what we consider evil. It is a positive and dynamic approach to such problems that confront us. We believe that each country has not only the right to freedom, but also to decide its own policy and way of life. Only thus can true freedom flourish and a people grow according to their own genius. We believe, therefore, in non-aggression and non-interference by one country in the affairs of another, and the growth of tolerance between them and the capacity for peaceful coexistence. We think that, by the free exchange of ideas and trade and other contacts between nations, each will learn from the other, and truth will prevail. We, therefore, endeavor to maintain friendly relations with all countries - even though we may disagree with them in their policies or structure of government. We think that, by this approach, we can serve not only our country, but also the larger causes of peace and good fellowship in the world.

Through the centuries, India has preached and practiced toleration and understanding, and has enriched human thought, art and literature, philosophy and religion. Her Sons journeyed far and wide, braving the perils of land and sea, not with thoughts of conquest or domination, but as messengers of peace or engaged in the commerce of ideas as well as of her beautiful products. During these millennia of history, India has experienced both good and ill but, throughout her checkered history, she has remembered the message of peace and tolerance. In our own time, this message was proclaimed by our great leader and master, Mahatma Gandhi, who led us to freedom by peaceful and yet effective action on a mass scale. Nine years ago, we won our independence through a bloodless revolution, in conditions of honor and dignity both to ourselves and to the erstwhile rulers of our country. We in India today are children of this revolution and have been conditioned by it. Although your revolution in America took place long ago and the conditions were different here, you will appreciate the revolutionary spirit which we have inherited and which still governs our activities.

Having attained political freedom, we are earnestly desirous of removing the many ills that our country suffers from, of eliminating poverty and raising the standards of our people, and giving them full and equal opportunities of growth and advancement.

India is supposed to be given to contemplation, and the American people have shown by their history that they possess great energy, dynamism and the passion to march ahead. Something of that contemplative spirit still remains in India. But, at the same time, the new India of today has also developed a certain dynamism and a passionate desire to raise the standards of her people. But with that desire is blended the wish to adhere to the moral and spiritual aspects of life. We are now engaged in a gigantic and exciting task of achieving rapid and large-scale economic development of our country. Such development, in an ancient and underdeveloped country such as India, is only possible with purposive planning. True to our democratic principles and traditions, we seek in free discussion and consultation, as well as in implementations the enthusiasm and the willing and active co-operation of our people. We completed our first Five-Year Plan eight months ago, and now we have begun, on a more ambitious scale, our second Five-Year Plan, which seeks a planned development in agriculture and industry, town and country, and between factory and small-scale and cottage production.

Reading and Discussion Questions

1. What arguments does Nehru give for India's non-aligned position?
2. How does he attempt to connect non-alignment with America's own past?

29.5 Juan Perón, excerpt from *The Voice of Peron*

The following are excerpts from speeches given by the Argentine dictator between 1946 and 1949, when he was head of state. Juan Perón (1896-1973) entered the Argentine government as a result of a coup in 1943 and became president in 1946. Developing an ardent following, particularly among urban workers, he launched extensive building projects and welfare programs. He was ousted in 1956, returning briefly thereafter, but a Perónist political movement remained an important force in Argentine politics for some time.

Source: Juan Perón, *The Voice of Perón* (Buenos Aires: Argentine government, 1950), 22, 36-7, 59, 64, 69-70, 71, 94, 10-11.

1. 1946

The Argentine Republic was born as a country of peace and work, endowed by nature with everything people may hope for to live happily and in peace; on this fact our international policy is based, we are inevitably heading for prosperity and greatness achieved partly by reason of our geographical situation and by our historical destiny. There is nothing we can envy others, since God gave us whatever we may wish for. Our policy is born of this aspect of our own natural greatness. We can never seek to take something from someone since we are surrounded on this earth by countries less fortunate than ours. For this reason, our international policy is a policy of peace, friendship, and the desire to trade honestly and freely, whenever we are offered the same freedom we grant, for in a world where absolute freedom of trade does not exist, it would be suicidal to profess this absolute liberty.

2. 1946

Social conscience has banished forever the selfish individualism that looked only for personal advantages, to seek the welfare of all through the collective action of unions. Without that social conscience modern peoples are driven to struggle and despair dragging their country to misery, war and distress. This magnificent spectacle of the awakening of a social conscience is condemned by men maintaining old standards, but they must not be blamed for they are the product of an unhappy era already surpassed by the Argentine Republic. They are the product of that individualistic and selfish age. They were born when gold was the only thing that mattered, when gold was handled without consulting the heart and therefore without understanding and realising that gold is not everything on this earth, that dividends are not of paramount importance.

3. 1946

The Five-Year Plan, as we have drawn it up, is simply the result of a careful study of all the Argentine problems, in the institutional order, in the field of national defence, and also in the field of national economy. We have considered each of these Argentine problems in detail, trying to discover their roots in order to find an adequate solution. Only a plan of vast proportions is in keeping with a great nation such as the Argentine Republic. The mediocre, those who lack courage and faith, always prefer small plans. Great nations, such as our own, with lofty ambitions and aspirations, must also envisage great plans. Nothing valuable can be achieved by planning trivialities.

4. 1946

Nowadays policy has changed: each person is at his post, working for the common patrimony. When something is achieved, it must benefit everyone; when suffering awaits us, all must share the sorrow. But let us advise those who still uphold ideas of the old politicians that today, Argentine men and Argentine women are aware of the existence of a movement supported by the whole country; that we all work and struggle for this joint movement; therefore, that any personal or group policy will be destroyed by us and also that our policy originates in this movement of union.

5. 1947

Encouraged by an overwhelming spirit of patriotism and steadily following the principles and standards of conduct set by precedent, an officer must apply all his strength of character and bring into play all his stalwart personality so that whatever may be the circumstances in which they find themselves, the Armed Forces will never cease to be an orderly and disciplined institution at the exclusive service of the Nation. He must be sure that they are never transformed into a constant danger which undervalues and hampers the will of a sovereign people.

6. 1948

To guide the masses one must first instruct and educate them, which can be done at meetings or at lectures on politics, to be given in our centres, not to tell them to vote for us, or that they must do this or that so that Peter or James will be elected to represent them. No, we must speak to them of what are their obligations, because in our country there is much talk of rights and little of moral obligations. We must talk somewhat more about the obligations of each citizen towards his country and towards his fellow countrymen, and forget for a time their rights since we have mentioned them often enough.

7. 1949

The Peronistic doctrine has to go forward with its fundamental idea; to free the people to prepare them to make the right use of this freedom. Neither can any Argentine, and still less a Peronist, use unfairly the individual freedom which the Magna Charter of the Republic offers him as a man of honour and not as a criminal. A Peronist must be a slave to the law because that is the only way in which he can eventually obtain his freedom. But it is not enough for a Peronist to be a slave of the law. He must also observe the Peronist code of ethics, because those who break laws are not the only criminals, those who abuse their freedom and who break the community laws of the land they live in to the detriment of their fellow beings, are also guilty.

8. 1949

Liberal Democracy, flexible in matters of political or economic retrocession, or apparent discretion, was not equally flexible where social problems were concerned. And the bourgeoisie after breaking their lines, have presented the spectacle of peoples who all rise at once so as to measure the might of their presence, the volume of their clamour, and the fairness of their claims. Popular expectation is followed by discontent. Hope placed in the power of law is transformed into resentment if these laws tolerate injustice. The State looks on impotently at a growing loss of prestige. Its institutions prevent it from taking adequate measures and there are signs of a divorce between its interpretation and that of the nation which it professes to represent. Having lost prestige it becomes ineffectual, and is threatened by rebellion, because if society does not find in the ruling powers the instrument with which to achieve its happiness it will devise in its unprotected state, the instrument with which to overthrow them.

9. 1949

The ambition for social progress has nothing to do with its noisy partisan exploitation, neither can it be achieved by reviling and lowering the different types of men. Mankind needs faith in his destiny and in what he is doing and to possess sufficient insight to realise that the transition from the "I" to the "we" does not take place in a flash as the extermination of the individual, but as a renewed avowal of the existence of the individual functioning in the community. In that way the phenomenon is orderly and takes place during the years in the form of a necessary evolution which is more in the nature of "coming of age" than that of a mutiny.

10. 1949

We are building cities, we are constructing gaspipe lines 1,800 kilometers long; we are building an aerodrome which may quite possibly be the largest and best-equipped in the world and we are acquiring a merchant fleet which is already beginning to take its place among the most important on the high seas.

By this I mean to point out that I was not just being vainglorious three years ago when I took over the Government and said that the Country was sick and tired of little things, and I wanted to make it sick and tired of big things.

11. 1949

The "caudillo" [name given to South American autocratic political leaders] improvises while the statesman makes plans and carries them out. The "caudillo" has no initiative, the statesman is creative. The "caudillo" is only concerned with measures which are applicable to the reigning circumstances whereas the statesman plans for all time; the deeds of the "caudillo" die with him, but the statesman lives on in his handiwork. For that reason the "caudillo" has no guiding principles or clear-cut plan while the statesman works methodically, defeating time and perpetuating himself in his own creations. "Caudillismo" is a trade, but statecraft is an art.

12. 1949

The politician of the old school made posts and favouritism a question of politics, because as he achieved nothing of general usefulness, he had at least to win the good will of those who would support him in the field of politics. The natural consequences of this nepotism were political cliques; one politician dominated one clique and another a different one. They fought among themselves until one of the cliques came out on top and from them emerged the general staff bent not on fulfilling their public office with self-denial and sacrifice, but on making the most of their position to use the Nation as a huge body at the service of their own interests and to throw away the wealth of the country with [no] sense of order and the fitness of things...

13. 1949

The revolutionary idea would not have been able to materialise along constitutional lines if it had not been able to withstand the criticism, the violent attacks and even the strain on principles when they run up against the rocks which appear, every day in the path of a ruler. The principles of the revolution would not have been able to be upheld if they had not been the true reflection of Argentine sentiments.

The guiding principles of our movement must have made a very deep impression on the national conscience for the people in the last elections to have consecrated them by giving us full power to make reforms.

Reading and Discussion Questions

1. Which other twentieth-century ideologies does Peronism most resemble?
2. What about Peronism makes it a uniquely Latin American phenomena?

29.6 Jomo Kenyatta, from *Facing Mt. Kenya: The Tribal Life of the Gikuyu*

Born in 1893, Kenyatta early campaigned for land rights for his Gikuyu tribe in Kenya. He spent sixteen years in England, studying at the University of London and linking with other African leaders. In 1946 he and Kwame Nkrumah, later the first leader of independent Ghana, formed the Pan-African Federation. Kenyatta returned to Kenya in 1946 and was jailed for a role in a violent uprising against white settlers. Released in 1961, he negotiated independence arrangements with the British while also reconciling two main tribal factions in Kenya. Kenyatta stands as one of the earliest and most revered African nationalist leaders.

Source: Jomo Kenyatta, *Facing Mt. Kenya: The Tribal Life of the Gikuyu* (London: Sedser and Warburg, 1936), 47-52.

And the Europeans, having their feet firm on the soil, began to claim the absolute right to rule the country and to have the ownership of the lands under the title of "Crown Lands," where the Gikuyu, who are the original owners, now live as "tenants at will of the Crown." The Gikuyu lost most of their lands through their magnanimity, for the Gikuyu country was never wholly conquered by force of arms, but the people were put under the ruthless domination of European imperialism through the insidious trickery of hypocritical treaties.

The relation between the Gikuyu and the Europeans can well be illustrated by a Gikuyu story which says: That once upon a time an elephant made a friendship with a man. One day a heavy thunderstorm broke out, the elephant went to his friend, who had a little hut at the edge of the forest, and said to him: "My dear good man, will you please let me put my trunk inside your hut to keep it out of this torrential rain?" The man, seeing what situation his friend was in, replied: "My dear good elephant, my hut is very small, but there is room for your trunk and myself. Please put your trunk in gently." The elephant thanked his friend, saying: "You have done me a good deed and one day I shall return your kindness." But what followed? As soon as the elephant put his trunk inside the hut, slowly he pushed his head inside, and finally flung the man out in the rain, and then lay down comfortably inside his friend's hut, saying: "My dear good friend, your skin is harder than mine, and as there is not enough room for both of us, you can afford to remain in the rain while I am protecting my delicate skin from the hailstorm."

The man, seeing what his friend had done to him, started to grumble, the animals in the nearby forest heard the noise and came to see what was the matter. All stood around listening to the heated argument between the man and his friend the elephant. In this turmoil the lion came along roaring, and said in a loud voice: "Don't you all know that I am the King of the Jungle! How dare anyone disturb the peace of my kingdom?" On hearing this the elephant, who was one of the high ministers in the jungle kingdom, replied in a soothing voice, and said: "My Lord, there is no disturbance of the peace in your kingdom. I have only been having a little discussion with my friend here as to the possession of this little hut which your lordship sees me occupying." The lion, who wanted to have "peace and tranquillity" in his kingdom, replied in a noble voice, saying: "I command my ministers to appoint a Commission of Enquiry to go thoroughly into this matter and report accordingly." He then turned to the man and said: "You have done well by establishing friendship with my people, especially with the elephant who is one of my honourable ministers of state. Do not grumble any more, your hut is not lost to you. Wait until the sitting of my Imperial Commission, and there you will be given plenty of opportunity to state your case. I am sure that you will be pleased with the findings of the Commission." The man was very pleased by these sweet words from the King of the Jungle, and innocently waited for his opportunity, in the belief, that naturally, the hut would be returned to him.

The elephant, obeying the command of his master, got busy with other ministers to appoint the Commission of Enquiry. The following elders of the jungle were appointed to sit in the Commission: (1) Mr. Rhinoceros; (2) Mr. Buffalo; (3) Mr. Alligator; (4) The Rt. Hon. Mr. Fox to act as chairman; and (5) Mr. Leopard to act as Secretary to the Commission. On seeing the personnel, the man protested and asked if it was not necessary to include in this Commission a member from his side. But he was told that it was impossible, since no one from his side was well enough educated to understand the intricacy of jungle law. Further, that there was nothing to fear, for the members of the Commission were all men of repute for their impartiality in justice, and as they were gentlemen chosen by God to look after the interests of races less adequately endowed with teeth and claws, he might rest assured that they would investigate the matter with the greatest care and report impartially.

The Commission sat to take the evidence. The Rt. Hon. Mr. Elephant was first called. He came along with a superior air, brushing his tusks with a sapling which Mrs. Elephant had provided, and in an authoritative voice said: "Gentlemen of the Jungle, there is no need for me to waste your valuable time in relating a story which I am sure you all know. I have always regarded it as my duty to protect the interests of my friends, and this appears to have caused the misunderstanding between myself and my friend here. He invited me to save his hut from being blown away by a hurricane. As the hurricane had gained access owing to the unoccupied space in the hut, I considered it necessary, in my friend's own interests, to turn the undeveloped space to a more economic use by sitting in it myself; a duty which any of you would undoubtedly have performed with equal readiness in similar circumstances."

After hearing the Rt. Hon. Mr. Elephant's conclusive evidence, the Commission called Mr. Hyena and other elders of the jungle, who all supported what Mr. Elephant had said. They then called the man, who began to give his own account of the dispute. But the Commission cut him short, saying: "My good man, please confine yourself to relevant issues. We have already heard the circumstances from various unbiased sources; all we wish you to tell us is whether the undeveloped space in your hut was occupied by anyone else before Mr. Elephant assumed his position?" The man began to say: "No, but - " But at this point the Commission declared that they had heard sufficient evidence from both sides and retired to consider their decision. After enjoying a delicious meal at the expense of the Rt. Hon. Mr. Elephant, they reached their verdict, called the man, and declared as follows: "In our opinion this dispute has arisen through a regrettable misunderstanding due to the backwardness of your ideas. We consider that Mr. Elephant has fulfilled his sacred duty of protecting your interests. As it is clearly for your good that the space should be put to its most economic use, and as you yourself have not yet reached the stage of expansion which would enable you to fill it, we consider it necessary to arrange a compromise to suit both parties. Mr. Elephant shall continue his occupation of your hut, but we give you permission to look for a site where you can build another hut more suited to your needs, and we will see that you are well protected."

The man, having no alternative, and fearing that his refusal might expose him to the teeth and claws of members of the Commission, did as they suggested. But no sooner had he built another hut than Mr. Rhinoceros charged in with his horn lowered and ordered the man to quit. A Royal Commission was again appointed to look into the matter, and the same finding was given. This procedure was repeated until Mr. Buffalo, Mr. Leopard, Mr. Hyena and the rest were all accommodated with new huts. Then the man decided that he must adopt an effective method of protection, since Commissions of Enquiry did nor seem to be of any use to him. He sat down and said: "Ng'enda thi mieagaga motegi," which literally means "there is nothing that treads on the earth that cannot be trapped," or in other words, you can fool people for a time, but not for ever.

Early one morning, when the huts already occupied by the jungle lords were all beginning to decay and fall to pieces, he went out and built a bigger and better hut a little distance away. No sooner had Mr. Rhinoceros seen it than he came rushing in, only to find that Mr. Elephant was already inside, sound asleep. Mr. Leopard next came in at the window, Mr. Lion, Mr. Fox, and Mr. Buffalo entered the doors, while Mr. Hyena howled for a place in the shade and Mr. Alligator basked on the roof. Presently they all began disputing about their rights of penetration, and from disputing they came to fighting, and while they were all embroiled together the man set the hut on fire and burnt it to the ground, jungle lords and all. Then he went home, saying: "Peace is costly, but it's worth the expense," and lived happily ever after.

There certainly are some progressive ideas among the Europeans. They include the ideas of material prosperity, of medicine, and hygiene, and literacy which enables people to take part in world culture. But so far the Europeans who visit Africa have not been conspicuously zealous in imparting these parts of their inheritance to the Africans, and seem to think that the only way to do it is by police discipline and armed force. They speak as if it was somehow beneficial to an African to work for them instead of for himself, and to make sure that he will receive this benefit they do their best to take away his land and leave him with no alternative. Along with his land they rob him of his government, condemn his religious idea, and ignore his fundamental conceptions of justice and morals, all in the name of civilisation and progress.

If Africans were left in peace on their own lands, Europeans would have to offer them the benefits of white civilisation in real earnest before they could obtain the African labour which they want so much. They would have to offer the African a way of life which was really superior to the one his fathers lived before him, and a share in the prosperity given them by their command of science. They would have to let the African choose what parts of European culture could be beneficially transplanted, and how they could be adapted. He would probably not choose the gas bomb or the armed police force, but he might ask for some other things of which he does not get so much today. As it is, by driving him off his ancestral lands, the Europeans have robbed him of the material foundations of his culture, and reduced him to a state of serfdom incompatible with human happiness. The African is conditioned, by the cultural and social institutions of centuries, to a freedom of which Europe has little conception, and it is not in his nature to accept serfdom forever. He realises that he must fight unceasingly for his own complete emancipation, for without this he is doomed to remain the prey of rival imperialisms, which in every successive year will drive their fangs more deeply into his vitality and strength.

Reading and Discussion Questions
1. What is the moral of Kenyatta's Gikuyu story?
2. What, in Kenyatta's view, have the Europeans robbed Africans of?

29.7 Babies Being Weighed, North Korea, 1955

This photograph dates to the period just after the Korean War (1950-53) when North Korea was still recovering from the effects of the conflict. Even though food shortages were—and still are—a constant feature of life in North Korea, this photo portrays a different image. The chubby babies suggest abundance, in keeping with North Korea's official propaganda that the country was a "paradise for children".

Reading and Discussion Questions
1. Why would a communist country like North Korea take pride in showing off its health-care system?
2. Do you believe a maternity hospital such as the one depicted here was available to all members of North Korean society?

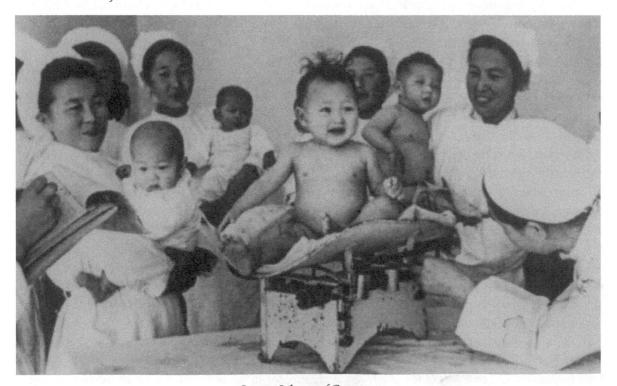

Source: Library of Congress

The End of the Cold War, Western Social Transformation, and the Developing World

Chapter 30

1963-1991

The period from 1963 through 1991 was an era of great social change mixed with some of history's worst examples of political tyranny. Cold War struggles saw increased tension in the 1960s shift to detente in the 1970s only to be followed by an all-out arms race and the subsequent fall of the Soviet Union in the 1980s. African nations endured genocide and destruction of natural resources associated with the growing pains of becoming independent countries. South Africa after years of apartheid rule now had free elections and equal representation in government. Civil rights made great strides in the United States during the 1960s with President Johnson's signing of the Civil Rights Act. The United States involvement in Vietnam sparked protests at universities around the world. South Vietnamese treatment of its many religious groups created protests with Buddhist monks. Students in China demanded freedom in 1989 at Tiananmen Square. However, despite protests, war, and political strife, the world made many advances and gave hope for the future.

30.1 The U.S. Civil Rights Act of 1964

In the United States, the struggle for civil rights gained momentum because of Cold War ideology. Soviet propaganda made much of the fact that proponents of democracy often marginalized a portion of their free society such as African Americans and women. In order to present a consistent picture to the world, the United States needed to address these issues. This focus toward equality for all coincided with the general mood of the sixties, which, paradoxically, ran counter to Western materialism and Capitalism. The Vietnam War, in which the United States sought to prevent the spread of Communism, became a focus of protests. Universities in particular became hotbeds of revolutionary ideology as students in the United States, France, Italy, and West Germany expressing solidarity with those in the developing world who championed socialism against global capitalism.

In a television and radio address, President Lyndon B. Johnson (1908-1973) explained the importance and reasoning behind the Civil Rights Bill that he signed on July 2, 1964. He insisted that the idea of "separate but equal," facilities for whites and blacks was not only an immoral and outdated policy, but also counterproductive to the image that the United States wanted to exude in the fight against communism. Communist countries used the racial problems in the United States in propaganda campaigns, insisting that Americans do not hold true to their own democratic values. Johnson believed that In order to promote freedom and prosperity to the world, it was imperative that the United States allow all its citizens to enjoy equally the same liberties and promise for the future.

The Civil Rights Bill outlawed racial discrimination in public places such as theaters, restaurants, parks, hotels and offered equal employment regardless of race.

Source: Lyndon Baines Johnson, " Remarks Upon Signing the Civil Rights Bill." 2 July 1964 *Public Papers of the Presidents of the United States: Lyndon B. Johnson, 1963-64*. Volume II, entry 446, pp. 842-844. Washington, D. C.: Government Printing Office, 1965.

My fellow Americans:

I am about to sign into law the Civil Rights Act of 1964. I want to take this occasion to talk to you about what that law means to every American.

One hundred and eighty-eight years ago this week a small band of valiant men began a long struggle for freedom. They pledged their lives, their fortunes, and their sacred honor not only to found a nation, but to forge an ideal of freedom--not only for political independence, but for personal liberty--not only to eliminate foreign rule, but to establish the rule of justice in the affairs of men.

That struggle was a turning point in our history. Today in far corners of distant continents, the ideals of those American patriots still shape the struggles of men who hunger for freedom.

This is a proud triumph. Yet those who founded our country knew that freedom would be secure only if each generation fought to renew and enlarge its meaning. From the minutemen at Concord to the soldiers in Viet-Nam, each generation has been equal to that trust.

Americans of every race and color have died in battle to protect our freedom. Americans of every race and color have worked to build a nation of widening opportunities. Now our generation of Americans has been called on to continue the unending search for justice within our own borders.

We believe that all men are created equal. Yet many are denied equal treatment.

We believe that all men have certain unalienable rights. Yet many Americans do not enjoy those rights.

We believe that all men are entitled to the blessings of liberty. Yet millions are being deprived of those blessings--not because of their own failures, but because of the color of their skin.

The reasons are deeply imbedded in history and tradition and the nature of man. We can understand--without rancor or hatred--how this all happened.

But it cannot continue. Our Constitution, the foundation of our Republic, forbids it. The principles of our freedom forbid it. Morality forbids it. And the law I will sign tonight forbids it.

Reading and Discussion Questions

1. In his speech the President declares, "without rancor or hatred." What is it that the President is anticipating by making this statement?
2. President Johnson makes an odd comparison between the minutemen at Concord and Vietnam. What is the commonality that the President is looking for by making this comparison?
3. Why would it be important for the President of the United States to explain his reasoning for signing a bill like this into law at this point in time?

30.2 National Organization for Women, Statement of Purpose

The Civil Rights movement stimulated women, gays, Native Americans, Hispanics, people with disabilities, and other groups to take action. In 1966, a group of feminist leaders founded NOW to fight for equal rights with men.

Source: National Organization for Women, Statement of Purpose, 1966.

We, men and women who hereby constitute ourselves as the National Organization for Women, believe that the time has come for a new movement toward true equality for all women in America, and toward a fully equal partnership of the sexes, as part of the worldwide revolution of human rights now taking place within and beyond our national borders.

The purpose of NOW is to take action to bring women into full participation in the mainstream of American society now, exercising all the privileges an responsibilities thereof in truly equal partnership with men.

WE BELIEVE the time has come to move beyond the abstract argument, discussion, and symposia over the status and special nature of women which have raged in America in recent years; the time has come to confront, with concrete action, the conditions that now prevent women from enjoying the equality of opportunity and freedom of choice which is their right, as individual Americans, and as human beings.

NOW is dedicated to the proposition that women, first and foremost, are human beings, who, like all other people in our society, must have the chance to develop their fullest human potential. We believe that women can achieve such equality only by accepting to the full the challenges and responsibilities they share with all other people in our society, as part of the decision-making mainstream of American political, economic, and social life.

WE ORGANIZE to initiate or support action, nationally, or in any part of this nation, by individuals or organizations, to break through the silken curtain of prejudice and discrimination against women in government, industry, the professions, the churches, the political parties, the judiciary, the labor unions, in education, science, medicine, law, religion, and every other field of importance in American society...

Despite all the talk about the status of American women in recent years, the actual position of women in the United States has declined, and is declining, to an alarming degree throughout the 1950's and 1960's... Working women are becoming increasingly - not less - concentrated on the bottom of the job ladder. As a consequence full-time women workers today earn on the average only 60% of what men earn, and that wage gap has been increasing over the past twenty-five years in every major industry group.

Further, with higher education increasingly essential in today's society, too few women are entering and finishing college or going on to graduate or professional school...

In all the professions considered of importance to society, and in the executive ranks of industry and government, women are losing ground. Where they are present it is only a token handful.

Official pronouncement of the advance in the status of women hide not only the reality of this dangerous decline, but the fact that nothing is being done to stop it. The excellent reports of the President's Commission on the Status of Women and of the State Commissions have not been fully implemented. Such Commissions have power only to advise. They have no power to enforce their recommendations; nor have they the freedom to organize American women and men to press for action on them. The reports of these commissions have, however, created a basis upon which it is now possible to build.

Discrimination in employment on the basis of sex is now prohibited by federal law, in Title VII of the Civil Rights Act of 1964...Until now, too few women's organizations and official spokesmen have been willing to speak out against these dangers facing women. Too many women have been restrained by the fear of being called "feminist."

There is no civil rights movement to speak for women, as there has been for Negroes and other victims of discrimination. The National Organization for Women must therefore begin to speak.

WE BELIEVE that the power of American law, and the protection guaranteed by the U.S. Constitution to the civil rights of all individuals, must be effectively applied and enforced to isolate and remove patterns of sex discrimination, to ensure equality of opportunity in employment and education, and equality of civil and political rights and responsibilities on behalf of women, as well as for Negroes and other deprived groups.

WE REALIZE that women's problems are linked to many broader questions of social justice; their solution will require concerted action by many groups...

WE DO NOT ACCEPT the token appointment of a few women to high-level positions in government and industry as a substitute for a serious continuing effort to recruit and advance women according to their individual abilities. To this end, we urge American government and industry to mobilize the same resources of ingenuity and command with which they have solved problems of far greater difficulty than those now impeding the progress of women.

WE BELIEVE that this nation has a capacity at least as great as other nations, to innovate new social institutions which will enable women to enjoy true equality of opportunity and responsibility in society, without conflict with their responsibilities as mothers and homemakers...

WE REJECT the assumption that these problems are the unique responsibility of each individual woman, rather than a basic social dilemma which society must solve...

WE BELIEVE that it is an essential for every girl to be educated to her full potential of human ability as it is for every boy - with the knowledge that such education is the key to effective participation in today's economy and that, for a girl as for a boy, education can only be serious where there is expectation that it will be used in society...

WE REJECT the current assumptions that a man must carry the sole burden of supporting himself, his wife, and family, and that a woman is automatically entitled to lifelong support by a man upon her marriage, or that marriage, home, and family are primarily woman's world and responsibility - hers to dominate - his to support. We believe that a true partnership between the sexes demands a different concept of marriage, and equitable sharing of the responsibilities of home and children and of the economic bur-dens of their support. We believe that proper recognition should be given to the economic and social value of homemaking and child care...

WE BELIEVE that women must now exercise their political rights and responsibilities as American citizens. They must refuse to be segregated on the basis of sex into separate-and-not-equal ladies' auxiliaries in the political parties, and they must demand representation according to their numbers in the regularly constituted party committees - at local, state, and national levels - and in the informal power structure, participating fully in the selection of candidates and political decision making, and running for office themselves...

NOW WILL HOLD ITSELF INDEPENDENT OF ANY POLITICAL PARTY in order to mobilize the political power of all women and men intent on our goals...

WE BELIEVE that women will do most to create a new image of women by acting now, and by speaking out in behalf of their own equality, freedom, and human dignity - not in pleas for special privilege, nor in enmity toward men, who are also victims of the current, half-equality between the sexes - but in an active, self-respecting partnership with men. By so doing, women will develop confidence in their own ability to determine actively, in partnership with men, the conditions of their life, their choices, their future, and their society.

Reading and Discussion Questions

1. Compare NOW's statement of purpose with Olympe de Gouges, Declaration of the Rights of Women and the Female Citizen in Chapter 22. How are the two similar? How are they different? In the nearly 200 years that separates the two documents, what has changed?

2. Have the goals set forth in this statement of purpose been realized? What about this statement makes it a product of Western civilization?

30.3 The Yom Kippur/Ramadan War

Leonid Brezhnev (1906-1982) came into power in the Soviet Union in 1964. After the Cuban Missile Crisis, both Soviet and American leaders recognized the need for safeguards to prevent nuclear escalation. In the late 1960s, these safeguards (backed by treaties and early warning systems) allowed for a decrease of tension, or "détente," between the two superpowers. The calm interlude of the Cold War ended abruptly in the fall of 1973.

During the Six Day War of 1967, Israeli troops captured the Sinai Peninsula from Egypt. Unwilling to accept the terms of their defeat, the Egyptian government launched a surprise attack upon Israel on October 6, 1973, which coincided with the Jewish celebration of Yom Kippur and the Muslim holy month of Ramadan. During the Cold War, even an essentially regional conflict intensified tensions on an international scale. Arab nations supported Egypt while the United States and western European countries garnered support for Israel. When the United States provided weapons to Israel, the Soviet Union quickly countered with similar offerings to Egypt. With the potential for the border dispute to become a proxy war between the two superpowers, Secretary of State Henry Kissinger raised America's nuclear threat level because of the tensions. The Disengagement Treaty of 1974 between Israel and Egypt asked for a separation of forces along a 20 miles wide, non-militarized zone that served as a buffer against future invasion. Negotiations between the disputing countries were overseen by the United Nations, along with help from both the United States and the Soviet Union.

Source: Egyptian-Israeli Agreement on Disengagement of Forces in Pursuance of the Geneva Peace Conference, January 18, 1974. In *The October War: A Retrospective* edited by Richard B. Parker (Gainesville: University Press of Florida, 2001), 352-354.

A. Egypt and Israel will scrupulously observe the cease-fire on land, sea, and air called for by the UN Security Council and will refrain from the time of the signing of this document from all military or para-military actions against each other.

B. The military forces of Egypt and Israel will be separated in accordance with the following principles:

1. All Egyptian forces on the east side of the Canal will be deployed west of the line designated as Line A on the attached map. All Israeli forces, including those west of the Suez Canal and the Bitter Lakes, will be deployed east of the line designated as Line B on the attached map.

2. The area between the Egyptian and Israeli lines will be a zone of disengagement in which the United Nations Emergency Force (UNEF) will be stationed. The UNEF will continue to consist of units from countries that are not permanent members of the Security Council.

3. The area between the Egyptian line and the Suez Canal will be limited in armament and forces.

4. The area between the Israeli line (Line B on the attached map) and the line designated as Line C on the attached map, which runs along the western base of the mountains where the Gidi and Mitla Passes are located, will be limited in armament and forces.

5. The limitations referred to in paragraphs 3 and 4 will be inspected by UNEF. Existing procedures of the UNEF, including the attaching of Egyptian and Israeli liaison officers to UNEF, will be continued.

6. Air forces of the two sides will be permitted to operate up to their respective lines without interference from the other side.

C. The detailed implementation of the disengagement of forces will be worked out by military representatives of Egypt and Israel, who will agree on the stages of this process. These representatives will meet no later than 48 hours after the signature of this agreement at Kilometre 101 under the aegis of the United Nations for this purpose. They will complete this task within five days. Disengagement will begin within 48 hours after the completion of the work of the military representatives and in no event later than seven days after the signature of this agreement. The process of disengagement will be completed not later than 40 days after it begins.

D. This agreement is not regarded by Egypt and Israel as a final peace agreement. It constitutes a first step toward a final, just and durable peace according to the provisions of Security Council Resolution 338 and within the framework of the Geneva Conference.

   For Egypt: General Abdul Gani al Garnasy

   For Israel: Lt. Gen. David Elazar, Chief of Staff of the Israeli Army

Reading and Discussion Questions

1.   What is the purpose of this demilitarized zone and why was this important to peace negotiations?
2.   What is meant by the term "disengagement" in the agreement, and how did it lead to some of the most important aspects of the agreement?
3.   Could the creation of a demilitarized zone be an ongoing concern for Israel and Arab countries? And if so why?

30.4 Post-Colonialism in Africa

As Cold War issues consumed most of the world, Africa became a locus of civil war and strife. After years of colonial rule, African countries fought for independence and underwent subsequent turmoil associated with development in the midst of domestic and international conflict. Entire populations were destroyed in order to maintain political power through fear and iron-clad rule.

Many African nations experienced economic and social catastrophe due to years of imperialism, depletion of natural resources, lack of entrepreneurial innovation, and failed political regimes. One by one military groups overthrew governments and replaced corrupt leaders only with other corrupt leaders, who heralded promises to promote civil rights and lead the country to prosperity. These promises were often left in the ashes of a destroyed economy and in the memories of murdered relatives and friends. Zimbabwe (formerly known as Rhodesia) achieved independence in 1980 and Robert Mugabe was elected its first president. He made many promises of freedom and prosperity though time would tell his true intent. Power and wealth became Mugabe's main purpose, outweighing any concerns for the people of his nation. Fear of being overthrown like most corrupt leaders in Africa, Mugabe unleashed a murderous campaign against anyone that spoke out against his government. Years after Mugabe began his rule, newspapers would speak of his injustice and crimes against the people he swore to protect and help.

Source: Robert Mugabe "Address to the Nation by the Prime Minister Elect." 4 March 1980. (Causeway, Zimbabwe: Ministry of Information, Immigration, and Tourism, 1980), 2-3.

Only a government that subjects itself to the rule of law has any moral right to demand of its citizen's obedience to the rule of law.

   Our Constitution equally circumscribes the powers of the government by declaring certain civil rights and freedoms as fundamental. We intend to uphold these fundamental rights and freedoms to the full...

   I urge you, whether you are black or white, to join me in a new pledge to forget our grim past, forgive others and forget, join hands in a new amity, and together, as Zimbabweans trample upon racialism, tribalism and regionalism, and work hard to reconstruct and rehabilitate our society as we reinvigorate our economic machinery.

The need for peace demands that our forces be integrated as soon as possible so we can emerge with a single national army. Accordingly, I shall authorize General Walls, working in conjunction with the ZANLA and ZIPRA commanders, to preside over the integration process. We shall also happily continue to enjoy the assistance of the British military instructors.

Finally, I wish to assure all the people that my government will strive to bring about meaningful change to their lives. But everyone should exercise patience, for change cannot occur overnight. For now, let us be united in our endeavor to lead the country to independence. Let us constitute a oneness derived from our common objectives and total commitment to build a great Zimbabwe that will be the pride of all Africa.

Let us deepen our sense of belonging and engender a common interest that knows no race, color or creed. Let us truly become Zimbabweans with a single loyalty.

The gap continues to widen between international guarantees of human rights for the people of Zimbabwe and the living reality of the abuse they endure. The government's grave attacks against its citizens show an increasingly desperate president undermining human rights and the rule of law in order to maintain power. This systematic oppression of an already impoverished people is being supplemented by a widespread government policy of subverting the press, the judicial system and the economy. The end result is a country in ruin. Zimbabwe's annual inflation rate is over 620 percent and climbing. The unemployment rate exceeds 70 percent. The World Health Organization reports that one in four Zimbabweans is HIV positive; 4,000 of them die every week. The country's agricultural output has been so ravaged by the government's policies that Zimbabwe now has the highest number of citizens starving to death in Africa.

Source: "International Justice: The World vs. Robert Mugabe," *New York Times*, published April 2, 2004.

Reading and Discussion Questions

1. Robert Mugabe promised his people certain things in his 1980 speech, but according to the New York *Times* article he went in a different direction. How does the newspaper article account of Mugabe's regime compare to the initial promises made by the president?
2. Crimes against humanity are most often associated with genocide, but according to the readings what else could be considered crimes against humanity?
3. The New York *Times* article explores the high percentage of the population that is HIV positive in Zimbabwe. How could this be contributed to Mugabe's poor leadership?

30.5 The Arms Race Between the USSR and the USA

In this 1985 speech, Mikhail Gorbachev addressed his concerns about the growing nuclear arms race between his Soviet Union and the United States. He used the platform to promote Soviet willingness to negotiate arms treaties and expressed his misgivings about Ronald Reagan's new "Star Wars" space-based missile defense program. The economic situation in the Soviet Union became a concern for Gorbachev after fighting a losing war in Afghanistan (December, 1979 to February, 1989). New advancements in weapons technology forced the Soviet Union into a costly arms race with the United States. Coupled with the disastrous consequences of their command-style economy, which could no longer support technological innovation, Soviet leaders commenced rethinking the arms race.

Source: Mikhail Gorbachev, "Speech of the General Secretary of the [Warsaw Pact] Political Consultative Committee," Sofia, October 22, 1985. Trans. unknown. Archive of the Gorbachev Foundation, Moscow.

Dear comrades!

Twice this year have we had the opportunity to conduct multilateral discussions on the international situation — in Moscow and in Warsaw. Life itself has confirmed our evaluations and conclusions. Mankind is facing a historic transitional period, during which both the arms race and military threat will be stopped or the forces pushing humanity towards nuclear catastrophe will prevail. The present world situation remains tense and perilous. There have been no serious moves in the disarmament sphere. Preparations for war continue. The U.S. is carrying out its gigantic space weapons program and constantly designs and manufactures new weapons. The military potential of the other members of NATO is increasing as well. American first-strike missiles are being placed in Western Europe. It is a reason for special concern that the arms race is a basis on which the USA and its closest allies build their adventuristic strategic policy concepts. They are planning to win over socialism through war or military blackmail. Exactly this was on Reagan's mind when, in a speech held at the British Parliament, he proclaimed an "Anti-Communist crusade". In the end of 70s-beginning of 80s US top echelons started hoping that they would be able to use their considerable technical and technological advantage against the socialist economies. Washington's conclusion regarding problems with economic development of our countries has also played its role nowadays, only our community [of socialist states] can prevent a nuclear war. Our community has done much to keep Europe peaceful, to prevent the nuclear catastrophe. But the complexity of today's situation suggests the necessity of finding new steps, new solutions which could lead to the end of the arms race. And the Soviet Union is making and proposing such steps. The Soviet Union has voluntarily taken the obligation not to be the first country to send arms into space. Unilaterally, we have declared a moratorium on nuclear explosions and on the deployment of medium-range nuclear weapons in Europe. Moreover, we have cut the number of our nuclear weapons. Due to common effort, we have managed to raise such questions as nonuse of power, creation of nuclear-free zones, removal from Europe of chemical weapons, and creation of corridors where such weapons would not be placed. The states of the socialist community, acting individually and collectively, have proposed a program of integrated measures, the realization of which would create a breakthrough in international affairs, and make them turn toward détente. The first two rounds of the Soviet-American talks in Geneva have shown that the USA did not seriously consider preventing the arms race either in space or on Earth. The talks were used by the US to cover up their actions, aimed at gaining military superiority. Now we have proposed a new set of initiatives — almost entirely on disarmament questions. We have stated that we are ready to cut in half the number of Soviet and American nuclear weapons which could reach another country's territory, if space weapons are prohibited.

Reading and Discussion Questions

1. Gorbachev appears to lay all the blame for failed nuclear talks at the feet of the United States. Why would it be important for the Soviet leader to present this image to the world as well as his countryman?
2. Gorbachev sees only two options for the future in his speech. The first is negotiations toward arms disarmament or reduction. What was the second option and why does the Soviet leader feel it is important to express this option in the manner that he does?
3. Gorbachev uses the expression "military blackmail" in his speech. What does the Soviet leader mean by this statement and how does he come to this conclusion?

30.6 The Tiananmen Square Massacre, 1989: a Poet Remembers

As the Soviet Union began to crumble in 1989, political conflict among Communist party elites, intellectuals, workers, and students in China culminated in June of that year when an estimated 600-1,000 democracy activists were massacred in Tiananmen Square, Beijing. Several thousand were arrested, though the exact figure will likely never be known. Following are the last two sections of a lengthy prose poem by an anonymous poet from the provinces, completed just after the massacre and smuggled out of China. In the poet's own recording of it, smuggled out with the words, he at times screams, weeps, and repeats phrases again and again, conveying a mood of hysteria. Writers connected with this poem and its distribution in a number of cities throughout China were reportedly arrested in May and June of 1990.

"The Howl"

But another sort of slaughter takes place at Utopia's core
The prime minister catches cold, the people cough, martial law is
declared again and again
The toothless old machinery of the state rolls on toward those with
the courage to resist the sickness
Unarmed hooligans fall by the thousands, ironclad professional
killers swim in a sea of blood, set fires beneath tightly closed
windows, wipe their army regulation boots on the skirts of dead
maidens. They're incapable of trembling
These heartless robots are incapable of trembling!
Their electronic brains possess only one program, an official
document full of holes
In the name of the motherland slaughter the Constitution! Replace
the Constitution and slaughter righteousness! In the name of
mothers throttle children! In the name of children sodomize
fathers! In the name of wives murder husbands! In the name of the
citizens blow up cities! OPEN FIRE! FIRE!FIRE!FIRE! Upon the
elderly! Upon the children! OPEN FIRE on women! On students!
Workers! Teachers! OPEN FIRE on peddlers! OPEN FIRE!
BLAST AWAY! Take aim at those angry faces. Horrified faces.
Convulsing faces. Empty all barrels at despairing and peaceful
faces! FIRE AWAY to your heart's content! These faces that come
on like a tide and in the next moment are dead are so beautiful!
These faces that will be going up to heaven and down to hell are so
beautiful! Beautiful. A beauty that turns men into beasts! A beauty
that lures men on to ravage, vilify, possess, despoil! Do away with
all beauty! Do away with flowers! Forests.Campuses.Love.
Guitars and pure clean air! Do away with flights of folly! OPEN
FIRE! BLAST AWAY! IT FEELS SO GOOD! SOOO GOOD!
Just like smoking dope. Taking a crap. Back on base giving the old

lady a good fuck! OPEN FIRE! ALL BARRELS! BLAST AWAY!
FEELS GOOD! SOOO GOOD! Smash open a skull! Fry his
scalp! Spill the brains out. Spill the soul out. Splatter on the
overpass. Gatehouse.Railings. Splatter on the road! Splatter
toward the sky where the drops of blood become stars! Stars on the
run! Stars with legs! Sky and earth have changed places. Mankind
wears bright shining hats. Bright shining metal helmets. A troop of
soldiers comes charging out of the moon. OPEN FIRE! ALL
BARRELS! BLAST AWAY! SUCH A HIGH! Mankind and the
stars fall together. Flee together. Can't make out one from the
other. Chase them up to the clouds! Chase them into the cracks of
the earth and into their flesh and WASTE THEM! Blow another
hole in the soul! Blow another hole in the stars! Souls in red skirts!
Souls with white belts! Souls in running shoes doing exercises to the
radio! Where can you run? We will dig you out of the mud. Tear
you out of the flesh. Scoop you out of the air and water. OPEN
FIRE! BLAST AWAY! IT FEELS GOOD! SOOO GOOD! The
slaughter takes place in three worlds. On the wings of birds. In the
stomachs of fish. In the fine dust. In countless species of living
things. LEAP! HOWL! FLY! RUN! You can't pass over wall after
wall of fire. Can't swim across pool after pool of blood. IT FEELS
SO GOOD! Freedom feels SO GOOD! Snuffing out freedom feels
SO GOOD! Power will always triumph. Will be passed down
forever from generation to generation. Freedom will also be
resurrected. Generation after generation. Like that dim light just
before the dawn. No. There's no light. At Utopia's core there can
never be light. Our hearts are pitch black. Black.Scalding. Like a
crematorium. Phantoms of the burnt dead. We will survive. The
government that dominates us will survive. Daylight comes
quickly. IT FEELS SO GOOD! SOOOO GOOD! The butchers
are still howling! Children.Children with cold bodies. Children
whose hands grasp stones. Let's go home. Girls, your lips drawn
and pale. Let's go home. Brothers and sisters, your shattered bodies
littering the earth. Let's go home. We walk noiselessly. Walk three
feet above the ground. Forward, on and on, there must be a place
to rest. There must be a place where sounds of gunfire and
explosions can't be heard. We yearn to hide within a stalk of grass.
A leaf.Uncle.Auntie.Grandpa.Granny.Daddy.Mommy. How
much farther till we're home? We have no home. Everyone knows.
The Chinese have no home. Home is a gentle desire. Let us die in
this desire! OPEN FIRE! BLAST AWAY! FIRE! Let us die in
freedom. Righteousness.Equality.Universal love. Peace. In these
vague desires. Let us become these desires. Stand on the horizon.

Attract more of the living to death! It rains. Don't know which is falling, raindrops or transparent ashes. Run quickly, mommy! Run quickly, son! Run quickly, elder brother! Run quickly, little brother! The butchers will not let up. An even more terrifying day approaches.

OPEN FIRE! BLAST AWAY! FIRE! IT FEELS GOOD! FEELS SOOO GOOD!

Cry CryCryCryCrycrycrycrycrycrycrycry

Before you've been surrounded and annihilated, while you still have the strength left to suckle, crycrycry

Let your sobs cast you off, fuse into radio, television, radar, testify to the slaughter again and again

Let your sobs cast you off, fuse into plant life, semi-vegetable life and microorganisms, blossom into flower after flower, year after year mourning the dead, mourning yourself

Let your sobs be distorted, twisted, annihilated by the tumult of the sacred battle

The butchers come from the east of the city, from the west, from the south, from the north

Metal helmets glint in the light. They're singing—

The sun rises in the east, the sun rises in the west, the sun rises in the south and north

Putrid, sweltering summer, people and ghosts sing—

Don't go to the east, don't go to the west, don't go to the south and north

In the midst of brilliance we stand blind

On a great road but we cannot walk

In the midst of a cacophony all are mute

In the midst of heat and thirst all refuse to drink

People who misunderstand the times, people who think they're surrounded, people who plot to shoot down the sun

You can only cry, you're still crying, crycrycrycrycrycrycry! CRY! CRY! CRY!

You've been smothered to death, baked to death, your whole body is on fire! And yet you're crying

You get up on the stage and act out a farce, you're paraded before the crowds in the streets, and yet you're crying

Your eyeballs explode, scald the surrounding crowd, and yet you're crying

You offer a bounty on yourself, track yourself down, frame yourself, you say you were mistaken, this accursed epoch is all wrong! And yet you're crying

You are trampled, you cry

You are pulverized, you cry

A dog licks up the paste, inside a dog's belly you cry! CRYCRYCRY!

In this historically unprecedented slaughter only the sons of bitches can survive.

Reading and Discussion Questions

1. What kind of imagery does the poet use to describe the massacre at Tiananmen Square? What relationship does Nature have to the slaughter?
2. The poet refers twice to "Utopia's core". To what is he referring?

A Fragile Democratic– Chapter
Capitalist World Order 31

1991-Present

The term "globalization" originated in the late 20th century to describe the international interdependence between trade, politics, and culture that characterizes the modern era, particularly in the era of freer international trade that developed following World War II. Critics of globalization condemn the process of extending global trade because they believe it undermines simple ways of life, places the world's poor in a state of dependence upon wealthy societies, brings about environmental destruction, and shifts power away from traditional political institutions to multinational corporations. As many faults as there may be with globalization, those who oppose it have failed to stem its expansion largely because of its material benefits. Never before have so many opportunities been available to so many people, nor have so many people been able to raise themselves up from the brutal poverty, slavery, and short life-spans that shaped the premodern world. Prior to 1800 the per capita global wage rate remained less than $10.00 per person in real wages. After 1800, real wages precipitously climbed to nearly ten times that amount by the late 20th century.

However, globalization as it is often defined is not a recent phenomenon. Global trading networks have existed for thousands of years. The exchange of ideas, religion, consumer goods, and political alliances is not confined to the modern age. But the extent of such exchange and the proportion of human participation clearly escalated after World War II due to lower trade barriers between nations and improvements upon electric forms of communication.

The positive changes associated with globalization came with a price as resistance movements took advantage of another form of globalization—the international exchange of ideas. Socialism, Islam, and Christianity gained the most from the exchange of ideas; though, it is still too soon to determine which gained the most. It appears, however, that socialism made the greatest mark upon global society if only temporarily. Relatively few societies endorsed complete central planning of their economy. Those that did endured considerable violence and social turmoil that eventually eliminated large populations. Scholars estimate that more people died at the hands of their own totalitarian governments during the 20th century than in all wars during the period. Some societies quickly turned against central planning as was the case of China, which implemented agricultural reform by the 1970s. Still, in the short span of a generation from the Cultural Revolution, millions still lost their lives.

Most democratic societies refused to abandon capitalism and sought to mollify what was perceived to be its most harmful effects by strengthening social safety nets and creating welfare states. Education, health care, transportation, the arts, labor relations, and other areas of life came under control of governments as politicians sought to encourage endeavors they believed capitalism failed to equitably deliver. To fund the benefits of welfare states, political leaders that benefited from voters without taxable wealth could not be completely tapped without serious economic consequences. As a result, nation states escalated issuing public debt instruments through their treasuries and central banks. Combined with innovations in international financial institutions, government, or "sovereign," debt became a chief means of financing welfare programs, military expenditures, and even encouraging economic growth. The sustainability of sovereign debt depending upon several factors including the ability of governments to maintain regular interest payments, the relative strength of the world's regional economies and a thriving birthrate. In the early 21st century, several factors pointed to diminished efficacy of sovereign debt as well as the social services and military expenditures it funded. The financial interconnectivity among central banks, financial markets, and international trade hastened economic corrections.

In the midst of global economic and political changes, innovation continued. Perhaps the most important was the invention of the World Wide Web, which revolutionized the way human beings communicated. Ironically, the internet threatened the ability of modern states to monopolize information and contributed to the overthrown of several regimes, including the "Arab Spring" uprising in 2011. The internet also enhanced productivity in many areas of business, expanded intellectual discourse, and provided access to information previously reserved to the most powerful members of society. Where the Modern Era began with intellectuals, explorers, religious leaders, and the politically connected developing sophisticated means of collecting and analyzing information, it does appear the era will end as those capabilities are obtained by the masses.

31.1   Tim Berners-Lee, "Enquire Within Upon Everything"

Like many great inventions in human history, several widely varying innovations came together to produce the World Wide Web. The original "Internet" began as an easy means of exchanging scientific information between researchers for the United States Department of Defense. It offered little incentive for public use and remained confined to only a small number of people. Several computer communications companies like CompuServe and America Online harnessed aspects of the Internet to provide online services to their customers. However, when Time Berners-Lee developed a new protocol based on hyperlinks and independent websites with u unique addresses. the World Wide Web was born. Perhaps not since Gutenberg invented the printing press had such large numbers of people so quickly embraced new forms of information. Not only did the World Wide Web revolutionize commerce and advertising, it produced profound effects in politics and popular culture where long established authorities found their legitimacy steadily shrink.

Source: Tim Berners-Lee, *Weaving the Web* (HarperCollins, 1999), pp. 1-3.

When I first began tinkering with a software program that eventually gave rise to the idea of the World Wide Web, I named it Enquire, short for *Enquire Within upon Everything*, a musty old book of Victorian advice I noticed as a child in my parents' house outside London. With its title suggestive of magic, the book served as a portal to a world of information, everything from how to remove clothing stains to tips on investing money. Not a perfect analogy for the Web, but a primitive starting point.

What that first bit of Enquire code led me to was something much larger, a vision encompassing the decentralized, organic growth of ideas, technology, and society. The vision I have for the Web is about anything being potentially connected with anything. It is a vision that provides us with new freedom, and allows us to grow faster than we ever could when we were fettered by the hierarchical classification systems into which we bound ourselves. It leaves the entirety of our previous ways of working as just one tool among many. It leaves our previous fears for the future as one set among many. And it brings the workings of society closer to the workings of our minds.

Unlike *Enquire Within upon Everything*, the Web that I have tried to foster is not merely a vein of information to be mined, nor is it just a reference or research tool. Despite the fact that the ubiquitous *www* and *.com* now fuel electronic commerce and stock markets all over the world, this is a large, but just one, part of the Web. Buying books from Amazon.com and stocks from E-trade is not all there is to the Web. Neither is the Web some idealized space where we must remove our shoes, eat only fallen fruit, and eschew commercialization.

The irony is that in all its various guises - commerce, research, and surfing - the Web is already so much a part of our lives that familiarity has clouded our perception of the Web itself. To understand the Web in the broadest and deepest sense, to fully partake of the vision that I and my colleagues share, one must understand how the Web came to be. . . .

Journalists have always asked me what the crucial idea was, or what the singular event was, that allowed the Web to exist one day when it hadn't the day before. They are frustrated when I tell them there was no "Eureka!" moment. It was not like the legendary apple falling on Newton's head to demonstrate the concept of gravity. Inventing the World Wide Web involved my growing realization that there was a power in arranging ideas in an unconstrained, weblike way. And that awareness came to me through precisely that kind of process. The Web arose as the answer to an open challenge, through the swirling together of influences, ideas, and realizations from many sides, until, by the wondrous offices of the human mind, a new concept jelled. It was a process of accretion, not the linear solving of one well-defined problem after another.

Reading and Discussion Questions

1. To what degree did the World Wide Web's formation result from an accidental convergence of many different technologies?
2. How would such technology undermine the legitimacy of established authorities and institutions?

31.2 "Death by Government"

While the modern era produced economic, political, and social innovations that raised the standard of living of most of the world's population beyond what it previously experienced in such a short amount of time, it also co-incides with the largest mass murders and genocides ever recorded. To make matters worse, tyrannical campaigns only increased with intensity and bloodshed as modernity ensued, leaving many to wonder if true progress was being achieved. Mass murder of tens of thousands of people at a time was known in the ancient world and during the medieval period. By comparison, one of the most horrific examples of mass murder in the early stages of the modern era was the French Revolution. During its peak—the Reign of Terror—the French state executed 20,000 political prisoners and nobility. But another 115,000 were killed during the genocidal campaign of the revolutionaries against the Vendee region of France. While high, such figures pale in comparison to the tens of millions killed during the 20th century in genocidal campaigns, political crafted famines, police state tactics, and under authoritarian regimes. R.J. Rummell spent his career compiling evidence of what he calls "death by government" and often claimed democracies produced the most peaceful form of government, a position challenged by the early 21st century. The following table *excludes* human beings killed in military combat and war.

Source: RJ Rummell

Reading and Discussion Questions

1. What are the commonalities among the countries with the highest death tolls?
2. What impact did mass genocides have upon the legitimacy of the governments that initiated them?

20th Century Democide					
		DEMOCIDE (OOO)[1]			ANNUAL
REGIMES	YEARS	TOTAL	DOMESTIC	GENOCIDE	RATE% [2]
MEGAMURDERERS	1900-87	151,491	116,380	33,476	[4]
DEKA-MEGAMURDERERS	1900-87	128,168	100,842	26,690	0.18 [4]
U.S.S.R	1917-87	61,911	54,769	10,000	0.42
China (PRC)	1949-87	35,236	35,236	375	0.12
Germany	1933-45	20,946	762	16,315	0.09
China (KMT)	1928-49	10,075	10,075	Nil	0.07 [5]
LESSER MEGAMURDERERS	1900-87	19,178	12,237	6,184	1.63 [4]
Japan	1936-45	5,964	Nil	Nil	Nil
China (Mao Soviets) [3]	1923-49	3,466	3,466	Nil	0.05 [5]
Cambodia	1975-79	2,035	2,000	541	8.16
Turkey	1909-18	1,883	1,752	1,883	0.96
Vietnam	1945-87	1,670	944	Nil	0.10
Poland	1945-48	1,585	1,585	1,585	1.99
Pakistan	1958-87	1,503	1,503	1,500	0.06
Yugoslavia (Tito)	1944-87	1,072	987	675	0.12
SUSPECTED MEGAMURDERERS	1900-87	4,145	3,301	602	0.24 [4]
North Korea	1948-87	1,663	1,293	Nil	0.25
Mexico	1900-20	1,417	1,417	100	0.45
Russia	1900-17	1,066	591	502	0.02
CENTI-KILOMURDERERS	1900-87	14,918	10,812	4,071	0.26 [4]
Top 5	1900-87	4,074	2,192	1,078	0.89 [4]
China (Warlords)	1917-49	910	910	Nil	0.02
Turkey (Atatürk)	1919-23	878	703	878	2.64
United Kingdom	1900-87	816	Nil	Nil	Nil
Portugal (Dictatorship)	1926-82	741	Nil	Nil	Nil
Indonesia	1965-87	729	579	200	0.02
LESSER MURDERERS	1900-87	2,792	2,355	1,019	0.1 [4]
WORLD TOTAL	1900-87	169,202	129,547	38,566	0.1 [6]

1. Includes genocide, politicide, and mass murder, excludes war-dead. These are the most probably mid-estimates in low to high ranges. Figures may not sum due to round off.
2. The percent of a population killed in democide per year of the regime
3. Guerrilla period.
4. Average
5. The rate is the average of that for three successive periods.
6. The world annual rate is calculated for the 1944 global population.

31.3   Rachel Carson, from *Silent Spring*

First published in 1962, Silent Spring by Rachel Carson (1907-1964) alerted a large audience to the environmental and human dangers of reckless use of pesticides, causing a storm of controversy and eventually legislation in the USA banning use of the pesticide DDT. It also led to the creation of the Environmental Protection Agency. Silent Spring remains to this day a cornerstone of the environmental movement.

Source: Rachel Carson, *Silent Spring* (Boston: Houghton Mifflin, 1962) pp. 5-6.

From Chapter Two: The Obligation to Endure

The history of life on earth has been a history of interaction between living things and their surroundings. To a large extent, the physical form and the habits of the earth's vegetation and its animal life have been molded by the environment. Considering the whole span of earthly time, the opposite effect, in which life actually modifies its surroundings, has been relatively slight. Only within the moment of time represented by the present century has one species - man - acquired significant power to alter the nature of his world.

During the past quarter century this power has not only increased to one of disturbing magnitude but it has changed in character. The most alarming of all man's assaults upon the environment is contamination of air, earth, rivers, and sea with dangerous and even lethal materials. This pollution is for the most part irrevocable; the chain of evil it initiates not only in the world that must support life but in living tissues is for the most part irreversible. In this now universal contamination of the environment, chemicals are the sinister and little-recognized partners of radiation in changing the very nature of the world - the very nature of its life. Strontium 90, released through nuclear explosions into the air, comes to earth in rain or drifts down as fallout, lodges in the soil, enters into the grass or corn or wheat grown there, and in time takes up its abode in the bones of a human being, there to remain until his death. Similarly, chemicals sprayed on croplands or forests or gardens lie long in soil, entering into living organisms, passing from one to another in a chain of poisoning and death. Or they pass mysteriously by underground streams until they emerge and, through the alchemy of air and sunlight, combine into new forms that kill vegetation, sicken cattle, and work unknown harm on those who drink from once pure wells. As Albert Schweitzer has said, "Man can hardly even recognize the devils of his own creation."

Reading and Discussion Questions
1.   How does Carson situate the environmental movement in the larger context of human history? Of global history?
2.   Do Carson's arguments, made over 50 years ago, still endure today?

31.4 The Sovereign Debt Crisis

European governments pioneered welfare states and social safety nets during the early 20th century. However, many of these services rested on three key factors: economic prosperity, strict limits on the beneficiaries of those policies, and nearly population expansion. Of the three, only economic prosperity continued by the beginning of the 21st century, and even then, it came in sporadic sputters rather than from a consistent flow. Voters demanded the expansion of public services as well as the number of beneficiaries. Perhaps most important, modern welfare states originated at a time when birth rates were high and few people lived long enough to enjoy retirement or require long term healthcare. Welfare networks depended upon large numbers of workers funding schemes to assist low numbers of indigent and retired workers. Shrinking birth rates in Europe coupled with a "greying" global population placed great strain on the ability of modern governments to fund their services. Most countries resorted to issuing public debt instruments, usually marketed by their central banks. As public debt emissions expanded in the 1980s, governments (again through their central banks) often purchased other country's debt in order to maximize currency exchange rates and indirectly subsidize their export sectors. Investors and traders combined public debt offerings with new financial instruments that collected massive amounts of private debt into pools. The pools were widely seen as safe havens for commercial bankers and investors who believed governments were "too big to fail" and this offered a sure return of their investment. The global financial collapse in 2008 heightened the risk of public debt securities and hastened demographic pressures on public services. In 2010 auditors determined that the ability of the Greek government to continue to service its public debt instruments was unsustainable. While

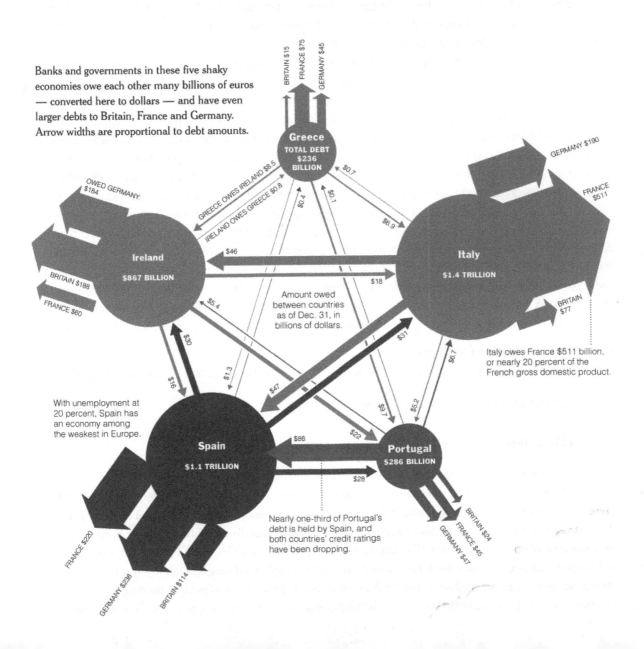

tiny in comparison to other sovereign debt, potential default on Greek debt threatened to cascade across the global economy triggering commercial bank failures and global recession.

Source: *New York Times*, May 5, 2010.

Reading and Discussion Questions

1. Why would sovereign debt default in a country as tiny as Greece trigger financial shocks in larger European economies?
2. If international monetary authorities fail to resolve the Greek sovereign debt crisis, what larger troubles are they sure to face?
3. At what point is a government no longer "too big to fail"?

31.5 James Tooley, from *The Beautiful Tree*

James Tooley (1959-), A British educator and theorist, has spent much of his career studying education in developing countries in Asia and Africa. The following description recounts Tooley's first encounter with private schools created to teach the poor of Hyderabad, India. It also illustrates the growing strain of modern states to educate large populations and in places like India, where population growth exceeds the administrative and financial capacity of state institutions. Ironically, Tooley's story shows the tension between two fixtures of the modern era: an insistence that education produces progressive benefits and the modern nation-state, whose legitimacy rests largely on providing public services like education. Eventually the modern era will pass, and some of the ideas and institutions that produced the era will fade into the past. At issue, is what will remain the era that follows and what will disappear.

Source: James Tooley, *The Beautiful Tree* (Cato Institute, 2009), 8.

There seemed to be a private school on almost every street corner, just as in the richer parts of the city.

I visited so many, being greeted at narrow entrances by so many students, who marched me into tiny playgrounds, beating their drums, to a seat in front of the school, where I was welcomed in ceremonies officiated by senior students, while school managers garlanded me with flowers, heavy, prickly and sticky around my neck in the hot sun, which I bore stoically as I did the rounds of the classrooms. . . .

Through a narrow metal gate, I entered a small courtyard, where Wajid had provided some simple slides and swings for the children to play on. By the far wall were hutches of pet rabbits for the children to look after. Wajid's office was to one side, the family's rooms on the other. We climbed a narrow, dark, dirty staircase to enter the classrooms.

They too were dark, with no doors, and noise from the streets easily penetrated the barred but unglazed windows. The children all seemed incredibly pleased to see their foreign visitor and stood to greet me warmly.

The walls were painted white but were discolored by pollution, heat, and the general wear and tear of children. From the open top floor of his building, Wajid pointed out the locations of five other private schools, all anxious to serve the same students in his neighborhood.

Wajid was quietly unassuming, but clearly caring and devoted to his children. He told me that his mother founded Peace High School in 1973 to provide "a peaceful oasis in the slums" for the children. Wajid, her youngest son, began teaching in the school in 1988, when he was himself a 10th-grade student in another private school nearby.

Having then received his bachelor's in commerce at a local university college and begun training as an accountant, his mother asked him to take over the school in 1998, when she felt she must retire from active service. She asked him to consider the "less blessed" people in the slums, and that his highest ambition should be to help them, as befitting his Muslim faith.

This seemed to have come as a blow to his ambitions. His elder brothers had all pursued careers, and several were now living overseas in Dubai, London and Paris, working in the jewelry business. But Wajid felt obliged to follow his mother's wishes and so began running the school. He was still a bachelor, he told me, because he wanted to build up his school. Only when his financial prospects were certain could he marry.

The school was called a high school, but like others bearing this name, it included kindergarten to 10th grade. Wajid had 285 children and 13 teachers when I first met him, and he also taught mathematics to the older children.

His fees ranged from 60 rupees to 100 rupees per month ($1.33 to $2.22 at the exchange rates then), depending on the children's grade, the lowest for kindergarten and rising as the children progressed through school.

These fees were affordable to parents, he told me, who were largely day laborers and rickshaw pullers, market traders and mechanics — earning perhaps a dollar a day. Parents, I was told, valued education highly and would scrimp and save to ensure that their children got the best education they could afford.

Reading and Discussion Questions

1. What advantages do the private schools of Hyderabad offer to those who live in its slums? Why would poor in the area send their children to such schools?
2. As modern states face diminishing resources and funding, what segments of their populations are likely to fair the worst?